TEACHINGS

of

THOMAS S. MONSON

TEACHINGS

of

THOMAS S. MONSON

COMPILED BY LYNNE F. CANNEGIETER

DESERET
BOOK

Library of Congress Cataloging-in-Publication Data

Monson, Thomas S., 1927–   author.
   Teachings of Thomas S. Monson / Compiled by Lynne Cannegieter.
      pages   cm
   Includes bibliographical references and index.
   ISBN 978-1-60908-890-3 (hardbound : alk. paper)
   1. Church of Jesus Christ of Latter-day Saints—Doctrines.   2. Mormon
Church—Doctrines.   I. Cannegieter, Lynne, compiler.   II. Title.
   BX8635.3.M66 2011
   230'.9332—dc23   2011029267

Printed in the United States of America
Worzalla Publishing Co., Stevens Point, WI

10   9   8   7   6   5   4   3   2   1

CONTENTS

PREFACE

President Thomas S. Monson was set apart as President of The Church of Jesus Christ of Latter-day Saints on February 3, 2008, after having served in the Quorum of the Twelve Apostles and the First Presidency of the Church for more than forty-four years. In the nearly five decades since his call as an apostle at age thirty-six, he has become known for the personal accounts he often uses to illustrate his teachings. Many of those heart-warming accounts appear in his official biography, *To the Rescue,* by Heidi S. Swinton.

This book, however, has a different focus. As a companion volume to the biography, its purpose is to highlight President Monson's doctrinal teachings on a variety of subjects, focusing on the core of the topic and featuring *what* he has taught rather than *how* he has taught it. His insights on communication, discipleship, home and family, service, and Jesus Christ, to name just a few of the dozens of topics treated herein, invite us to examine our own lives and move us to reach higher.

An interesting facet of this approach to excerpting the prophet's words is that it emphasizes how frequently he teaches from the scriptures. A scripture index has been included to provide easy access to his teachings relative to a number of scriptural passages.

The quotations in this volume have been selected from a variety of sources, including general conference addresses, devotionals, firesides, miscellaneous talks, and transcripts of training meetings, some of them previously unpublished. For consistency, minor stylistic changes have been made in a few cases to reflect current usage. Italics and boldface type appear as they did in the original sources. A full citation appears after each excerpt to provide context. The teachings are presented alphabetically by topic; however, in recognition that ideas over-lap and that one quotation will sometimes touch on several themes, a subject index has been provided to make the materi-als even more accessible.

One of the great blessings of membership in The Church of Jesus Christ of Latter-day Saints is the steady leadership of prophets, seers, and revelators in an often chaotic modern world. It is our belief that as we read the prophet's words, tes-timonies will grow, and we can catch a vision of our Father in Heaven's eternal purpose that will provide the guidance, stabil-ity, and hope we need in our lives.

TEACHINGS

of

THOMAS S. MONSON

AARONIC PRIESTHOOD
(SEE ALSO PRIESTHOOD)

I sincerely hope that each deacon, teacher, and priest is aware of the significance of his priesthood ordination and the privilege which is his to fulfill a vital role in the life of every member through his participation in administration and passing of the sacrament each Sunday. ("The Priesthood—A Sacred Trust," *Ensign,* May 1994, 49)

An anxious mother of a prospective missionary once asked me what I would recommend her son learn before the arrival of his missionary call. I am certain she anticipated a profound response which would contain the more familiar requirements for service of which we are all aware. However, I said, "Teach your son how to cook, but more particularly, teach him how to get along with others. He will be happier and more productive if he learns these two vital skills."

Young men, you are preparing for your missions when you learn your duties as deacons, teachers, and priests and then perform those duties with determination and love, knowing you are on the Lord's errand. ("Who Honors God, God Honors," *Ensign,* November 1995, 49)

Those who hold the Melchizedek Priesthood are not the only resource with the strength to lift, the wisdom to guide, and the ability to save. Many of you young men comprise the presidencies of quorums of deacons, quorums of teachers, and hold leadership positions assisting the bishops in guiding quorums of priests. As you magnify your callings with respect to aiding those over whom you preside, heavenly help will be forthcoming. Remember that throughout the ages of time, our Heavenly Father has shown His confidence in those of tender years. ("The Upward Reach," *Ensign*, November 1993, 48)

———

I feel we have the duty to encourage our bishoprics in their responsibilities to the Aaronic Priesthood. If I were a bishop today, I would turn to my second counselor and say, "Brother Hemingway, your responsibility pertains to the ten deacons that we have in our ward. Your charge is to love them, to testify to them, and to ensure that when they are fourteen they are ordained teachers." I would turn to my first counselor, Brother Balmforth, and I would say, "Don, your responsibility is to look after the eleven boys in our ward who are teachers. Use your own ingenuity, but ensure that when those young men are sixteen, they are ready and worthy to be ordained priests." I would also tell my counselors, "The nine whom we have as priests will be my responsibility, as the scripturally mandated president of the priests quorum, to ensure that when they are in their nineteenth year, they will be ordained elders." I believe we will have success when we emphasize this responsibility with the bishoprics and point out the scriptural mandate. ("The Need to Add Men to the Melchizedek Priesthood," Regional Representatives Seminar, April 6, 1984)

———

The scripture outlines the duties of the president of the deacons quorum, the teachers quorum, the priests quorum. I recall that when I was the second counselor in our deacons quorum presidency, I was considered a ward officer. At ward conference, when we sat on the front row of our ward officer's meeting, I remember the stake presidency saying, "We will now call on Thomas Monson, the second counselor in the presidency of the deacons quorum of this ward, to give an account of his steward-ship before the priesthood leadership of this ward." Twelve years old, shaking like a leaf, I had to go forward to the same pulpit and give an account of my stewardship as the second counselor in the deacons quorum. We were taught responsibility, depend-ability, and accountability. We have not tapped that resource to a sufficient degree. Let us teach our bishoprics to harness the energy of the deacons quorum presidency, the teachers quorum presidency, and the leadership of the priests quorum. ("The Need to Add Men to the Melchizedek Priesthood," Regional Representatives Seminar, April 6, 1984)

———

When I was ordained a deacon[, our] bishopric stressed the sacred responsibility which was ours to pass the sacrament. Emphasized was proper dress, a dignified bearing and the im-portance of being clean "inside and out." As we were taught the procedure in passing the sacrament, we were told how we should assist a particular brother who was afflicted with a pal-sied condition, that he might have the opportunity to partake of the sacred emblems.

How I remember being assigned to pass the sacrament to the row where Louis sat. I was fearful and hesitant as I ap-proached this wonderful brother, and then I saw his smile and the eager expression of gratitude that showed his desire to par-take. Holding the tray in my left hand, I took a piece of bread and pressed it to his lips. The water was later served in the same way. I felt I was on holy ground. And indeed I was. The privilege to pass the sacrament to Louis made better deacons of us all. ("A Deacon Today—An Elder Tomorrow," Priesthood Restoration Commencement Satellite Broadcast, May 5, 1991)

———

Some of you are called to serve the young men who hold the Aaronic Priesthood. These precious young men come in all sizes and with varying dispositions and different backgrounds. Yours is the privilege to know them individually and to motivate and lead each youth in his quest to qualify for the Melchizedek Priesthood, a successful mission, a temple marriage, a life of service, and a testimony of truth.

Let us remember that a boy is the only known substance from which a man can be made. . . .

A proper perspective of our young men is absolutely essential for those called to serve them. They are young, pliable, eager, and filled with unlimited energy. Sometimes they make mistakes. I remember a meeting where we of the First Presidency and the Twelve were reviewing a youthful mistake made by a missionary. The tone was serious and rather critical, when Elder LeGrand Richards said, "Now brethren, if the good Lord wanted to put a forty-year-old head on a nineteen-year-old body, He would have done so. But He didn't. He placed a nineteen-year-old head on a nineteen-year-old body, and we should be a bit more understanding." The mood of the group changed, the problem was solved, and we moved on with the meeting.

The years in the Aaronic Priesthood are growing years. They are years of maturing, learning, developing. They are years of emotional highs and lows, a period when wise counseling and proper example by an inspired leader can work wonders and lift lives. ("Called to Serve," *Ensign,* November 1991, 46)

———

As bearers of the Aaronic Priesthood, you have weekly, if not daily, opportunities to serve with love. I hope each of you will live the teachings of the Lord and keep His commandments so you can qualify to be worthy to fill a mission. I want each of you to have in your life the promise of the Lord: "I will go before your face. I will be on your right hand and on your left, and my Spirit shall be in your hearts, and mine angels round about you, to bear you up" (D&C 84:88). Until that day dawns, you will have the privilege as a deacon, as a teacher, as a priest to prepare for such divine service. ("Preparation Precedes Performance," Priesthood Commemoration Satellite Broadcast, May 2, 1993)

———

In a very real sense, all of you who hold the Aaronic Priesthood are entering into the most exciting and challenging period of your young lives, even the race of life. Danger abounds, enemies lurk; but God is near to guide your way and insure your victory. May I suggest four guides which, when followed, will assure your success in every endeavor you undertake:

1. Grow in wisdom.
2. Walk by faith.
3. Teach through testimony.
4. Serve with love.

("Preparation Precedes Performance," Priesthood Commemoration Satellite Broadcast, May 2, 1993)

———

We must provide for our young men of the Aaronic Priesthood faith-building experiences. They seek to have the opportunity we have had to feel the Spirit of the Lord helping them. ("The Call to Serve," *Ensign*, November 2000, 48)

———

In my office I have two small earthen containers. One is filled with water I retrieved from the Dead Sea. The other contains water from the Sea of Galilee. Occasionally I will shake one of the bottles to insure that the water has not diminished. When I follow this practice, my mind turns to these two different bodies of water. The Dead Sea is void of life. The Sea of Galilee is filled with life and with memories of the mission of the Lord Jesus Christ.

There is another body of water found throughout the Church today. I speak of the pool of prospective elders in each ward and each stake. Picture in your mind a river of water gushing into the pool. Then consider a trickle of water emerging from that stagnated pool—a trickle which represents those going forward into the Melchizedek Priesthood. The pool of prospective elders is becoming larger and wider and deeper more rapidly than any of us can fully appreciate.

It is essential, even critical, that we study the Aaronic Priesthood pathway, since far too many boys falter, stumble, then fall without advancing into the quorums of the Melchizedek Priesthood, thereby eroding the active priesthood base of the Church and curtailing the activity of loving wives and precious children.

What can we as leaders do to reverse this trend? The place to begin is at the headwaters of the Aaronic Priesthood stream. There is an ancient proverb which purports to correctly determine the sanity of an individual. A person is shown a stream of water flowing into a stagnant pond. He is given a bucket and asked to commence to drain the pond. If he first takes steps to effectively dam the inflow to the pond, he is adjudged sane. If, on the other hand, he ignores the inflow and tries to empty the pond bucket by bucket, he is designated as insane.

The bishop, by revelation, is the president of the Aaronic Priesthood and is president of the priests quorum in his ward. He cannot delegate these God-given responsibilities. However, he can place accountability with those called as quorum advisers, men who can touch the lives of boys.

The bishop's counselors, other ward officers and teachers, and particularly the fathers and the mothers of our young men can be of immeasurable help. Also very effective can be the service rendered by Aaronic Priesthood quorum presidencies.

This, then, is our goal: to save every young man, thereby assuring a worthy husband for each of our young women, strong Melchizedek Priesthood quorums, and a missionary force trained and capable of accomplishing what the Lord expects. ("The Priesthood—Mighty Army of the Lord," *Ensign,* May 1999, 48)

———

Many of our Aaronic Priesthood young men have a limited understanding of what it means to hold the priesthood and of their duties. Some do not take seriously, or do not understand fully, the necessity of being worthy in order to exercise their priesthood. They live in a world where they are surrounded by outside influences which can be enticing to them but which, if followed, could lead them from the path of righteousness. It is often difficult for us to compete with what they see as exciting and fun outside the bounds of gospel teachings. At their ages, the thrill of the moment often supersedes, in their mnds, the blessings of righteous living. . . .

Emphasis should be placed on what it means for these young men to be bearers of the priesthood of God. They need to be guided to a spiritual awareness of the sacredness of their ordained callings. Their duties should be reviewed, and the fulfillment of those duties stressed. They should be given opportunity to magnify their callings in the priesthood. (General Authority Training Meeting, March 11, 2011)

———

It is essential for the young men who hold the Aaronic Priesthood to take more responsibility for increasing the numbers of active quorum members. Priesthood advisers can do much; the young men, themselves, can often do even more, if they will put forth the effort. . . .

There are quorum members and those who should be quorum members who await a helping hand, an encouraging word, and a personal testimony of truth expressed from a heart filled with love and a desire to lift and build. (General Authority Training Meeting, March 11, 2011)

ABUSE

———

If only all children had loving parents, safe homes, and caring friends, what a wonderful world would be theirs. Unfortunately, not all children are so bounteously blessed. Some children witness their fathers savagely beating their mothers, while others are on the receiving end of such abuse. What cowardice, what depravity, what shame! . . .

A district judge, in a letter to me, declared, "Sexual abuse of children is one of the most depraved, destructive, and demoralizing crimes in civilized society. There is an alarming increase of reported physical, psychological, and sexual abuse of children. Our courts are becoming inundated with this repulsive behavior."

The Church does not condone such heinous and vile conduct. Rather, we condemn in the harshest of terms such treatment of God's precious children. Let the child be rescued, nurtured, loved, and healed. Let the offender be brought to justice, to accountability, for his actions and receive professional treatment to curtail such wicked and devilish conduct. When you and I know of such conduct and fail to take action to eradicate it, we become part of the problem. We share part of the guilt. We experience part of the punishment. ("Precious Children—A Gift from God," *Ensign,* November 1991, 69)

———

A physician revealed to me the large number of children who are brought to the emergency rooms of local hospitals in your city and mine. In many cases guilty parents provide fanciful accounts of the child falling from his high chair or stumbling over a toy and striking his head. Altogether too frequently it is discovered that the parent was the abuser and the innocent child the victim. Shame on the perpetrators of such vile deeds. God will hold such strictly accountable for their actions. ("A Little Child Shall Lead Them," *Ensign,* May 1990, 53)

ADVERSITY

———

As we ponder the events that can befall all of us—even sickness, accident, death, and a host of lesser challenges—we can say, with Job of old, "Man is born unto trouble" (Job 5:7). Needless to add, that reference to man in the King James Version of the book of Job encompasses women as well. It may be safely assumed that no person has ever lived entirely free of suffering and tribulation. Nor has there ever been a period in human history that did not have its full share of turmoil, ruin, and misery.

When the pathway of life takes a cruel turn, there is the temptation to think or speak the phrase, "Why me?" Self-incrimination is a common practice, even when we may have had no control over our difficulty. Socrates is quoted as saying: "If we were all to bring our misfortunes into a common store, so that each person should receive an equal share in the distribution, the majority would be glad to take up their own and depart."

However, at times there appears to be no light at the tunnel's end—no dawn to break the night's darkness. We feel surrounded by the pain of broken hearts, the disappointment of shattered dreams, and the despair of vanished hopes. We join in uttering the biblical plea, "Is there no balm in Gilead?" (Jeremiah 8:22). We are inclined to view our own personal misfortunes through the distorted prism of pessimism. We feel abandoned, heartbroken, alone. . . .

Whenever we are inclined to feel burdened down with the blows of life's fight, let us remember that others have passed the same way, have endured, and then have overcome. ("Meeting Life's Challenges," *Ensign,* November 1993, 70)

———

Life is a school of experience, a time of probation. We learn as we bear our afflictions and live through our heartaches. . . .

There seems to be an unending supply of trouble for one and all. Our problem is that we often expect instantaneous solutions, forgetting that frequently the heavenly virtue of patience is required.

Do any of the following challenges sound familiar to you?

- Handicapped children
- The passing of a loved one
- Employment downsizing
- Obsolescence of one's skills
- A wayward son or daughter
- Mental and emotional illness
- Accidents
- Divorce

- Abuse
- Excessive debt

The list is endless. In the world of today there is at times a tendency to feel detached—even isolated—from the Giver of every good gift. We worry that we walk alone. You ask, "How can we cope?" What brings to us ultimate comfort is the gospel.

From the bed of pain, from the pillow wet with tears, we are lifted heavenward by that divine assurance and precious promise "I will not fail thee, nor forsake thee" (Joshua 1:5).

Such comfort is priceless as we journey along the pathway of mortality, with its many forks and turnings. Rarely is the assurance communicated by a flashing sign or a loud voice. Rather, the language of the Spirit is gentle, quiet, uplifting to the heart, and soothing to the soul. ("Look to God and Live," *Ensign,* May 1998, 52–53)

If we do not have a deep foundation of faith and a solid testimony of truth, we may have difficulty withstanding the harsh storms and icy winds of adversity which inevitably come to each of us.

Mortality is a period of testing, a time to prove ourselves worthy to return to the presence of our Heavenly Father. In order for us to be tested, we must face challenges and difficulties. These can break us, and the surface of our souls may crack and crumble—that is, if our foundations of faith, our testimonies of truth are not deeply imbedded within us.

We can rely on the faith and testimony of others only so long. Eventually we must have our own strong and deeply placed foundation, or we will be unable to withstand the storms of life, which *will* come. Such storms come in a variety of forms. We may be faced with the sorrow and heartbreak of a wayward child who chooses to turn from the pathway leading to eternal truth and rather travel the slippery slopes of error and disillusionment. Sickness may strike us or a loved one, bringing suffering and sometimes death. Accidents may leave their cruel marks of remembrance or may snuff out life. . . .

How can we build a foundation strong enough to withstand such vicissitudes of life? How can we maintain the faith and testimony which will be required, that we might experience the joy promised to the faithful? Constant, steady effort is necessary. Most of us have experienced inspiration so strong that it brings tears to our eyes and a determination to ever remain faithful. I have heard the statement, "If I could keep these feelings with me always, I would never have trouble doing what I should." Such feelings, however, can be fleeting. The inspiration we feel . . . may diminish and fade as . . . we face the routines of work, of school, of managing our homes and families. Such can easily take our minds from the holy to the mundane, from that which uplifts to that which, if we allow it, will chip away at our testimonies, our strong foundations.

Of course we do not live in a world where we experience nothing but the spiritual, but we can fortify our foundations of faith, our testimonies of truth, so that we will not falter, we will not fail. ("How Firm a Foundation," *Ensign*, November 2006, 62, 67)

———

You may at times have cried out in your suffering, wondering why our Heavenly Father would allow you to go through whatever trials you are facing.

On one occasion, a father accompanied his small daughter to nursery school and watched through a one-way glass window as she and her friends played with the toys which were provided. More than once this father was ready to enter the room, eager to save his daughter from the dangers of choice and discovery. His desire to protect her, however, was tempered by the instinct of a loving father, who knows that scraped knees, tears, and bruised feelings are often necessary parts of growth and development.

We all have treasured memories of certain days in our lives—days when all seemed to go well for us, when much was accomplished or when relationships were pleasant and loving. It's not difficult to be happy on such perfect days. We wish all days could be so memorable for their perfection.

Our mortal life, however, was never meant to be easy or consistently pleasant. Our Heavenly Father, who gives us so much to delight in, also knows that we learn and grow and become refined through hard challenges, heartbreaking sorrows, and difficult choices. Each one of us experiences dark days when our loved ones pass away, painful times when our health is lost, feelings of being forsaken when those we love seem to have abandoned us. These and other trials present us with the real test of our ability to endure. . . .

You may have heard the account of an elderly jeweler who proudly showed his grandson how to polish gemstones by placing them in a tumbler where repeated exposure to abrasive materials revealed each stone's true beauty. He pointed out to the boy that, as with the stones, we can become better, more polished and more beautiful by those things we suffer, endure and overcome. ("Joy in the Journey," BYU Women's Conference, May 2, 2008)

AGENCY
(SEE ALSO CHOICE AND ACCOUNTABILITY)

———

I am so grateful to a loving Heavenly Father for His gift of agency, or the right to choose. President David O. McKay, ninth President of the Church, said, "Next to the bestowal of life itself, the right to direct that life is God's greatest gift to man" (*Teachings of Presidents of the Church: David O. McKay* [2003], 208).

We know that we had our agency before this world was and that Lucifer attempted to take it from us. He had no confidence in the principle of agency or in us and argued for imposed salvation. He insisted that with his plan none would be lost, but he seemed not to recognize—or perhaps not to care—that in addition, none would be any wiser, any stronger, any more compassionate, or any more grateful if his plan were followed.

We who chose the Savior's plan knew that we would be embarking on a precarious, difficult journey, for we walk the ways of the world and sin and stumble, cutting us off from our Father. But the Firstborn in the Spirit offered Himself as a sacrifice to atone for the sins of all. Through unspeakable suffering He became the great Redeemer, the Savior of all mankind, thus making possible our successful return to our Father.

The prophet Lehi tells us: "Wherefore, men are free according to the flesh; and all things are given them which are expedient unto man. And they are free to choose liberty and eternal life, through the great Mediator of all men, or to choose captivity and death, according to the captivity and power of the devil; for he seeketh that all men might be miserable like unto himself" (2 Nephi 2:27). ("The Three Rs of Choice," *Ensign,* November 2010, 67)

AMERICA
(THE UNITED STATES)

The Lord gave a divine promise to the ancient inhabitants of this favored country (the United States): "Behold, this is a choice land, and whatsoever nation shall possess it shall be free from bondage, and from captivity, and from all other nations under heaven, if they will but serve the God of the land, who is Jesus Christ" (Ether 2:12).

Are we today serving the God of the land, even the Lord Jesus Christ? Do our lives conform with His teachings? Are we entitled to His divine blessings?

Too many Americans have been screaming ever louder for more and more of the things we cannot take with us and paying less and less attention to the real sources of the very happiness we seek. We have been measuring our fellow man more by balance sheets and less by moral standards. We have developed frightening physical power and fallen into pathetic spiritual weakness. We have become so concerned over the growth of our earning capacity that we have neglected the growth of our character.

As we view the disillusionment that engulfs countless thousands today, we are learning the hard way what an ancient prophet wrote out for us over three thousand years ago: "He that loveth silver shall not be satisfied with silver; nor he that loveth abundance with increase" (Ecclesiastes 5:10).

The revered American president Abraham Lincoln accurately described our plight: "We have been the recipients of the choicest bounties of heaven; we have been preserved these many years in peace and prosperity. We have grown in numbers, wealth, and power as no other nation has ever grown; but we have forgotten God. We have forgotten the gracious hand which preserved us in peace and multiplied and enriched and strengthened us. We have vainly imagined, in the deceitfulness of our hearts, that all these blessings were produced by some superior wisdom and virtue of our own. Intoxicated with unbroken succession, we have become too self-sufficient to feel the necessity of preserving and redeeming grace, to proud to pray to God that made us" ("Proclamation Appointing a National Fast Day," Washington, D.C., March 30, 1864).

Can we extricate ourselves from this frightful condition? Is there a way out? If so, what is the way?

We can solve this perplexing dilemma by adopting the counsel given by Jesus to the inquiring lawyer who asked, "Master, which is the great commandment in the law?

"Jesus said unto him, Thou shalt love the Lord thy God with all thy heart, and with all thy soul, and with all thy mind. This is the first and great commandment. And the second is like unto it, Thou shalt love thy neighbour as thyself" (Matthew 22:36–39). ("America Needs You," *Church of the Air*, October 4, 1964)

———

✗ For many years the code 911 has been the telephone number dialed to report any emergency. Children have memorized the number, and it has been well known by one and all that when 911 was dialed, help would soon be on its way.

Then came September 11th, 2001, and nine-eleven took on another meaning and has a universal and everlasting place in the annals of history and in the hearts of millions. As with December 7, 1941, it too has become a day of infamy.

Early on the morning of September 11, 2001, men and women left their homes for work, mothers prepared their children for school, commuters filled the freeways. Then everything changed. The unthinkable occurred. An insidious attack, planned and executed by evil minds, wreaked havoc in America. Indiscriminately, men, women, and children were slaughtered, including those who responded to the call to rescue. No dastardly deed has been so rapidly and graphically reported.

Amidst the fear, the sorrow, the pain and the suffering, a mighty miracle occurred. Experienced was a fusion of faith— even a pattern of prayer—as Americans turned not to dial 911, but rather dropped to their knees and looked heavenward

to God for help. ("Nine-One-One," September 11 Memorial
Observance, September 11, 2002)

———

I never entered the classrooms of learning there where students are taught concerning the Declaration of Independence,
the Bill of Rights, the Constitution and other monumental
foundation principles but what I had the feeling that I was
walking on sacred ground. ("God Bless America," Freedoms
Foundation Utah Chapter Constitution Day, September 17,
2002)

———

One of the most famous enlistment posters of World War
II was one depicting Uncle Sam pointing his long finger and
directing his piercing eyes at the viewer. The words read,
"America Needs You." America truly does need you and me
to lead out in a mighty crusade of righteousness. We can help
when we love God and with our families serve Him; and when
we love our neighbor as ourselves. ("Duty—Honor—Country,"
National Boy Scouts of America Duty to God Breakfast, May
29, 2003)

ANGER

———

Recently as I watched the news on television, I realized that
many of the lead stories were similar in nature in that the tragedies reported all basically traced back to one emotion: *anger.*
The father of an infant had been arrested for physical abuse

of the baby. It was alleged that the baby's crying had so infuriated him that he had broken one of the child's limbs and several ribs. Alarming was the report of growing gang violence, with the number of gang-related killings having risen sharply. Another story that night involved the shooting of a woman by her estranged husband, who was reportedly in a jealous rage after finding her with another man. Then, of course, there was the usual coverage of wars and conflicts throughout the world.

I thought of the words of the Psalmist: "Cease from anger, and forsake wrath" (Psalm 37:8). ("School Thy Feelings, O My Brother," *Ensign,* November 2009, 62)

———

We've all felt anger. It can come when things don't turn out the way we want. It might be a reaction to something which is said of us or to us. We may experience it when people don't behave the way we want them to behave. Perhaps it comes when we have to wait for something longer than we expected. We might feel angry when others can't see things from our perspective. There seem to be countless possible reasons for anger. . . .

The Apostle Paul asks in Ephesians, chapter 4, verse 26 of the Joseph Smith Translation: "Can ye be angry, and not sin? let not the sun go down upon your wrath." I ask, is it possible to feel the Spirit of our Heavenly Father when we are angry? I know of no instance where such would be the case. . . .

To be angry is to yield to the influence of Satan. No one can *make* us angry. It is our choice. If we desire to have a proper spirit with us at all times, we must choose to refrain from becoming angry. I testify that such is possible.

Anger, Satan's tool, is destructive in so many ways. ("School Thy Feelings, O My Brother," *Ensign,* November 2009, 67–68)

———

We are all susceptible to those feelings which, if left unchecked, can lead to anger. We experience displeasure or irritation or antagonism, and if we so choose, we lose our temper and become angry with others. Ironically, those others are often members of our own families—the people we really love the most. . . .

May we make a conscious decision, each time such a decision must be made, to refrain from anger and to leave unsaid the harsh and hurtful things we may be tempted to say. ("School Thy Feelings, O My Brother," *Ensign*, November 2009, 68–69)

ATONEMENT
(SEE ALSO JESUS CHRIST)

———

Among all the facts of mortality, none is so certain as its end. Death comes to all; it is our "universal heritage; it may claim its victim[s] in infancy or youth, [it may visit] in the period of life's prime, or its summons may be deferred until the snows of age have gathered upon the . . . head; it may befall as the result of accident or disease, . . . or . . . through natural causes; but come it must" (James E. Talmage, *Jesus the Christ*, 3rd ed. [1916], 20). It inevitably represents a painful loss of association and, particularly in the young, a crushing blow to dreams unrealized, ambitions unfulfilled, and hopes vanquished.

What mortal being, faced with the loss of a loved one or, indeed, standing himself or herself on the threshold of infinity, has not pondered what lies beyond the veil which separates the seen from the unseen?

✹ Centuries ago the man Job—so long blessed with every material gift, only to find himself sorely afflicted by all that can befall a human being—sat with his companions and uttered the timeless, ageless question, "If a man die, shall he live again?"(Job 14:14). Job spoke what every other living man or woman has pondered. . . .

I'd like to consider Job's question—"If a man die, shall he live again?"—and provide the answer which comes not only from thoughtful consideration but also from the revealed word of God. . . .

More than 2,000 years ago, Christ, our Savior, was born to mortal life in a stable in Bethlehem. The long-foretold Messiah had come.

There was very little written of the boyhood of Jesus. I love the passage from Luke: "And Jesus increased in wisdom and stature, and in favour with God and man" (Luke 2:52). And from the book of Acts, there is a short phrase concerning the Savior which has a world of meaning: "[He] went about doing good" (Acts 10:38).

He was baptized by John in the river Jordan. He called the Twelve Apostles. He blessed the sick. He caused the lame to walk, the blind to see, the deaf to hear. He even raised the dead to life. He taught, He testified, and He provided a perfect example for us to follow.

And then the mortal mission of the Savior of the world drew to its close. A last supper with His Apostles took place in an upper room. Ahead lay Gethsemane and Calvary's cross.

No mere mortal can conceive the full import of what Christ did for us in Gethsemane. He Himself later described the experience: "[The] suffering caused myself, even God, the greatest of all, to tremble because of pain, and to bleed at every pore, and to suffer both body and spirit"(D&C 19:18).

Following the agony of Gethsemane, now drained of strength, He was seized by rough, crude hands and taken before Annas, Caiaphas, Pilate, and Herod. He was accused and cursed. Vicious blows further weakened His pain-wracked body. Blood ran down His face as a cruel crown fashioned of sharp thorns was forced onto His head, piercing His brow. And then once again He was taken to Pilate, who gave in to the cries of the angry mob: "Crucify him, crucify him" (Luke 23:21).

He was scourged with a whip into whose multiple leather strands sharp metals and bones were woven. Rising from the cruelty of the scourge, with stumbling steps He carried His own cross until He could go no farther and another shouldered the burden for Him.

Finally, on a hill called Calvary, while helpless followers looked on, His wounded body was nailed to a cross. Mercilessly He was mocked and cursed and derided. And yet He cried out, "Father, forgive them; for they know not what they do" (Luke 23:34).

The agonizing hours passed as His life ebbed. From His parched lips came the words, "Father, into thy hands I commend my spirit: and having said thus, he gave up the ghost" (Luke 23:46).

As the serenity and solace of a merciful death freed Him from the sorrows of mortality, He returned to the presence of His Father.

At the last moment, the Master could have turned back. But He did not. He passed beneath all things that He might save all things. His lifeless body was hurriedly but gently placed in a borrowed tomb.

No words in Christendom mean more to me than those spoken by the angel to the weeping Mary Magdalene and the other Mary when, on the first day of the week, they approached the tomb to care for the body of their Lord. Spoke the angel:

"Why seek ye the living among the dead?

"He is not here, but is risen" (Luke 24:5–6).

Our Savior lived again. The most glorious, comforting, and reassuring of all events of human history had taken place—the victory over death. The pain and agony of Gethsemane and Calvary had been wiped away. The salvation of mankind had been secured. The Fall of Adam had been reclaimed. ("He Is Risen!" *Ensign,* May 2010, 87–89)

———

All that we hold dear, even our families, our friends, our joy, our knowledge, our testimonies, would vanish were it not for our Father and His Son, the Lord Jesus Christ. . . .

This precious Son, our Lord and Savior, atoned for our sins and the sins of all. That memorable night in Gethsemane His suffering was so great, His anguish so consuming that He pleaded, "Father, if it be possible, let this cup pass from me: nevertheless not as I will, but as thou wilt" (Matthew 26:39). Later, on the cruel cross, He died that we might live, and live everlastingly. Resurrection morning was preceded by pain, by suffering in accordance with the divine plan of God. Before Easter there had to be a cross. The world has witnessed no greater gift, nor has it known more lasting love. ("Gifts," *Ensign,* May 1993, 62–63)

———

Our Mediator, our Redeemer, our Brother, our Advocate with the Father died for our sins and the sins of all mankind. The Atonement of Jesus Christ is the foreordained but voluntary act of the Only Begotten Son of God. He offered His life as a redeeming ransom for us all.

His mission, His ministry among men, His teachings of truth, His acts of mercy, His unwavering love for us prompts our gratitude and warms our hearts. ("They Showed the Way," *Ensign,* May 1997, 52)

ATTITUDE

Too many people shrink from reality and recoil from discomfort. The tendency of the discontented is to look back at everything with nostalgia and of the timid to look ahead at everything with fear. I hope you will join with the Roman poet and declare, "Let ancient times delight other folk; I rejoice that I was not born till now" (Ovid). ("The Race for Eternal Life," Ricks College Baccalaureate, May 10, 1967)

Attitude can make all the difference in our lives, and we control our attitude. It can make us miserable or happy, content or dissatisfied. To a great degree, it can make us strong or weak. ("Three Bridges to Cross," Dixie State College Commencement, May 6, 2011)

Most of you have heard of John James Audubon, the famous ornithologist, naturalist and painter who was noted for his expansive studies to document all types of American birds. His detailed illustrations depicted the birds in their natural habitat. When I was about ten years old, I served as the president of the Junior Audubon Club at the Grant Elementary School in Salt Lake City. I've always loved birds and have enjoyed being able to identify them.

Well, John James Audubon once left a box containing over 200 of his beautiful drawings of birds at home when he went on a business trip. Upon his return he found that a pair of rats had entered the box and chewed through the paper, destroying years of work. He was devastated and spent weeks nearly paralyzed by grief. One day he awaked and realized that his attitude would have to change. He picked up his notebook and pencils and went out into the woods. "I felt pleased," he said, "that I might now make better drawings than before." ("Three Bridges to Cross," Dixie State College Commencement, May 6, 2011)

———

So much in our life depends on our attitude. The way we choose to see things or to behave or to respond to others makes all the difference. To do the very best we can, and then to choose to be happy about our circumstances, whatever they may be, can bring peace and contentment. "Happiness is an attitude. We either make ourselves miserable, or happy and strong. The amount of work is the same" (Francesca Reigler).

Charles Swindoll—author, educator and Christian pastor—said this about attitude: "The longer I live, the more I realize the impact of attitude on life. Attitude, to me, is more important . . . than the past, . . . than money, than circumstances, than failures, than successes, than what other people think or say or do. It is more important than appearance, giftedness or skill. It will make or break a company, a church, a home." He continued, "The remarkable thing is we have a choice every day regarding the attitude we will embrace for that day. We cannot change our past; we cannot change the fact that people will act in a certain way. We cannot change the inevitable. The only thing we can do is [to change] our attitude." He concluded, "I am convinced that life is 10% what happens to me and 90% how I react to it. . . . We are in charge of our attitudes."

We all know people who seem to "roll with the punches" so to speak, who are pleasant and cheerful through almost any challenge. Generally these are the people with whom we like to spend our time, for they make us feel better about circumstances and about ourselves. It seems that good things gravitate to them, for they don't let less-than-ideal circumstances stand in their way. They choose to find joy everywhere and to leave it behind them when they go.

We, too, can choose to have a positive attitude. We can't direct the wind, but we can adjust the sails. In other words, we can choose to be happy and positive, regardless of what comes our way. The definition of an optimist, according to one man, is "someone who isn't sure whether life is a tragedy or a comedy but is tickled silly just to be in the play" (Robert Brault, at www.robertbrault.com).

We know that some people are more talented than others. Some are more educated. Regardless of where we fit in the scheme of things, we all have the capacity to be great, for we are only limited by how we choose, how resolute we are—in other words, by our attitude. . . .

We have but one chance at this life. For maximum happiness, peace and contentment, may we choose a positive attitude. ("In Quest of the Abundant Life," Weber State University Commencement, April 23, 2010)

———

Some spurn effort and substitute an alibi. We hear the plea, "I was denied the advantages others had in their youth." And then we remember the caption which Webster, the cartoonist, placed under a sketch of Abraham Lincoln's log cabin: "Ill-housed, ill-fed, ill-clothed."

Others say, "I am physically limited." History is replete with people possessing physical limitations. Homer could have sat at the gates of Athens, have been pitied and fed by coins from the rich. He, like Milton the poet, and Prescott the historian, had good alibis—they were blind. Demosthenes, greatest of all great orators, had a wonderful alibi—his lungs were weak, his voice hoarse and unmusical and he stuttered. Beethoven was stone deaf at middle age. They all had good alibis—but they never used them. ("In Quest of the Abundant Life," Utah State University Baccalaureate, June 2, 1967)

———

There is no deafness so permanent as the deafness which will not hear. There is no blindness so incurable as the blindness which will not see. There is no ignorance so deep as the ignorance that will not know. ("Thou Art a Teacher Come from God," Conference Report, October 1970, 108)

———

Our individual journey through life will be marked by sorrow and joy, sickness and health—even by *failure* and *accomplishment*. Failure, that monstrous scoundrel who would thwart your progress, stifle your initiative, and destroy your dreams, has many faces. Can you recognize them?

There is the *Face of Fear.* Fear erects barriers which separate us from our objectives. We become content with mediocrity, when in reality excellence is within our grasp. The comment of the crowd causes us to withdraw from the race, and we retreat to the supposed safety of a sheltered life. . . .

Failure has yet another face, even the *Face of Idleness.* To daydream, to loaf, to wish without work is to fall into the power of its hypnotic trance. So subtle, so inviting is the appeal of idleness that one does not know he has yielded his powers to such a deceitful face. "There has never lived a person who was an idler in his own eyes."

Consider the *Face of Doubt.* It too is one of failure's many masks. Doubt destroys. It chips away at your confidence, undermines your testimony, and erodes your resistance to evil. Shun its winsome smile.

No enumeration of failure's many faces would be complete without the *Face of Sin.* This culprit plays for keeps. The stakes are high. Paul declared, "The wages of sin is death" (Romans 6:23). And who can disregard the word of the Lord, "That which breaketh a law, and abideth not by law, but seeketh to become a law unto itself, and willeth to abide in sin, and altogether abideth in sin, cannot be sanctified by law, neither by mercy, justice, nor judgment" (D&C 88:35).

Thus are the faces of failure: The *Face of Fear,* the *Face of Idleness,* the *Face of Doubt,* and the *Face of Sin.* Let us never for a moment cast even a glance toward such a face. ("Attitudes of Accomplishment," BYU Devotional, May 19, 1970)

Some . . . young people . . . don't know who they are, what they can be or even want to be. They are afraid, but they don't know of what. They are angry, but they don't know at whom. They are rejected, and they don't know why. All they want is to be somebody.

Others are stooped with age, burdened with care, or filled with doubt—living lives far below the level of their capacities.

All of us are prone to excuse our own mediocre performance. We blame our misfortunes, our disfigurements, or our so-called handicaps. Victims of our own rationalization, we say silently to ourselves: "I'm just too weak," or "I'm not cut out for better things." Others soar beyond our meager accomplishments. Envy and discouragement then take their toll. . . .

To live greatly, we must develop the capacity to face trouble with courage, disappointment with cheerfulness, and triumph with humility. You ask, "How might we achieve these goals?" I answer, "By getting a true perspective of who we really are!" We are sons and daughters of a living God in whose image we have been created. ("Yellow Canaries with Gray on Their Wings," *Ensign,* July 1973, 42, 43)

———

Sometimes, my dear sisters, you feel inadequate and ineffective because you can't do all that you feel you should. Rather than continually dwelling on what still needs to be done, pause occasionally and reflect on all that you do and have done. It is most significant.

The good you have done, the kind words you have spoken, the love you have shown to others, can never be fully measured. ("Joy in the Journey," BYU Women's Conference, May 2, 2008)

BALANCE

———

We find in the Church many people who so love Church experiences and so much love Church activity that they devote all of their waking hours to their assignments in the kingdom. We have had bishops who have failed because they have not provided for their families. We have had bishops who have been rejected by their companies because they have attempted to intermix the daily work with the assignment in building the kingdom of God. Let me give you an example.

I never set apart a bishopric but what I don't talk to the wives and say, "There will be individuals in every ward who will call the bishop at all hours of the night and day. You have to have the wisdom to handle those telephone calls in a proper manner. For example, if someone calls and says, "I want to talk to the bishop, " you would be wise to say, "Fine. Leave your number and I will have my husband get in touch with you at 5:30 this evening when he returns from the office." Then again the person may say, "But it's an emergency." At that time the wise wife can say, "Oh, I am sorry to hear that but if you will leave your number I will get in touch with the bishop and have him call you right away." . . .

I would like to testify that it's a wise person who knows how to have balance in his life. There's time for business, there's time for family, there's time for wife, there's time for self, there's time for Christ. We need to have this kind of balance if we are to find wisdom and hence be successful. (BYU College of Business, March 14, 1973)

⚡ BISHOPS ⚡

As a young bishop in 1950, I talked to my former stake president and asked him if he had some suggestions on how I might qualify to be a good bishop. That was my desire. He sat back in his chair and made this statement: "You have what I consider to be the most difficult ward in the Church." It was big—about 1,100 members, about 86 widows, and the largest welfare load of any ward to my knowledge.

He then turned to me and said, "First and foremost among your responsibilities will be to care for the poor; second, to have no favorites, and third, to tolerate no iniquity." ("A Progress Report," Friday Evening Leadership Meeting, April 6, 1984)

One of the titles of . . . these bishops is "Presiding High Priest." As such, he presides at sacrament meeting, priesthood meeting, ward council meetings and at all other ward services and activities. By these and other means he watches over both the spiritual and temporal affairs of the ward. He is also responsible for the doctrine which is taught in the ward.

A bishop must know his people, their names, their circumstances, their challenges and goals, their abilities. A wise bishop knows the names of the children in the ward as well, and he remembers them on their birthdays. He also is mindful of the widow and those who, for whatever reason, are not found as regular attenders in the meetings. He leads with kindness, patience and genuine love. By so doing, the Lord magnifies him in the eyes of his people and brings forth opportunities for the less active to return to Church activity and to the fellowship of the ward family. Frequently the children will lead their parents back to Church activity and service.

In reaching out to his ward members, a bishop finds that the heavenly virtue of patience is required. ("The Bishop and the Spiritual and Temporal Well-Being of the Saints," Worldwide Leadership Training Satellite Broadcast, June 19, 2004)

———

The bishop is responsible for the Aaronic Priesthood. He, of course, is president of the Aaronic Priesthood in the ward and hence his duty is to see that every boy is ordained a deacon at the right age, as well as a teacher, a priest, and an elder. The bishop cannot let these precious youth slip through his fingers. The two words, "labor" and "love," will work wonders in achieving this objective. For those who are behind schedule, I leave the challenge, "Reach out to rescue."

Appoint as advisers to the Aaronic Priesthood quorums brethren who can relate to these young men—who can give them encouragement in the performance of their responsibilities and prepare them to serve at the sacrament table, as home teachers in the case of teachers and priests, and to qualify for missions.

It is in these formative years that the course of a lifetime is determined. It is the time to instill within these young men a desire to "stay on the Lord's side of the line," as President George Albert Smith was known to say. A bishop, himself, must be on the Lord's side of the line with them—an exemplar in keeping the commandments of God, presiding in righteousness in his own family.

A wise bishop will help to guide each Aaronic Priesthood holder to a spiritual awareness of the sacredness of his ordained calling. ("The Bishop and the Spiritual and Temporal Well-Being of the Saints," Worldwide Leadership Training Satellite Broadcast, June 19, 2004)

—

The bishop is in charge of unit finances. He receives tithes and offerings, and he supervises the unit budget and expenditures. He is also to make certain that records are properly and appropriately kept. The bishop is the one who must determine how Church commodities and funds are used to provide for the temporal needs of the members.

Of course the bishop uses the financial clerk to assist in this regard, as well as his counselors. But he is responsible to see that the tithes and offerings of the people are properly recorded so that there is order in all things. . . .

Closely allied to the responsibilities for finances is that of keeping accurate records. It is essential that we know how we're doing and where we need improvement. This knowledge can come only if we keep attendance and related records. I am a firm believer that where performance is measured, performance improves. Where performance is measured and reported back, the rate of improvement accelerates. ("The Bishop and the Spiritual and Temporal Well-Being of the Saints," Worldwide Leadership Training Satellite Broadcast, June 19, 2004)

BLESSINGS

———

We need not feel that we must be without fault in order to receive the blessings of God. He will take us from where we stand now if we will come to Him, and He will build us upward, not only spiritually, but He will build us up with confidence within ourselves. ("The Three R's of Choice," BYU Devotional, November 5, 1963)

———

When we encounter challenges and problems in our lives, it is often difficult for us to focus on our blessings. However, if we reach deep enough and look hard enough, we will be able to feel and recognize just how much we have been given. ("The Divine Gift of Gratitude," *Ensign*, November 2010, 89)

———

An angel wife and mother who, without stint, sacrifices her own comfort for the blessing of her eternal companion; neighbors with hands that help, hearts that feel, and whose feet and talents all come quickly to rescue—are manifested blessings of the Lord's promises. ("Christ at Bethesda's Pool," *Ensign*, November 1996, 18)

———

Our Heavenly Father knows who we are, His sons and His daughters. He wants to bring into our lives the blessings for which we qualify, and He can do it. He can accomplish anything. ("They Will Come," *Ensign*, May 1997, 45)

———

It is the celestial glory which we seek. It is in the presence of God we desire to dwell. It is a forever family in which we want membership. Such blessings are earned. A high report card of mortality qualifies us to graduate with honors. ("An Invitation to Exaltation," Satellite Broadcast, March 4, 1984)

BOOKS AND READING

———

Do you remember those days of long ago when you read a book just for the pure pleasure of reading, rather than as a class assignment and the inevitable report your studies required? ("In Search of Treasure," BYU Devotional, March 11, 1997)

———

Reading "out of the best books" stretches our mental muscles and expands our horizons. It takes us out of our mundane worlds and lets us travel as far as our imaginations and the picture painting words of the authors can carry us. Reading keeps us vibrant, it keeps us alive and makes us far more interesting to our marriage mates and our families. It is also a form of insurance against mental aging. We are only as old as we think we are. Some people say that one way to keep alive is to keep interested in many things, and the way to keep interested is to read widely and wisely. ("Constant Truths in Changing Times," BYU Commencement, May 26, 1967)

Reading is one of the true pleasures of life. In our age of mass culture, when so much that we encounter is abridged, adapted, adulterated, shredded and boiled down, and commercialism's loudspeakers are incessantly braying, it is mind-easing and mind-inspiring to sit down privately with a good book. It is ennobling when that book contains the revealed word of God. ("Constant Truths in Changing Times," BYU Commencement, May 26, 1967)

CHANGE
(SEE ALSO REPENTANCE)

We can turn from the paths which would lead us down and, with a song in our hearts, follow a star and walk toward the light. We can quicken our step, bolster our courage, and bask in the sunlight of truth. We can hear more clearly the laughter of little children. We can dry the tear of the weeping. We can comfort the dying by sharing the promise of eternal life. ("Now Is the Time," *Ensign,* November 2001, 60)

Those who have felt the touch of the Master's hand somehow cannot explain the change which comes into their lives. There is a desire to live better, to serve faithfully, to walk humbly, and to live more like the Savior. Having received their spiritual eyesight and glimpsed the promises of eternity, they echo the words of the blind man to whom Jesus restored sight, " . . . one thing I know, that, whereas I was blind, now I see"

(John 9:25). ("The Precious Gift of Sight," Conference Report, April 1965, 46)

———

Two fundamental reasons largely account for . . . changes of attitudes, of habits, of actions.

First, men have been shown their eternal possibilities and have made the decision to achieve them. Men cannot really long rest content with mediocrity once they see excellence is within their reach.

Second, other men and women and, yes, young people have followed the admonition of the Savior and have loved their neighbors as themselves and helped to bring their neighbors' dreams to fulfilment and their ambitions to realization. ("The Precious Gift of Sight," Conference Report, April 1965, 46)

———

The Master could be found mingling with the poor, the downtrodden, the oppressed, and the afflicted. He brought hope to the hopeless, strength to the weak, and freedom to the captive. He taught of the better life to come—even eternal life. This knowledge ever directs those who receive the divine injunction: "Follow thou me." It guided Peter. It motivated Paul. It can determine our personal destiny. Can we make the decision to follow in righteousness and truth the Redeemer of the world? With his help a rebellious boy can become an obedient man, a wayward girl can cast aside the old self and begin anew. Indeed, the gospel of Jesus Christ can change men's lives. ("Yellow Canaries with Gray on Their Wings," *Ensign,* July 1973, 43)

CHARACTER

———

Perhaps the word "character" best describes one who is true to himself. For character takes no account of what you are thought to be, but what you are. Character is having an inner light and the courage to follow its dictates.

One who is true to himself develops the attributes needed to survive errors, to keep marching on a road that seems to be without end, and to rise above disappointment and distress. ("Yesterday, Today, and Tomorrow," Weber State College Baccalaureate, May 31, 1968)

———

Your decision to think right, choose right, and do right will rarely if ever be the easiest course to follow. Truth has never been so popular as error. Be ready to withstand the ridicule and mockery of the uninformed, the uncultured, the uninspired. However, men and women of character stand ready to respect a man of principle, a man of courage, a man of faith. ("Learning the ABC's at BYU," BYU Devotional, February 8, 1966)

CHARITY

———

What *is* charity? The prophet Mormon teaches us that "charity is the pure love of Christ" (Moroni 7:47). In his farewell message to the Lamanites, Moroni declared, "Except ye have charity ye can in nowise be saved in the kingdom of God" (Moroni 10:21).

I consider charity—or the "pure love of Christ"—to be the opposite of criticism and judging. In speaking of charity, I do not . . . have in mind the relief of the suffering through the giving of our substance. That, of course, is necessary and proper. . . . I have in mind the charity that manifests itself when we are tolerant of others and lenient toward their actions, the kind of charity that forgives, the kind of charity that is patient.

I have in mind the charity that impels us to be sympathetic, compassionate, and merciful, not only in times of sickness and affliction and distress but also in times of weakness or error on the part of others.

There is a serious need for the charity that gives attention to those who are unnoticed, hope to those who are discouraged, aid to those who are afflicted. True charity is love in action. The need for charity is everywhere.

Needed is the charity which refuses to find satisfaction in hearing or in repeating the reports of misfortunes that come to others, unless by so doing, the unfortunate one may be benefitted. The American educator and politician Horace Mann once said, "To pity distress is but human; to relieve it is godlike" (*Lectures on Education* [1845], 297).

Charity is having patience with someone who has let us down. It is resisting the impulse to become offended easily. It is accepting weaknesses and shortcomings. It is accepting people as they truly are. It is looking beyond physical appearances to attributes that will not dim through time. It is resisting the impulse to categorize others.

Charity, that pure love of Christ, is manifest when a group of young women from a singles ward travels hundreds of miles to attend the funeral services for the mother of one of their Relief Society sisters. Charity is shown when devoted visiting teachers return month after month, year after year to the same uninterested, somewhat critical sister. It is evident when an elderly widow is remembered and taken to ward functions and to Relief Society activities. It is felt when the sister sitting alone in Relief Society receives the invitation, "Come—sit by us."

In a hundred small ways, all of you wear the mantle of charity. Life is perfect for none of us. Rather than being judgmental and critical of each other, may we have the pure love of Christ for our fellow travelers in this journey through life. May we recognize that each one is doing her best to deal with the challenges which come her way, and may we strive to do *our* best to help out. ("Charity Never Faileth," *Ensign*, November 2010, 124–25)

⚔CHASTITY ⚔

Almost everywhere we turn, there are those who would have us believe that what was once considered immoral is now acceptable. I think of the scripture, "Wo unto them that call evil good, and good evil, that put darkness for light, and light for darkness" (2 Nephi 15:20). . . . We are reminded in the Book of Mormon that chastity and virtue are precious above all things. ("True to the Faith," *Ensign*, May 2006, 18)

You live in a world where moral values have, in great measure, been tossed aside, where sin is flagrantly on display, and where temptations to stray from the strait and narrow path surround you. Many are the voices telling you that you are far too provincial or that there is something wrong with *you* if you still believe there is such a thing as immoral behavior. . . .

Great courage will be required as you remain chaste and virtuous amid the accepted thinking of the times.

In the world's view today there is little thought that young men and young women will remain morally clean and pure before marriage. Does this make immoral behavior acceptable? Absolutely not!

The commandments of our Heavenly Father are not negotiable! ("May You Have Courage," *Ensign,* May 2009, 125)

CHILDREN

It is our solemn duty, our precious privilege—even our sacred opportunity—to welcome to our homes and to our hearts the children who grace our lives. ("Precious Children—A Gift from God," *Ensign,* November 1991, 67)

Children seem to be endowed with abiding faith in their Heavenly Father and His capacity and desire to answer their sweet prayers. It has been my personal experience that when a child prays, God listens. ("Precious Children—A Gift from God," *Ensign,* November 1991, 69)

May the laughter of children gladden our hearts. May the faith of children soothe our souls. May the love of children prompt our deeds. "Children are an heritage of the Lord" (Psalm 127:3). May our Heavenly Father ever bless these sweet souls, these special friends of the Master. ("Precious Children—A Gift from God," *Ensign,* November 1991, 70)

———

When we realize just how precious children are, we will not find it difficult to follow the pattern of the Master in our association with them. Not long ago, a sweet scene took place at the Salt Lake Temple. Children, who had been ever so tenderly cared for by faithful workers in the temple nursery, were now leaving in the arms of their mothers and fathers. One child turned to the lovely women who had been so kind to them and, with a wave of her arm, spoke the feelings of her heart as she exclaimed, "Goodnight, angels." ("A Little Child Shall Lead Them," *Ensign,* May 1990, 53)

———

Our children today are growing up surrounded by voices urging them to abandon that which is right and to pursue, instead, the pleasures of the world. Unless they have a firm foundation in the gospel of Jesus Christ, a testimony of the truth, and a determination to live righteously, they are susceptible to such influences. It is our responsibility to fortify and protect them.

To an alarming extent, our children today are being educated by the media, including the Internet. . . . The messages portrayed on television, in movies, and in other media are very often in direct opposition to that which we want our children to embrace and hold dear. It is our responsibility not only to teach them to be sound in spirit and doctrine but also to help them stay that way, regardless of the outside forces they may encounter. This will require much time and effort on our part— and in order to help others, we ourselves need the spiritual and moral courage to withstand the evil we see on every side. ("Three Goals to Guide You," *Ensign,* November 2007, 118–19)

———

In a Latter-day Saint home, children are not simply tolerated, but welcomed; not commanded, but encouraged; not driven, but guided; not neglected, but loved. ("Timeless Truths for a Changing World," BYU Women's Conference, May 4, 2001)

CHOICE AND ACCOUNTABILITY

———

We have the right to choose; likewise, we have the responsibility to choose. We cannot be neutral. There is no middle ground. The Lord knows this; Lucifer knows this. So there is a great campaign being waged today. On the one hand, Lucifer has attractively painted his road signs. You have read them; you have seen them. They are bright; they are attractive. They read something like this: "Eat, drink, and be merry, for tomorrow we die" (2 Nephi 28:7). Another may read: "It's the popular thing to do." And another: "Just this once won't matter."

On the other hand, the Lord has prepared His road signs for our guidance. They read: "Fear God and keep his commandments" (Ecclesiastes 12:13). Another: "Whatsoever ye sow, that shall ye also reap" (D&C 6:33). And yet another: "There is a law, irrevocably decreed in heaven before the foundations of this world, upon which all blessings are predicated—And when we obtain any blessing from God, it is by obedience to that law upon which it is predicated" (D&C 130:20–21). ("The Three R's of Choice," BYU Devotional, November 5, 1963)

———

No decision that Latter-day Saints must make is minor or unimportant, for every decision has a bearing upon our eternal welfare. I would urge you to stay close to the Lord. Call upon Him for guidance and for help in the choices which are placed before you. The results of these choices can be good, or they can be very damaging. They can have a bearing upon another's spiritual welfare through eternity, as well as directing one's own spiritual attainment. ("The Three R's of Choice," BYU Devotional, November 5, 1963)

———

If we choose to do that which is right, if we will be responsible in our choices, then the results of our choices will bring joy and happiness to our souls, for the Lord has told us, "I, the Lord, am merciful and gracious unto those who fear me, and delight to honor those who serve me in righteousness and in truth unto the end" (D&C 76:5).

I pray that our choice today will be that of serving the Lord in truth and in righteousness unto the end, that our Savior, our Mediator, our Lord Jesus Christ, of whom I testify . . . will be by our side and direct us throughout our lives and into eternity. ("The Three R's of Choice," BYU Devotional, November 5, 1963)

———

Scarcely an hour of the day goes by but what we are called upon to make choices of one sort or another. Some are trivial, some more far-reaching. Some will make no difference in the eternal scheme of things, and others will make *all* the difference. ("The Three Rs of Choice," *Ensign,* November 2010, 67)

✗
___

Each of us has come to this earth with all the tools necessary to make correct choices. The prophet Mormon tells us, "The Spirit of Christ is given to every man, that he may know good from evil" (Moroni 7:16).

We are surrounded—even at times bombarded—by the messages of the adversary. Listen to some of them; they are no doubt familiar to you: "Just this once won't matter." "Don't worry; no one will know." "You can stop smoking or drinking or taking drugs any time you want." "Everybody's doing it, so it can't be that bad." The lies are endless.

. . . Lucifer, that clever pied piper, plays his lilting melody and attracts the unsuspecting away from the safety of their chosen pathway, away from the counsel of loving parents, away from the security of God's teachings. He seeks not just the so-called refuse of humanity; he seeks all of us, including the very elect of God. King David listened, wavered, and then followed and fell. So did Cain in an earlier era and Judas Iscariot in a later one. Lucifer's methods are cunning; his victims, numerous.

We read of him in 2 Nephi: "Others will he pacify, and lull them away into carnal security" (2 Nephi 28:21). "Others he flattereth away, and telleth them there is no hell . . . until he grasps them with his awful chains" (2 Nephi 28:22). "And thus the devil cheateth their souls, and leadeth them away carefully down to hell" (2 Nephi 28:21).

When faced with significant choices, how do we decide? Do we succumb to the promise of momentary pleasure? To our urges and passions? To the pressure of our peers?

Let us not find ourselves as indecisive as is Alice in Lewis Carroll's classic *Alice's Adventures in Wonderland*. You will remember that she comes to a crossroads with two paths before her, each stretching onward but in opposite directions. She is confronted by the Cheshire cat, of whom Alice asks, "Which path shall I follow?"

The cat answers, "That depends where you want to go. If you do not know where you want to go, it doesn't matter which path you take" (*Alice's Adventures in Wonderland* [1898], 89).

Unlike Alice, we all know where we want to go, and it *does* matter which way we go, for by choosing our path, we choose our destination. ("The Three Rs of Choice," *Ensign*, November 2010, 67–68)

———

Whether you wear a green T-shirt or a blue one makes no difference in the long run. However, whether you decide to push a key on your computer which will take you to pornography can make *all* the difference in your life. You will have just taken a step off the straight, safe path. If a friend pressures you to drink alcohol or to try drugs and you succumb to the pressure, you are taking a detour from which you may not return. Brethren, whether we are 12-year-old deacons or mature high priests, we are susceptible. May we keep our eyes, our hearts, and our determination focused on that goal which is eternal and worth any price we will have to pay, regardless of the sacrifice we must make to reach it.

No temptation, no pressure, no enticing can overcome us unless we allow such. If we make the wrong choice, we have no one to blame but ourselves. President Brigham Young once expressed this truth by relating it to himself. Said he: "If Brother Brigham shall take a wrong track, and be shut out of the Kingdom of heaven, no person will be to blame but Brother Brigham. I am the only being in heaven, earth, or hell, that can be blamed." He continued: "This will equally apply to every Latter-day Saint. Salvation is an individual operation" (*Discourses of Brigham Young* [1999], 390). ("The Three Rs of Choice," *Ensign*, November 2010, 68–69)

You have great expectations—not through the generosity of an unknown benefactor, but through the inspired plan of a loving Heavenly Father who knows the end from the beginning and who is mindful of each of you. Why? Because He is your Father. . . . He has made careful and elaborate plans to help you grow and to achieve. He refers to His blueprint as "The Plan of Salvation." You are provided the God-given blessing of free agency. The pathway is marked. The blessings and penalties are shown clearly. But the choice is up to you. Of course there will be opposition. There always has been and always will be. That evil one, even Satan, desires that you become his follower, rather than a leader in your own right.

He has evil and designing men as his agents. Together they conspire to make evil appear to be good. In a most enticing manner he cunningly invites: "This is the way to happiness; come." Yet, that still, small voice within you cautions: "Not so. This doesn't seem right." A choice has to be made. There are no minor or insignificant decisions in your life. . . . Whether you like it or not, you are engaged in the race of your life. At stake is eternal life—yours. ("Leadership—Our Challenge Today," Explorer-Ensign Leadership Conference, August 18, 1967)

The way to exaltation is not a freeway featuring unlimited vision, unrestricted speeds, and untested skills. Rather, it is known by many forks and turnings, sharp curves, and controlled speeds. Your driving skill will be put to the test. Are you ready? You're driving. You haven't passed this way before. Fortunately, the Master Highway Builder, even our Heavenly Father, has provided a road map showing the route to follow. He has placed markers along the way to guide you to your destination.

Perhaps you may recognize some of His signs:

Honor thy father and thy mother.
Search the scriptures, for they are
    they which testify of me.
Seek ye first the kingdom of God and
    His righteousness.
Be ye clean.

That evil one, too, has placed road signs to frustrate your progress and to lead you from the path of truth into detours of sin. His detours all lead to a dead end. Have you noticed his markers:

Times have changed.
My love is mine to give; my life is mine
    to live.
It can't hurt anyone but me.
Just this once won't matter.

Now we see coming into focus the responsibility to choose; that inevitable crisis at the crossroads of life. He who would lead you down waits patiently for the dark night, a wavering will, a confused conscience, a mixed-up mind. Are you prepared to make the decision at the crossroads? ("Decisions Determine Destiny," LDS Student Association Young Women's Meeting, Logan, Utah, May 16, 1968)

———

Our Heavenly Father has given to each of us the power to think and reason and decide. With such power, self-discipline becomes a necessity.

Each of us has the responsibility to choose. You may ask, "Are decisions really that important?" I say to you, decisions determine destiny. You can't make eternal decisions without eternal consequences. ("Pathways to Perfection," *Ensign,* May 2002, 100)

———

Each of us knows those who do not have sight. We also know many others who walk in darkness at noonday. Those in this latter group may never carry the usual white cane and carefully make their way to the sound of its familiar tap, tap, tap. They may not have a faithful seeing-eye dog by their side nor carry a sign about their neck which reads, "I am blind." But blind they surely are. Some have been blinded by anger, others by indifference, by revenge, by hate, by prejudice, by ignorance, by neglect of precious opportunities.

Of such the Lord said, " . . . their ears are dull of hearing, and their eyes they have closed; lest at any time they should see with their eyes, and hear with their ears, and should understand with their heart, and should be converted, and I should heal them" (Matthew 13:15). ("The Precious Gift of Sight," Conference Report, April 1965, 45)

CHRISTMAS

———

This is a glorious time of the year, simple in origin, deep in meaning, beautiful in tradition and custom, rich in memories, and charitable in spirit. It has an attraction to which our hearts are readily drawn. This joyful season brings to each of us a measure of happiness that corresponds to the degree in which we have turned our minds, feelings, and actions to the Spirit of Christmas. ("May We See and Follow That Blessed Star," Employees Christmas Devotional, December 9, 1964)

———

There is no better time than now, this very Christmas season, for all of us to rededicate ourselves to the principles taught by Jesus the Christ. It is the time to love the Lord our God with all our heart and our neighbors as ourselves. It is well to remember that he who gives money gives much, he who gives time gives more, but he who gives of himself gives all. ("May We See and Follow That Blessed Star," Employees Christmas Devotional, December 9, 1964)

———

Charles Dickens, in his immortal *A Christmas Carol*, depicted the sorrow of opportunities lost. Jacob Marley's ghost, speaking to Ebenezer Scrooge, said, "Not to know that any Christian spirit working kindly in its little sphere, whatever it may be, will find its mortal life too short for its vast means of usefulness. Not to know that no space of regret can make amends for one life's opportunities misused! Yet such was I! Oh! such was I!"

"At this time of the rolling year," he said, "I suffer most. Why did I walk through crowds of fellow-beings with my eyes turned down, and never raise them to that blessed Star which led the Wise Men to a poor abode? Were there no poor homes to which its light would have conducted me!"

As the Christmas season envelops us with all its glory, may we remember that if we but look, we, too, may see a bright, particular star to guide us to our Christmas opportunity in service to our fellow man. ("May We See and Follow That Blessed Star," Employees Christmas Devotional, December 9, 1964)

———

Christmas is a wonderful time of year. It is a season when there are more smiles, more cheerful greetings, more acts of thoughtful kindness, more sweet remembrances of cherished friends and loved ones than are found through the rest of the entire year. In the troubled times in which we live, this is truly a miracle.

What is it that brings such love into our hearts, such joy into our lives? It is, of course, the spirit of Christmas. To catch the real meaning of the Spirit of Christmas, we need only drop the last syllable, and it becomes the Spirit of Christ. And one of the ways in which we obtain the Christmas spirit—the Christ spirit—is by willingly giving of ourselves to others. ("The Spirit of Christmas," First Presidency Christmas Devotional, December 4, 1994)

——

We must not let the commercial aspects of the glorious Christmas season dominate our lives. "What did you get for Christmas?" This is the universal question among children for days following that most celebrated holiday of the year. A small girl might reply: "I received a doll, a new dress, and a fun game." A boy might respond: "I received a pocketknife, a train, and a truck with lights." Newly acquired possessions are displayed and admired as Christmas day dawns, then departs.

The gifts so acquired are fleeting. Dolls break, dresses wear out, and fun games become boring. Pocketknives are lost, trains do nothing but go in circles, and trucks are abandoned when the batteries which power them dim and die.

If we change but one word in our Christmas question, the outcome is vastly different. "What did you *give* for Christmas?" prompts stimulating thought, causes tender feelings to well up and memory's fires to glow ever brighter. ("The Gifts of Christmas," First Presidency Christmas Devotional, December 2, 1990)

The Spirit of Christmas illuminates the picture window of the soul, and we look out upon the world's busy life and become more interested in people than things. ("The Gifts of Christmas," First Presidency Christmas Devotional, December 2, 2001)

———

We must make Christmas real. It isn't just tinsel and ribbon, unless we have made it so in our lives. Christmas is the spirit of giving without a thought of getting. It is happiness because we see joy in people. It is forgetting self and finding time for others. It is discarding the meaningless and stressing the true values. It is peace because we have found peace in the Savior's teachings. It is the time we realize most deeply that the more love is expended, the more there is of it for others. ("The Spirit of Christmas," First Presidency Christmas Devotional, December 4, 1994)

———

Christmas is many things to many people—from the eager, materialistic grasping of a child for a present to the deep spiritual thankfulness of the mature heart for the gift of a Savior. If there is one common denominator, perhaps it is this: Christmas is *love*. Christmas is the time when the bonds of family love transcend distance and inconvenience. It is a time when love of neighbor rises above petty day-to-day irritations, and doors swing open to give and receive expressions of appreciation and affection.

If to our Christmas gift list is added the gift of service—not only to friends and family, but also to those who badly need help—then our giving can be complete. ("A Christmas Dress for Ellen," First Presidency Christmas Devotional, December 7, 1997)

———

I reflect on the contrasts of Christmas. The extravagant gifts, expensively packaged and professionally wrapped, reach their zenith in the famed commercial catalogs carrying the headline "For the person who has everything." In one such reading I observed a four-thousand-square-foot home wrapped with a gigantic ribbon and comparable greeting card which said, "Merry Christmas." Other items included diamond-studded clubs for the golfer, a Caribbean cruise for the traveler, and a luxury trip to the Swiss Alps for the adventurer. Such seemed to fit the theme of a Christmas cartoon which showed the Three Wise Men traveling to Bethlehem with gift boxes on their camels. One says, "Mark my words, Balthazar, we're starting something with these gifts that's going to get way out of hand!" . . .

For a few moments, may we set aside the catalogs of Christmas, with their gifts of exotic description. Let's even turn from the flowers for mother, the special tie for Father, the cute doll, the train that whistles, the long-awaited bicycle—even the "Star Trek" books and videos—and direct our thoughts to those God-given gifts that endure. I have chosen from a long list just four:

> 1. The gift of birth.
> 2. The gift of peace.
> 3. The gift of love.
> 4. The gift of life eternal.

("Gifts," *Ensign*, May 1993, 59, 60)

———

Why does peace come closer to reality at [the Christmas] season than at any other? Why is it that more friends are re-membered and more enemies forgiven at the Christmas season than at any other time? It is the Christmas Spirit. The miracle of Christmas weaves the magic of brotherhood, fills hearts with peace, and causes a weary world to pause, to remember, and to hope. ("Christmas Is Love," First Presidency Christmas Devotional, December 5, 2004)

———

As Christmas comes, let it be a time that lights the eyes of children and puts laughter on their lips. Let it be a time for lifting the lives of those who live in loneliness. Let it be a time for calling our families together, for feeling a closeness to those who are near to us and a closeness also to those who are absent.

Let it be a time of prayers for peace, for the preservation of free principles, and for the protection of those who are far from us. Let it be a time of forgetting self and finding time for others. Let it be a time for discarding the meaningless and for stressing the true values. Let it be a time of peace because we have found peace in His teachings. ("Christmas Is Love," First Presidency Christmas Devotional, December 5, 2004)

———

Probably no other time of the year yields as many poignant memories as does Christmas. The Christmases we remember best generally have little to do with worldly goods, but a lot to do with families, with love, and with compassion and caring. This thought provides hope for those of us who fear that the simple meaning of the holiday is diluted by commercialism, or by opposition from those with differing religious views, or just by getting so caught up in the pressures of the season that we lose that special spirit we could otherwise experience.

For many people, "overdoing it" is especially common at this time of the year. We may take on too much for the time and energy we have. Perhaps we don't have enough money to spend for those things we feel we must purchase. Often our efforts at Christmastime result in feeling stressed out, wrung out and worn out during a time when instead we should feel the simple joys of commemorating the birth of the Babe in Bethlehem.

Usually, however, the special spirit of the season somehow finds its way into our hearts and into our lives despite the difficulties and distractions which may occupy our time and energy. ("The Spirit of the Season," First Presidency Christmas Devotional, December 6, 2009)

———

Finding the real joy of the [Christmas] season comes not in the hurrying and the scurrying to get more done or in the purchasing of obligatory gifts. Real joy comes as we show the love and compassion inspired by the Savior of the World. . . .

At this joyous season, may personal discords be forgotten and animosities healed. May enjoyment of the season include remembrance of the needy and afflicted. May our forgiveness reach out to those who have wronged us, even as we hope to be forgiven. May goodness abound in our hearts and love prevail in our homes.

As we contemplate how we're going to spend our money to buy gifts this holiday season, let us plan also for how we will spend our time in order to help bring the true spirit of Christmas into the lives of others. ("The Spirit of the Season," First Presidency Christmas Devotional, December 6, 2009)

———

With the pure love of Christ, let us walk in His footsteps as we approach the season celebrating His birth. As we do so, let us remember that He still lives and continues to be the "light of the world," who promised, "He that followeth me shall not walk in darkness, but shall have the light of life" (John 8:12). . . .

With the spirit of Christ in our lives, we will have good will and love toward all mankind, not only during this season, but throughout the year as well. ("The Spirit of the Season," First Presidency Christmas Devotional, December 6, 2009)

CHURCH CALLINGS

Remember, you are entitled to our Father's blessings. He did not call you to your privileged post to build alone, without guidance, trusting to luck. On the contrary, He knows your skills, He realizes your devotion, and He will convert your supposed inadequacies to recognized strengths. As you plan your project, don't fall victim to the temptation that ensnared Laman and Lemuel. When they received the awesome assignment to obtain the plates of Laban, the record indicates that they murmured, saying that it was a hard thing which they had been commanded to do. And they lost their opportunity and their reward. Rather, let your attitude be that of their brother, Nephi: "I will go and do the things which the Lord hath commanded" (1 Nephi 3:5–7). ("Building Bridges," Address to YWMIA Executives, June 24, 1967)

What does it mean to magnify a calling? It means to build it up in dignity and importance, to make it honorable and commendable in the eyes of all men, to enlarge and strengthen it, to let the light of heaven shine through it to the view of other men. And how does one magnify a calling? Simply by performing the service that pertains to it. ("The Call of Duty," *Ensign,* May 1986, 38)

———

We do not covet a position. Our response is affirmative when called, and we serve faithfully until released. This connotes a certain trust in God, that He knows best. Those who go upon their knees regarding their assignments which come to them are entitled to the inspiration of our Heavenly Father. ("Traditions," Dixie College Homecoming, November 2, 1986)

———

I was happy to hear [President James E. Faust] was called at 17 to be in the presidency—or the superintendency, as we called it—of the Sunday School. I had the same experience, only mine was the Young Men's Mutual Improvement Association. I thought to myself, *We were both called at 17 and served in the presidency of an auxiliary organization.* I think it was of necessity in my case, for it was wartime. On the other hand, I think there's a lesson there—that we can trust in the performance of young people who are younger than we are and who have a life before them, and who need to begin the scholarship and the responsibility of looking after the work of the Lord in a called and sustained assignment. (General Authority Training Meeting, April 2, 2003)

———

I was called to serve as bishop of the Sixth-Seventh Ward in Salt Lake City in May of 1950. . . . As a new bishopric, our first objective was to provide an assignment for each member. To help achieve this goal, we printed a small pamphlet which related the pioneer history of the ward, the friendly nature of its membership, and the need for all to serve.

How?

1. A dignified call preceded by earnest prayer;
2. An explanation concerning what was expected;
3. The presentation of the pamphlet, which contained fundamentals for successful teaching, such as:

   • A personality filled with religious quality;
   • A genuine interest in people;
   • A knowledge of the gospel;
   • A wholesome attitude;
   • A utilization of good teaching methods. . . .

Explained to the newly called was the specific help which would be provided. The teaching improvement course was explained. Help from the ward auxiliary organization presidency was assured. The fact that the ward had a significant number of relatively transient members was not considered a deterrent at all. Rather, this provided an ideal opportunity to reach and teach many more of our Heavenly Father's children. (" 'A New Spirit Will I Put within You,'" Satellite Priesthood Leadership Training, June 21, 2003)

———

If any . . . feel unprepared, even incapable of responding to a call to serve, to sacrifice, to bless the lives of others, remember the truth: "Whom God calls, God qualifies." He who notes the sparrow's fall will not abandon the servant's need. ("Tears, Trials, Trust, Testimony," *Ensign*, May 1987, 44)

———

Miracles are everywhere to be found when priesthood callings are magnified. When faith replaces doubt, when selfless service eliminates selfish striving, the power of God brings to pass His purposes. ("A Deacon Today—An Elder Tomorrow," Priesthood Restoration Commencement Satellite Broadcast, May 5, 1991)

———

Every bishop can testify to the promptings which attend calls to serve in the Church. Frequently the call seems to be for the benefit not so much of those to be taught or led as for the person who is to teach or lead. ("Called to Serve," *Ensign,* November 1991, 47)

———

Balance is key to us in our sacred and solemn responsibilities in our own homes and in our Church callings. We must use wisdom, inspiration and sound judgment as we care for our families and fulfill our Church callings, for each is vitally important. We cannot neglect our families; we must not neglect our Church callings. ("Heavenly Homes—Forever Families," Worldwide Leadership Training Satellite Broadcast, February 11, 2006)

———

Young Women leaders, do you know your girls? Do you understand their problems and their perplexities, yearnings, ambitions and hopes? Do you know how far they have traveled, the troubles they have experienced, the burdens they have carried, the sorrows they have borne?

I encourage you to reach out to them and love them. . . .

As we succeed, as we bring a girl back into activity, we will be answering a mother's fervent prayer, a father's greatest desire. Our names will forever be honored by those whom we reach. ("Sugar Beets and the Worth of a Soul," Message to Young Women, August 2005)

———

We do not appoint ourselves to the positions we occupy; there is order in the Church. Calls to serve come through that priesthood channel as established by our Heavenly Father. When we remember this, we can then appreciate that we are on the Lord's errand and thus entitled to His divine help. We can, with effectiveness, serve God and serve our fellowmen. ("The Quest for Peace," Munich Area Conference, August 26, 1973)

COMMITMENT

———

Steadfastness of purpose provides a refreshing breeze amidst the stale winds of indecision and lethargy. ("Constant Truths in Changing Times," BYU Commencement, May 26, 1967)

———

Signs of national weakness pose threats to our quest for the perfect life—and these threats grow more prevalent as each day goes by. Some of them are:

1. The growing trend toward personal non-involvement;
2. The rising tide of mediocrity; and
3. The choice of security over opportunity.

Refuse to compromise with expedience. Maintain the courage to defy the consensus. Choose the harder right instead of the easier wrong. By so doing, you will not detour, but rather ever remain on the way to perfection. ("Constant Truths in Changing Times," BYU Commencement, May 26, 1967)

The battle for the souls of men rages daily. The forces of evil do not yield ground willingly. We must not flinch nor falter. United in the cause of truth we shall prevail. ("Duty Calls," Regional Representatives Seminar, March 30, 1990)

Today we have a rebirth of ancient Sodom and Gomorrah. From seldom read pages in dusty Bibles they come forth as real cities in a real world, depicting a real malady—pernicious permissiveness.

We have the capacity and the responsibility to stand as a bulwark between all we hold dear and the fatal contamination of such sin. An understanding of who we are and what God expects us to become will prompt us to pray—as individuals and as families. Such a return reveals the constant truth, "Wickedness never was happiness" (Alma 41:10).

May each of us seek the good life—even life everlasting, with mother, father, brothers, sisters, husband, wife, sons and daughters, together forever.

Remember the Savior's words spoken to the Nephites: "Ye must watch and pray always lest ye enter into temptation; for Satan desireth to have you" (3 Nephi 18:18).

Let us join in the fervent declaration of Joshua: "Choose you this day whom ye will serve . . . but as for me and my house, we will serve the Lord" (Joshua 24:15). Let us shun those things which will drag us down. Let our hearts be pure. Let our lives be clean. ("I Will Serve the Lord," BYU Devotional, January 20, 2004)

Four pledges for the new year. I will listen, I will learn, I will labor, I will love. As we fulfill these pledges, we can have the guidance of our Heavenly Father and in our own lives experience true joy. Now, I don't simply mean that we should make a wish, or that we should dream a dream, but rather determine to do that which we pledge to accomplish. We can, if we will. . . . Now, shall we go forward with such resolutions? Can we change our practices if such need changing? I declare that we can. ("A Time to Choose," BYU Devotional, January 16, 1973)

———

It's important that we are fortified with truth that we might turn our backs to the adversary, that there will be no equivocation, that each man will make up his mind what to say and what to do under any circumstance. ("Truth, Service, Love," Copenhagen Area Conference, August 5, 1976)

COMMUNICATION

———

Listening is not a passive activity. To actively listen to another person requires willpower, concentration and great mental effort. Its rewards are great, because only then do you really learn to understand. ("Building Bridges," Address to YWMIA Executives, June 24, 1967)

———

Communication between people has been a principal problem throughout recorded history. It is complicated further when translation is involved.

A few years ago this country had some diplomatic problems which resulted in riots and general civil disturbance. Just when it appeared that agreement had been reached between Panama, the Canal Zone, and the United States, diplomatic relations came apart because the parties differed on the meaning of a single word. In the English language text, the two parties agreed to "discuss" differences.

The Spanish language text used the word *negociar*—"to negotiate." Americans assumed that negotiation meant (according to Funk and Wagnalls Standard College Dictionary) "a conference or discussion designed to produce an agreement." They felt this was synonymous with "discussion."

Panamanians thought that "to negotiate" implies a willingness to *renegotiate* existing treaties. It took months, patience, and the services of communications experts to bring about the ultimate understanding.

In another instance, the realization that the question of war or peace could depend upon effective communication brought about the establishment of the "hot line" between the world's nuclear capitals—Washington and Moscow—to avoid an inadvertent pushing of the panic button.

We have a communication problem as we wage war against the powers of the adversary and strive to help members of the Church to live by gospel principles. ("How to Communicate Effectively," General Authority Training Meeting, December 1967)

Effective communication always includes the three C's:

> CLEAR
> CONCISE
> CONFIRM

("How to Communicate Effectively," General Authority Training Meeting, December 1967)

———

To be concise means to express much in few words. The amount of time spent in communicating an idea may vary depending on the complexity of the subject matter and the previous knowledge of members of the audience. But communication is improved when each word, each sentence, each paragraph is meaningful and pertinent to the objective. ("How to Communicate Effectively," General Authority Training Meeting, December 1967)

———

Fragmentary listening, misinterpretation of ideas, mistaken meanings of words may cause misunderstandings. It is important, therefore, to have a method of checkup, feedback, and correction of mistaken impressions whenever possible. One labor negotiator found a very effective way to cool down heated arguments and improve communication in labor and management disputes. The referee made a rule that the representative of labor could not present his viewpoint until he could explain management's viewpoint to the satisfaction of the management representative and vice versa. ("How to Communicate Effectively," General Authority Training Meeting, December 1967)

———

Here are some of the methods that have been used successfully to improve communication skills:

1. *Improve your vocabulary* by keeping a dictionary available when reading or writing. Check words about which you have a question to see if your understanding of their meaning is the same as the dictionary definition. The listening vocabulary should be greater than the one you use to speak or write so you can learn on a higher level than that on which you speak or write.

2. *Read aloud* (as a drill) when the opportunity to do so presents itself. This strengthens the voice and makes it more clear. It helps the reader to enunciate words more clearly, carefully, and naturally. It helps to prevent speech mannerisms and monotonous patterns because the reader has an opportunity to use other people's word combinations. The reader should also practice voice inflection and develop a wider range of tones to make the voice more interesting. ("How to Communicate Effectively," General Authority Training Meeting, December 1967)

When we let the Lord be our guide in developing communication skills, He can help us to be humble, to present ourselves to the right people at the proper time and in an atmosphere where we will be trusted and worthy of a listening ear. When communication skills are accompanied by spirituality, the Lord can work through His servants to accomplish His purposes. ("How to Communicate Effectively," General Authority Training Meeting, December 1967)

What we say and how we say it tend to reflect what we are. In the life of the Apostle Peter, when he attempted to distance himself from Jesus and pretended to be other than what he was, his tormenters detected his true identity with the penetrating statement, "Thy speech bewrayeth thee" (Matthew 26:73). The words we utter will reflect the feelings of our hearts, the strength of our character, and the depth of our testimonies. ("The Upward Reach," *Ensign,* November 1993, 49)

———

[I] emphasize the responsibility to bridge the communications gap which often separates parents and their children.

For some this will be the minor task of closing a narrow fissure, while for others it will consist of crossing a chasm as wide as a canyon. All of us are active participants; none escapes. For the challenge to communicate is the dilemma of our age—even the opportunity of our generation. ("I Love You," MIA June Conference, June 28, 1968)

COMPASSION

———

Jesus provided us many examples of compassionate concern. The crippled man at the pool of Bethesda; the woman taken in adultery; the woman at Jacob's well; the daughter of Jairus; Lazarus, brother of Mary and Martha . . . each needed help.

To the cripple at Bethesda, Jesus said, "Rise, take up thy bed, and walk" (John 5:8). To the sinful woman came the counsel, "Go, and sin no more" (John 8:11). To help her who came to draw water, He provided a well of water, "springing up into everlasting life" (John 4:14). To the dead daughter of Jairus came the command, "Damsel, I say unto thee, arise" (Mark 5:41). To the entombed Lazarus, "Come forth"(John 11:43).

The Savior has always shown unlimited capacity for compassion. . . .

One may well ask the penetrating question: *These accounts pertain to the Redeemer of the world. Can there actually occur in my own life, on my own Jericho road, such a treasured experience?*

I phrase my answer in the words of the Master, "Come and see" (John 1:39). ("Compassion," *Ensign,* May 2001, 18)

———

We have no way of knowing when our privilege to extend a helping hand will unfold before us. The road to Jericho each of us travels bears no name, and the weary traveler who needs our help may be one unknown. ("Compassion," *Ensign*, May 2001, 18)

———

What power, what tenderness, what compassion did our Master . . . demonstrate! We, too, can bless if we will but follow His noble example. Opportunities are everywhere. Needed are eyes to see the pitiable plight and ears to hear the silent pleadings of a broken heart. Yes, and a soul filled with compassion, that we might communicate not only eye to eye or voice to ear but, in the majestic style of the Savior, even heart to heart. ("Meeting Life's Challenges," *Ensign*, November 1993, 71)

———

Consider . . . the aged, the widowed, the sick. All too often they are found in the parched and desolate wilderness of isolation called loneliness. When youth departs, when health declines, when vigor wanes, when the light of hope flickers ever so dimly, the members of these vast "lost battalions" can be rescued by the hand that helps and the heart that knows compassion. ("In Remembrance," Freedom Festival, Provo, Utah, June 28, 1998)

———

As I ponder [the Savior's] words, I can almost hear the shuffle of sandaled feet, the murmurs of astonishment from listeners as they echo from Capernaum's peaceful scene. Here multitudes crowded around Jesus, bringing the sick to be healed. A palsied man picked up his bed and walked, and a Roman centurion's faith restored his servant's health.

Not only by precept did Jesus teach, but also by example. He was faithful to his divine mission. He stretched forth his hand, that others might be lifted toward God.

At Galilee there came to him a leper who pleaded: "Lord, if thou wilt, thou canst make me clean. And Jesus put forth his hand, and touched him, saying, I will; be thou clean. And immediately his leprosy was cleansed" (Matthew 8:2–3). The hand of Jesus was not polluted by touching the leper's body, but the leper's body was cleansed by the touch of that holy hand.

In Capernaum, at the house of Peter, yet another example was provided. The mother of Peter's wife lay sick of a fever. The sacred record reveals that Jesus came "and took her by the hand, and lifted her up; and immediately the fever left her. . . ." (Mark 1:31). . . .

The beloved apostles noted well his example. He lived not so to be ministered unto, but to minister; not to receive, but to give; not to save his life, but to pour it out for others.

If they would see the star which should at once direct their feet and influence their destiny, they must look for it, not in the changing skies or outward circumstance, but each in the depth of his own heart and after the pattern provided by the Master.

Reflect for a moment on the experience of Peter at the gate Beautiful of the temple. One sympathizes with the plight of the man lame from birth who each day was carried to the temple gate that he might ask alms of all who entered. That he asked alms of Peter and John as these two brethren approached indicates that he regarded them no differently from scores of others who must have passed by him that day. Then Peter's majestic yet gentle command: "Look on us" (Acts 3:4). The record states that the lame man gave heed unto them, expecting to receive something from them.

The stirring words Peter then spoke have lifted the hearts of honest believers down through the stream of time, even to this day: "Silver and gold have I none; but such as I have give I thee: In the name of Jesus Christ of Nazareth rise up and walk."

Frequently we conclude the citation at this point and fail to note the next verse: "And he took him by the right hand, and lifted him up: . . . he . . . stood, and walked, and entered with them into the temple" (Acts 3:6–8).

A helping hand had been extended. A broken body had been healed. A precious soul had been lifted toward God.

Time passes. Circumstances change. Conditions vary. Unaltered is the divine command to succor the weak and lift up the hands which hang down and strengthen the feeble knees. Each of us has the charge to be not a doubter, but a doer; not a leaner, but a lifter. ("With Hand and Heart," *Ensign*, December 1971, 131–32)

———

Each of us, in the journey through mortality, will travel his own Jericho Road. What will be your experience? What will be mine? Will I fail to notice him who has fallen among thieves and requires my help? Will you?

Will I be one who sees the injured and hears his plea, yet crosses to the other side? Will you?

Or will I be one who sees, who hears, who pauses, and who helps? Will you?

Jesus provided our watchword, "Go, and do thou likewise." When we obey that declaration, there opens to our eternal view a vista of joy seldom equaled and never surpassed.

Now the Jericho Road may not be clearly marked. Neither may the injured cry out, that we may hear. But when we walk in the steps of that good Samaritan, we walk the pathway that leads to perfection. ("Your Jericho Road," *Ensign*, May 1977, 71)

———

Frequently when we watch the news on television or pick up a newspaper, we learn of terrible human suffering as a result of tornadoes, floods, fires, drought, hurricanes, earthquakes, conflicts of war. I ask the question: Do we have a responsibility to do something about such suffering?

Long years ago a similar question was posed and preserved in Holy Writ, even the Bible, and I quote from the book of Genesis: "And Cain talked with Abel his brother: and it came to pass, when they were in the field, that Cain rose up against Abel his brother, and slew him. And the Lord said unto Cain, Where is Abel thy brother? And he said, I know not: Am I my brother's keeper?" (Genesis 4:8–9) The answer to that vital question is: *Yes, we are our brothers' keepers.* ("My Brother's Keeper," BYU Management Society, Bay Area Chapter, February 12, 1999)

———

Particularly among the young, there are those who are tragically involved in such things as drugs, immorality, gangs, and all the serious problems that go with them. In addition, there are those who are lonely, including widows and widowers, who long for the company and concern of others. May we ever be mindful of the needs of those around us and be ready to extend a helping hand and a loving heart. ("Until We Meet Again," *Ensign*, November 2008, 107)

CONSCIENCE

———

Doing what's right is the easiest thing to judge of all. Whenever you're about to do something and that little voice in your head stops you and asks the question, "Should I?" the chances are you shouldn't. We all have a conscience, and it's there for a purpose. We should always be guided by it, rather than running from it. ("Duty—Honor—Country," National Boy Scouts of America Duty to God Breakfast, May 29, 2003)

———

It has been said that conscience warns us as a friend before it punishes us as a judge. The expression of one young man is a sermon in itself. When asked when he was happiest, he replied, "I'm happiest when I don't have a guilty conscience." ("Happiness—The Universal Quest," Church Educational System Fireside, March 7, 1993)

———

In the private sanctuary of one's own conscience lies that spirit, that determination, to cast off the old person and to measure up to the stature of true potential. But the way is rugged and the course is strenuous. ("Happiness—The Universal Quest," Church Educational System Fireside, March 7, 1993)

CONVERSION

———

Come from your wandering way, weary traveler. Come to the gospel of Jesus Christ. Come to that heavenly haven called home. Here you will discover the truth. Here you will learn the reality of the Godhead, the comfort of the plan of salvation, the sanctity of the marriage covenant, the power of personal prayer. Come home. . . .

Many of you have traveled long in a personal quest for that which rings true. The Church of Jesus Christ of Latter-day Saints sends forth to you an earnest appeal. Open your doors to the missionaries. Open your minds to the word of God. Open your hearts—even your very souls—to the sound of that still, small voice which testifies of truth. As the prophet Isaiah promised: "Thine ears shall hear a word . . . , saying, This is the way, walk ye in it" (Isaiah 30:21). ("Dedication Day," *Ensign,* November 2000, 66)

CONTENTION
(SEE ALSO ANGER)

———

I would plead with you to rid from your lives any spirit of contention, any spirit wherein we might vie one with another for the spoils of life, but rather that we might cooperatively work with our brethren and with our sisters for the fruits of the gospel of Jesus Christ. ("The Spirit of Christmas," BYU Devotional, December 6, 1966)

———

Sometimes we can take offense so easily. On other occasions we are too stubborn to accept a sincere apology. Who will subordinate ego, pride, and hurt—then step forward with, "I am truly sorry! Let's be as we once were: friends. Let's not pass to future generations the grievances, the anger of our time." Let's remove any hidden wedges that can do nothing but destroy.

Where do [offenses] originate? Some come from unresolved disputes, which lead to ill feelings, followed by remorse and regret. Others find their beginnings in disappointments, jealousies, arguments, and imagined hurts. We must solve them—lay them to rest and not leave them to canker, fester, and ultimately destroy. ("Hidden Wedges," *Ensign,* May 2002, 20)

Courage

Some of us remember David as a shepherd boy divinely commissioned by the Lord through the prophet Samuel. Others of us know him as a mighty warrior, for doesn't the record show the chant of the adoring women following his many victorious battles, "Saul hath slain his thousands, and David his ten thousands" (1 Samuel 18:7)? Or perhaps we look upon him as the inspired poet or as one of Israel's greatest kings. Still others recall that he violated the laws of God and took that which belonged to another—the beautiful Bathsheba. He even arranged the death of her husband, Uriah.

I, however, like to think of David as the righteous lad who had the courage and the faith to face insurmountable odds when all others hesitated, and to redeem the name of Israel by facing that giant in his life—Goliath of Gath.

Well might we look carefully into our own lives and judge our courage, our faith. Is there a Goliath in your life? Is there one in mine? Does he stand squarely between you and your desired happiness? Oh, your Goliath may not carry a sword or hurl a verbal challenge of insult that all may hear and force you to decision. He may not be ten feet tall, but he likely will appear equally as formidable, and his silent challenge may shame and embarrass.

One man's Goliath may be the stranglehold of a cigarette or perhaps an unquenchable thirst for alcohol. To another, his Goliath may be an unruly tongue or a selfish streak which causes him to spurn the poor and the downtrodden.

Envy, greed, fear, laziness, doubt, vice, pride, lust, selfishness, discouragement—all spell Goliath.

The giant you face will not diminish in size or in power or strength by your vain hoping, wishing, or waiting for him to do so. Rather, he increases in power as his hold upon you tightens.

The poet Alexander Pope truly describes this truth:

"Vice is a monster of so frightful mien,

As, to be hated, needs but to be seen;

Yet seen too oft, familiar with her face,

We first endure, then pity, then embrace."

The battle for our immortal souls is no less important than the battle fought by David. The enemy is no less formidable, the help of Almighty God no farther away. What will our action be? Like David of old, "our cause is just." We have been placed upon earth not to fail or fall victim to temptation's snare, but rather to succeed. Our giant, our Goliath, must be conquered. . . .

May we ever remember that we do not go forth alone to battle against the Goliaths of our lives. As David declared to Israel, so might we echo the knowledge, " . . . the battle is the Lord's, and he will give [Goliath] into our hands" (1 Samuel 17:47).

The battle must be fought. Victory cannot come by default. So it is in the battles of life. . . . Our most significant opportunities will be found in times of greatest difficulty.

The vast, uncharted expanse of the Atlantic Ocean stood as a Goliath between Christopher Columbus and the new world. The hearts of his comrades became faint, their courage dimmed, hopelessness engulfed them; but Columbus prevailed with his watchword, "Westward, ever Westward, sail on, sail on."

Carthage jail; an angry mob with painted faces; certain death faced the Prophet Joseph Smith. But from the wellsprings of his abundant faith he calmly met the Goliath of death. "I am going like a lamb to the slaughter; but I am calm as a summer's morning; I have a conscience void of offense towards God, and towards all men" (D&C 135:4).

Gethsemane, Golgotha, intense pain and suffering beyond the comprehension of mortal man stood between Jesus the Master and victory over the grave. Yet He lovingly assured us, " . . . I go to prepare a place for you, . . . that where I am, there ye may be also" (John 14:2, 3).

And what is the significance of these accounts? Had there been no ocean, there would have been no Columbus. No jail, no Joseph. No mob, no martyr. No cross, no Christ!

Should there be a Goliath in our lives or a giant called by any other name, we need not "flee" or be "sore afraid" as we go up to battle against him. Rather we can find assurance and divine help in that inspired psalm of David: "The Lord is my shepherd; I shall not want . . .

"Yea, though I walk through the valley of the shadow of death, I will fear no evil: for thou art with me" (Psalm 23:1, 4). ("Meeting Your Goliath," Conference Report, October 1967, 130–31, 132–33)

———

Let us have the courage to defy the consensus, the courage to stand for principle. Courage, not compromise, brings the smile of God's approval. Courage becomes a living and an attractive virtue when it is regarded not only as a willingness to die manfully, but as the determination to live decently. A moral coward is one who is afraid to do what he thinks is right because others will disapprove or laugh. Remember that all men have their fears, but those who face their fears with dignity have courage as well. ("Courage Counts," *Ensign,* November 1986, 41)

———

May we muster courage at the crossroads, courage for the conflicts, courage to say "No," courage to say yes, for *courage counts.* ("Courage Counts," *Ensign,* November 1986, 42)

———

Some foolish persons turn their backs on the wisdom of God and follow the allurement of fickle fashion, the attraction of false popularity, and the thrill of the moment. Courage is required to think right, choose right, and do right, for such a course will rarely, if ever, be the easiest to follow. ("Pathways to Perfection," *Ensign,* May 2002, 100)

———

Do you remember the game of childhood, "Run Sheepie Run"? He who would look for the carefully hidden sheep would announce his search, "Ready or not, here I come!" So it is with the challenges of daily living—"Ready or not, here they come." How will you meet them? Bravely or cowardly? How will they leave you? Victorious or defeated? The outcome will depend largely on these seven guideposts: . . .

> Your Perspective
> Your Determination
> Your Courage
> Your Love
> Your Wisdom
> Your Humility
> Your Faith

("Return with Honor," BYU Devotional, January 19, 1971)

———

Courage is not so much the willingness to die manfully as to live decently. The greatest battle of life is fought within the silent chambers of one's own soul. ("Each Must Choose," Manchester Area Conference, August 29, 1971)

As I contemplate all that you face in the world today, one word comes to my mind. It describes an attribute needed by all of us but one which you—at this time of your life and in this world—will need particularly. That attribute is courage. . . .

- First, the courage to refrain from judging others;
- Second, the courage to be chaste and virtuous; and
- Third, the courage to stand firm for truth and righteousness.

("May You Have Courage," *Ensign*, May 2009, 124)

The philosophies of men surround us. The face of sin today often wears the mask of tolerance. Do not be deceived; behind that facade is heartache, unhappiness, and pain. You know what is right and what is wrong, and no disguise, however appealing, can change that. The character of transgression remains the same. If your so-called friends urge you to do anything you know to be wrong, *you* be the one to make a stand for right, even if you stand alone. Have the moral courage to be a light for others to follow. There is no friendship more valuable than your own clear conscience, your own moral cleanliness—and what a glorious feeling it is to know that you stand in your appointed place clean and with the confidence that you are worthy to do so. ("Examples of Righteousness," *Ensign*, May 2008, 65)

CREATION

If there is a design in this world in which we live, there must be a Designer. Who can behold the many wonders of the universe without believing that there is a design for all mankind? Who can doubt that there is a Designer?

In the book of Genesis we learn that the Grand Designer created the heaven and the earth: "And the earth was without form, and void; and darkness was upon the face of the deep."

"Let there be light," said the Grand Designer, "and there was light." He created a firmament. He separated the land from the waters and said, "Let the earth bring forth grass, . . . the fruit tree yielding fruit after his kind, whose seed is in itself."

Two lights He created—the sun and the moon. Came the stars by His design. He called for living creatures in the water and fowls to fly above the earth. And it was so. He made cattle, beasts, and creeping things. The design was nearly complete.

Last of all, He created man in His own image—male and female—with dominion over all other living things (see Genesis 1:1–27).

Man alone received intelligence—a brain, a mind, and a soul. Man alone, with these attributes, had the capacity for faith and hope, for inspiration and ambition.

Who could persuasively argue that man—the noblest work of the Great Designer, with dominion over all living things, with a brain and a will, with a mind and a soul, with intelligence and divinity—should come to an end when the spirit forsakes its earthly temple? ("He Is Risen!" *Ensign,* May 2010, 87–88)

———

God left the world unfinished for man to work his skill upon. He left the electricity in the cloud, the oil in the earth. He left the rivers unbridged, the forests unfelled and the cities unbuilt. God gives to us the challenge of raw materials, not the ease of finished things. He leaves the pictures unpainted and the music unsung and the problems unsolved, that we might know the joys and glories of creation. ("Your Future Awaits,"

BYU College of Engineering and Technology Convocation, April 25, 2003)

DEATH
(SEE ALSO RESURRECTION)

———

At some period in our mortal mission, there appears the faltering step, the wan smile, the pain of sickness—even the fading of summer, the approach of autumn, the chill of winter, and the experience we call death, which comes to all mankind. It comes to the aged as they walk on faltering feet. Its summons is heard by those who have scarcely reached midway in life's journey. Often it hushes the laughter of little children.

Throughout the world there is enacted daily the sorrowful scene of loved ones mourning as they bid farewell to a son, a daughter, a brother, a sister, a mother, a father, or a cherished friend. . . .

Let us remember that after the funeral flowers fade, the well wishes of friends become memories, and the prayers offered and words spoken dim in the corridors of the mind. Those who grieve frequently find themselves alone. Missed is the laughter of children, the commotion of teenagers, and the tender, loving concern of a departed companion. The clock ticks more loudly, time passes more slowly, and four walls can indeed a prison make.

I extol those who, with loving care and compassionate concern, feed the hungry, clothe the naked, and house the homeless. He who notes the sparrow's fall will not be unmindful of such service. ("Compassion," *Ensign,* May 2001, 19)

Frequently death comes as an intruder. It is an enemy that suddenly appears in the midst of life's feast, putting out its lights and gaiety. . . .

There is only one source of true peace. I am certain that the Lord, who notes the fall of a sparrow, looks with compassion upon those who have been called upon to part—even temporarily—from their precious [loved ones]. The gifts of healing and of peace are your greatest needs, and He, through His Atonement, has provided them for one and all.

The prayer of faith will calm grieving hearts. The peace promised by the Savior will bless your lives, for He declared: "Peace I leave with you, my peace I give unto you: not as the world giveth, give I unto you. Let not your heart be troubled, neither let it be afraid. . . . In my father's house are many mansions: if it were not so, I would have told you. I go to prepare a place for you. . . . that where I am, there ye may be also" (John 14:27, 2–3).

The psalmist provided this assurance: "Weeping may endure for a night, but joy cometh in the morning" (Psalm 30:5).

True joy is found in holy temples of our Heavenly Father. I can think of no greater incentive to inspire compliance with God's commandments and entry to His holy house than the beckoning love of those who have gone ahead and plead for us to follow. As we strive with determination to do so, no way will be too steep, no path too long. Jesus Christ, the Savior of the world, invites us to follow Him: "Come unto me, all ye that labour and are heavy laden, and I will give you rest. Take my yoke upon you, and learn of me; for I am meek and lowly in heart: and ye shall find rest unto your souls" (Matthew 11:28–29). ("And a Little Child Shall Lead Them," Funeral for five little girls, August 12, 1998)

Death lays its heavy hand upon those dear to us and at times leaves us baffled and wondering. In certain situations, as in great suffering and illness, death comes as an angel of mercy. But for the most part, we think of it as the enemy of human happiness. . . .

Out of the darkness and horror of Calvary came the voice of the Lamb, saying, "Father, into thy hands I commend my spirit" (Luke 23:46). And the dark was no longer dark, for He was with His Father. He had come from God, and to Him He had returned. So also those who walk with God in this earthly pilgrimage know from blessed experience that He will not abandon His children who trust in Him. ("Now Is the Time," *Ensign*, November 2001, 59)

We laugh, we cry, we work, we play, we love, we live. And then we die. Death is our universal heritage. All must pass its portals. . . . In the words of the Apostle Paul, "It is appointed unto men once to die" (Hebrews 9:27).

And dead we would remain but for one Man and His mission, even Jesus of Nazareth. ("I Know That My Redeemer Lives!" *Ensign*, May 2007, 24)

Debt

Perhaps no counsel has been repeated more often than how to manage wisely our income. Consumer debt in some nations of the world is at staggering levels. Too many in the Church have failed to avoid unnecessary debt. They have little, if any, financial reserve. The solution is to budget, to live within our means, and to save some for the future. (Address at Regional Representatives Seminar, April 4, 1986)

——

Feelings become strained, quarrels more frequent and nerves frayed when excessive debt knocks on the family door. . . .

When emergency situations arise, the difficulty may become drastic when resources are stretched to pay for the rent, food, and clothing and, in addition, to service debt. Resources channeled to make payment on debt do not put one crumb on the table, provide one degree of warmth in the house, or bring one thread into a garment. Many more people could ride out the storm-tossed waves in their economic lives if they had their year's supply of food and clothing and were debt-free. Today we find that many have followed this counsel in reverse: they have at least a year's supply of debt and are food-free. ("Timeless Truths for a Changing World," BYU Women's Conference, May 4, 2001)

——

We must learn to separate need from greed. . . . Enticements to embrace the demon of debt are thrust upon us many times each day. . . . We must not allow our yearnings to exceed our earnings. ("Peace, Be Still," *Ensign*, November 2002, 53, 54)

——

Credit card charges continue to soar. Exorbitant interest rates hit hard those who are slow to pay. Rather than reserving debt for essential items, such as a home or transportation, many charge everything. I even observed a young woman use a charge card to buy a chocolate malt and an order of french fries.

. . . [We] are urged by financial institutions, through radio, television and newspapers, to "take advantage of tax deductions by seeking a home-equity loan." The ease of obtaining such a loan is made most attractive. The repayment of the loan is made to appear simple, with interest-only payments being made for a number of years, if desired. The gullible, the spendthrift, the "live for today, tomorrow will take care of itself" advocates borrow to the hilt and buy, buy, and buy. Nowhere is there mentioned that this easily acquired loan represents a dreaded second mortgage on the very home in which the family lives. ("Prophets Speak—The Wise Obey," General Conference Friday Leadership Session, April 3, 1987)

———

We urge all Latter-day Saints to be prudent in their planning, to be conservative in their living, and to avoid excessive or unnecessary debt. The financial affairs of the Church are being managed in this manner, for we are aware that your tithing and other contributions have not come without sacrifice and are sacred funds. ("To Learn, to Do, to Be," *Ensign*, May 1992, 47)

———

One cannot continually spend more than he earns and remain solvent. This law applies to nations as well as to men. A worker cannot, in the long run, adhere to a philosophy of something for nothing as opposed to something for something. Nor can management dismiss as optional the necessity of an adequate corporate profit and a reasonable return to shareholders if our economy of free enterprise is to flourish. ("In Quest of the Abundant Life," Utah State University Baccalaureate, June 2, 1967)

———

We hear the radio and the television and see the newspaper advertising for all they are worth promoting the importance of buying immediately the product that is being advertised. I have watched television once in a while, and . . . I hear this comment: "Just phone now and give us the number of your credit card, and you will automatically receive this" or "receive that" without any problems. That's what they think! This illusion that credit cards can bring great joy and easy credit without problems is a fallacious idea.

The other one that bothers me is when the credit card advertisers will say something like this: "You may pay in full or, if you choose, the minimum payment is _____ ." By following that come-on and making the minimum payment, you just add to your long-term debt. The interest rate—don't you believe it when they say it is under 10%. It goes way over on that balance that you are projecting into an unforeseen future. So be careful of that. (General Authority Training Meeting, March 29, 2007)

———

Let us be content with what we have, and make sure that we are able, if we move a little beyond, that it is not beyond our financial reach. Then we will have happier marriages. We will have fewer bankruptcies. We will have people who have that smile of being out of debt or in controlled debt, without the specter of losing their home and all they have when the inability to pay dawns upon them. (General Authority Training Meeting, March 29, 2007)

Avoid the philosophy that yesterday's luxuries have become today's necessities. They aren't necessities unless we make them so. Many enter into long-term debt only to find that changes occur: people become ill or incapacitated, companies fail or downsize, jobs are lost, natural disasters befall us. For many reasons, payments on large amounts of debt can no longer be made. Our debt becomes as a Damocles sword hanging over our head and threatening to destroy us.

I urge you to live within your means. One cannot spend more than one earns and remain solvent. I promise you that you will then be happier than you would be if you were constantly worrying about how to make the next payment on nonessential debt. In the Doctrine and Covenants we read: "Pay the debt thou hast contracted. . . . Release thyself from bondage" (D&C 19:35). ("True to the Faith," *Ensign,* May 2006, 19)

This is a day of borrowing, this is a day where credit cards by the bushel are sent out in every mailing. You no doubt receive them. According to recent statistics, the average American has 10 credit cards. It's so easy to buy on time, without reading the small print. A fairly low interest rate may apply for the first 60 days or so, but one generally doesn't realize that after that period, the interest rate increases dramatically. As an example of how much interest one pays at such a rate, if a person owed just $500 in credit card debt, had a rate of 18.5% interest, and paid a minimum payment of $10 per month, it would take 7 years and 10 months to pay the debt in full. In addition to paying the principal of $500, one would have paid $430 in interest for the privilege of borrowing the $500. . . .

If you use a credit card, pay the remaining balance promptly. Don't stretch your payments out. ("I Will Serve the Lord," BYU Devotional, January 20, 2004)

DECISIONS
(SEE ALSO CHOICE AND ACCOUNTABILITY)

———

Perhaps the renowned author Charles Dickens, without really realizing his prophetic powers, described our day when he spoke of a period two centuries ago. His classic *A Tale of Two Cities* begins:

> It was the best of times, it was the worst of times;
> It was the age of wisdom, it was the age of foolishness;
> It was the epoch of belief, it was the epoch of incredulity;
> It was the season of Light, it was the season of Darkness;
> It was the spring of hope, it was the winter of despair;
> We had everything before us, we had nothing before us . . .

This is your world. Whether you like it or not, you are engaged in the race of your life. At stake is eternal life—yours. What shall be the outcome? Will you be a leader of men and a servant of God? Or will you be a servant of sin and a follower of Satan? ("Pathway to Eternal Life," LDS Student Association Fireside, November 5, 1967)

———

It has been said that history turns on small hinges, and so do people's lives. Decisions determine destiny. That is why it is worthwhile to look ahead, to set a course, to be at least partly ready when the moment of decision comes. ("Your Choice," BYU Devotional, March 10, 1998)

———

May I provide a simple formula by which you can measure the choices which confront you. It's easy to remember: "You can't be right by doing wrong; you can't be wrong by doing right." ("Pathways to Perfection," *Ensign*, May 2002, 100)

———

There is no resting place along the path called faithfulness. The trek is constant, and no lingering is allowed. It must not be expected that the road of life spreads itself in an unobstructed view before the person starting his journey. He must anticipate coming upon forks and turnings in the road. But he cannot hope to reach his desired journey's end if he thinks aimlessly about whether to go east or west. He must make decisions purposefully. ("Happiness—The Universal Quest," Church Educational System Fireside, March 7, 1993)

DISABILITIES

———

There are those situations where children come to mortality with a physical or mental handicap. Try as we will, it is not possible to know why or how such events occur. I salute those parents who without complaint take such a child into their arms and into their lives and provide that added measure of sacrifice and love to one of Heavenly Father's children.

[One] summer at Aspen Grove Family Camp, I observed a mother patiently feeding a teenage daughter injured at birth and totally dependent upon Mother. Mother administered each spoonful of food, each swallow of water, while holding steady the head and neck of her daughter. Silently I thought to myself, *For seventeen years, Mother has provided this service and all others to her daughter, never thinking of her own comfort, her own pleasure, her own food.* May God bless such mothers, such fathers, such children. And He will. ("Precious Children—A Gift from God," *Ensign,* November 1991, 68)

———

Mothers and fathers who anxiously await the arrival of a precious child sometimes learn that all is not well with this tiny infant. A missing limb, sightless eyes, a damaged brain, or the term "Down's syndrome" greets the parents, leaving them baffled, filled with sorrow, and reaching out for hope.

There follows the inevitable blaming of oneself, the condemnation of a careless action, and the perennial questions: "Why such a tragedy in our family?" "Why didn't I keep her home?" "If only he hadn't gone to that party." "How did this happen?" "Where was God?" "Where was a protecting angel?" *If, why, where, how*—those recurring words—do not bring back the lost son, the perfect body, the plans of parents, or the dreams of youth. Self-pity, personal withdrawal, or deep despair will not bring the peace, the assurance, or help which are needed. Rather, we must go forward, look upward, move onward, and rise heavenward.

It is imperative that we recognize that whatever has happened to us has happened to others. They have coped and so must we. We are not alone. Heavenly Father's help is near. ("Miracles—Then and Now," *Ensign,* November 1992, 68–69).

———

To all who have suffered silently from sickness, to you who have cared for those with physical or mental impairment, who have borne a heavy burden day by day, year by year, and to you noble mothers and dedicated fathers—I salute you and pray God's blessings to ever attend you. To the children, particularly they who cannot run and play and frolic, come the reassuring words: "Dearest children, God is near you, Watching o'er you day and night" (*Hymns,* no. 96).

There will surely come that day, even the fulfillment of the precious promise from the Book of Mormon:

"The soul shall be restored to the body, and the body to the soul; yea, and every limb and joint shall be restored to its body; yea, even a hair of the head shall not be lost; but all things shall be restored to their proper and perfect frame. . . .

"And then shall the righteous shine forth in the kingdom of God" (Alma 40:23, 25). ("Miracles—Then and Now," *Ensign*, November 1992, 70)

———

Have you experienced the frustration of wanting but not knowing how to help he who walks stiffly behind his seeing eye canine companion, or she who moves so slowly with the aid of a white cane? There are many who are lost in this trackless desert of darkness.

If you desire to see a rescue operation of a "lost battalion," visit your city's center for the blind and witness the selfless service of those who read to those who can't. Observe the skills which are taught the handicapped. Be inspired by the efforts put forth in their behalf to enable them to secure meaningful employment.

Those who labor so willingly and give so generously to those who have lost so tragically find ample reward in the light which they bring into the lives of so many. ("In Remembrance," Freedom Festival, Provo, Utah, June 28, 1998)

DISCIPLESHIP

———

By following this formula, . . . we can find faith, . . . learn love, . . . [and] choose Christ:

When you recognize sin, shun it.
When you make a mistake, admit it.
When you receive a gift, share it.
When you enjoy freedom, protect it.
When you have the truth, live it.
When you have a duty, do it.

("Honor Thy Father and Thy Mother," BYU Fourteen-Stake Fireside, December 3, 1978)

———

Down through the generations of time, the message from Jesus has been the same. To Peter and Andrew by the shores of the beautiful Sea of Galilee, He said, "Follow me" (Matthew 4:19). To Philip of old came the call, "Follow me" (John 1:43). To the Levite who sat at receipt of customs came the instruction, "Follow me" (Luke 5:21). And to you and to me, if we but listen, will come that same beckoning invitation, "Follow me." ("Models to Follow," *Ensign*, November 2002, 67).

———

Take the Lord as your guide. Do not lend a listening ear to the persuasive voice of that evil one who would entice you to depart from your standards, your home-inspired teachings, and your philosophy of life. Rather, remember that gentle and ever genuine invitation from the Redeemer, "Come, follow me" (Luke 18:22). Follow Him, and you will be acting wisely and will be blessed eternally. ("A Time to Choose," *Ensign*, May 1995, 98).

———

Two questions, spoken at an earlier time, roll as thunder to the ears of each of us: "What think ye of Christ?" and "What shall [we] do . . . with Jesus" (Matthew 22:42; 27:22). I proffer these three suggestions:

1. **Learn of Him.** "Learn of me," He pleaded, "for I am meek and lowly in heart: and ye shall find rest unto your souls" (Matthew 11:29).

2. **Believe in Him.** The writer of the proverb urged: "Trust in the Lord with all thine heart; and lean not unto thine own understanding. In all thy ways acknowledge him, and he shall direct thy paths" (Proverbs 3:5–6). His is the only name under heaven whereby we might be saved.

3. **Follow Him.** He brought reality to the word *compassion*. He showed us the way. He marked the path we should follow. Selfless service characterized His life.

By learning of Him, by believing in Him, by following Him, there is the capacity to become like Him. The countenance can change, the heart can be softened, the step can be quickened, the outlook enhanced. Life becomes what it should become. Change is at times imperceptible, but it does take place. ("The Way of the Master," *Ensign*, May 1996, 50–51)

———

Through the years, the offices I have occupied have been decorated with lovely paintings of peaceful and pastoral scenes. However, there is one picture that always hangs on the wall which I face when seated behind my desk. It is a constant reminder of Him whom I serve, for it is a picture of our Lord and Savior, Jesus Christ. When confronted with a vexing problem or difficult decision, I always gaze at that picture of the Master and silently ask myself the question, "What would He have me do?" No longer does doubt linger, nor does indecision prevail. The way to go is clear, and the pathway before me beckons. ("Windows," *Ensign*, November 1989, 69)

Develop a yearning to know the Lord, to understand His commandments and to follow Him. Then shadows of despair are dispelled by rays of hope, sorrow yields to joy, and the feeling of being lost in the crowd of life vanishes with the certain knowledge that our Heavenly Father is mindful of each of us. ("In Harm's Way," *Ensign,* May 1998, 47)

Before we can take Jesus as our companion, before we can follow Him as our guide, we must find Him. You ask, "How can we find Jesus?" I would like to suggest that, first of all, we need to make room for Him. . . .

As I drive through the many parts of this land, as I see the homes of America, I note that most homes have a room for Mary, a room for John—bedrooms, eating rooms, playrooms, sewing rooms—but I ask the fundamental question, "Is there room for the Son of Almighty God, our Savior, and our Redeemer?"

The invitation of the Lord is directed to each of us: "Behold, I stand at the door, and knock: if any man hear my voice, and open the door, I will come in to him" (Revelation 3:20).

. . . Make room for the Lord in your homes and in your hearts, and He will be a welcome companion. He will be by your side. He will teach you the way of truth. ("Great Expectations," BYU Devotional, May 11, 1965)

I like this thought: "Your mind is a cupboard, and you stock the shelves." Let us make certain that our cupboard shelves, and those of our family members, are stocked with the things which will provide safety to our souls and enable us to return to our Father in Heaven. Such shelves could well be stocked with gospel scholarship, faith, prayer, love, service, obedience, example, and kindness. ("Constant Truths for Changing Times," *Ensign*, May 2005, 19)

———

As members of The Church of Jesus Christ of Latter-day Saints, sacred covenants are to be revered by us, and faithfulness to them is a requirement for happiness. Yes, I speak of the covenant of baptism, the covenant of the priesthood, and the covenant of marriage as examples. ("Happiness—The Universal Quest," Church Educational System Fireside, March 7, 1993)

———

When we obey, as did Adam, endure as did Job, teach as did Paul, testify as did Peter, serve as did Nephi, give ourselves as did the prophet Joseph, respond as did Ruth, honor as did Mary, and live as did Christ, we are born anew. All power becomes ours. Cast off forever is the old self and with it defeat, despair, doubt, and disbelief. To a newness of life we come—a life of faith, hope, courage, and joy. No task looms too large. No responsibility weighs too heavily. No duty is a burden. All things become possible. ("My Personal Hall of Fame," *Ensign*, November 1974, 108)

———

How do we find the Lord? I believe we have to seek Him in simple things. I believe we have to seek Him in personal prayer. I believe we must seek Him in personal service. I believe we seek and find Jesus when we follow His example. ("Let Every

Man Learn His Duty," Dortmund Area Conference, August 3, 1976)

———

May we be persistent in those things which are good and noble. May we ever stay safely on the Lord's side of the line. May we be considerate, studious, responsive to the whisperings of the Holy Spirit. May we be dedicated to the gospel of Jesus Christ. May we love one another and always look for the best in people. May we do our best in all that we do. ("Principles from Prophets," BYU Devotional, September 15, 2009)

DRUGS

———

Drugs impair our ability to think, to reason, and to make prudent and wise choices. Often they result in violence, child and wife abuse, and they can provoke conduct which brings pain and suffering to those who are innocent. "Just say no to drugs" is an effective statement of one's determination. ("Peace, Be Still," *Ensign,* November 2002, 54)

———

Drugs and alcohol cloud thinking, remove inhibitions, fracture families, shatter dreams, and shorten life. They are everywhere to be found and are placed purposely in the pathway of vulnerable youth.

Each one of us has a body that has been entrusted to us by a loving Heavenly Father. We have been commanded to care for it. Can we deliberately abuse or injure our bodies without being held accountable? We cannot! . . . May we keep our bodies—our temples—fit and clean, free from harmful substances which destroy our physical, mental, and spiritual well-being. ("True to the Faith," *Ensign,* May 2006, 19)

DUTY

———

Duty is not merely doing the thing we ought to do, but doing it when we should, whether we like it or not. ("Meeting Your Goliath," Conference Report, October 1967, 132)

———

Time marches on. Duty keeps cadence with that march. Duty does not dim nor diminish. Catastrophic conflicts come and go, but the war waged for the souls of men continues without abatement. Like a clarion call comes the word of the Lord to you, to me, and to priesthood holders everywhere: "Wherefore, now let every man learn his duty, and to act in the office in which he is appointed, in all diligence" (D&C 107:99). ("The Call of Duty," *Ensign,* May 1986, 37)

———

May all of us and all with whom we have influence pray to God that no enemy will breech that portion of the line assigned to us. It matters little in which organization of the Church we are called to labor. We have been given a portion of the line to defend, and ours is the responsibility to do so. ("Timeless Truths for a Changing World," BYU Women's Conference, May 4, 2001)

———

You may well ask, "Where does the path of duty lie?" Brethren, I believe with all my heart that two markers define the path: the *duty to prepare* and the *duty to serve.* ("Duty Calls," *Ensign,* May 1996, 43)

———

I believe we should have an attitude of willingness— even anxiousness—to learn our duty, to do our duty and to put a touch of quality on the work we produce. (All-Church Coordinating Council, November 15, 1988)

EDUCATION

———

Life is a sea upon which the proud are humbled; the shirker is exposed and the leader is revealed. To sail it safely and reach your desired port, you need to keep your charts at hand and up to date. You need to learn by the experience of others, to stand firm for principles, to broaden your interests and to be reliable in your discharge of duty. And through your willingness to learn, education will be achieved. Henry Ford said, "An educated man is not one whose memory is trained to carry a few dates in history—he is one who can accomplish things. A man who cannot think is not an educated man, however many college degrees he may have acquired. Thinking is the hardest work anyone can do, which is probably the reason why we have so few thinkers." ("Builders of Boys," 47th Annual Scouters Convention, February 14, 1966)

—

"Seek ye out of the best books words of wisdom; seek learning, even by study and also by faith" (D&C 88:118). This is your day of preparation, that you might meet the days of decision which are before you.

Part of this seeking of wisdom pertains to your chosen field or profession. A sophisticated economy, based upon power tools and computers, upon engineer and the professional, has no room at the bottom for unskilled labor. "The uneducated need not apply" is the unseen sign on every employment door. "Out of school and out of work" could well apply to those who interrupt a vital training program before its conclusion. ("Building a House for Eternity," Special Priesthood Session, Logan Temple, May 4, 1967)

—

Study and prepare for your life's work in a field that you enjoy, because you are going to spend a good share of your life in that field. It should be one which will challenge your intellect and which will make maximum utilization of your talents and your capabilities. Finally, it should be a field that will supply sufficient remuneration to provide adequately for your companion and your children. Now that's a big order. But I bear testimony that these criteria are very important in choosing your life's work. ("Life's Greatest Decisions," Church Educational System Fireside Satellite Broadcast, September 7, 2003)

—

Someone has said that learning is not just an in-class activity, but an all-day, everywhere process. It is not all formal, rarely neat, and not at all cut-and-made-to-order. Maybe that is why it is so challenging. Schooling and education are not the same thing. Education is a process to which one is subjected throughout life. Schooling is only part of that process, covering but a fraction of a normal life span. ("Your Future Awaits," BYU College of Engineering and Technology Convocation, April 25, 2003)

————

Academic preparation . . . is so important because it is here that we learn the lessons which will help us meet the challenges of this changing world in which we live.

Just a generation ago, if your father or my father were applying for a position of responsibility in the business world, a foreman would no doubt say to him, "Are you willing to work hard? Are you healthy?" And if the answers to these questions were to be "Yes," chances are Dad would be hired.

This is not so today. That foreman has long ago been replaced by a personnel director who sits in a modern office and rather quizzically looks at you while he asks, "What skills do you have? What advantage will you be to our firm? May we have a look at your transcript of credits and see your grades?" It is here that we have an immediate application of [Amulek's] prophecy that we shall "have a bright recollection of all our guilt" (Alma 11:43). ("Great Expectations," BYU Devotional, May 11, 1965)

Credit hours, transcripts, satisfied requirements and diplomas do not an education make. Education is a process, not a completed act. The prescriptions of our times look as though you'll go through the motions of an education whether you want to or not. You don't need to ask anymore for an educational opportunity. You have only to knock to take advantage of it. But to achieve excellence, you must open the door to learning yourself. Contrary to what we'd like to believe, excellence in education is rarely unearned. In our quest for knowledge, there is no room for cheating, for dishonesty, for that which would degrade us or cause the loss of our precious self-respect. ("Learning the ABC's at BYU," BYU Devotional, February 8, 1966)

———

In academic preparation, I found it a good practice to read a text with the idea that I would be asked to explain that which the author wrote and its application to the subject it covered. Also, I tried to be attentive in any lecture in the classroom and to pretend that I would be called upon to present the same lecture to others. While this practice is very hard work, it certainly helps during test week! ("Three Gates to Open," BYU Devotional, November 14, 2006)

———

Your training, your experience, your knowledge are tools to be skillfully used. They have been self-acquired. Your conscience, your love, your faith are delicate and precious instruments to guide your destiny. They have been God-given. (BYU Commencement, April 22, 1998)

EFFORT
(SEE ALSO WORK)

———

"Thrust in thy sickle with thy might" was not an admonition reserved for missionary work alone. Our Father expects us to labor and to do so diligently and willingly. He counseled: "[I] the Lord requireth the heart and a willing mind" (D&C 64:34). ("Building Bridges," Address to YWMIA Executives, June 24, 1967)

———

We must make continuous effort. Have you noticed that many of the most cherished of God's dealings with His children have been when they were engaged in a proper activity? The visit of the Master to His disciples *on the way* to Emmaus, the good Samaritan *on the road* to Jericho, even Nephi *on his return* to Jerusalem, and Father Lehi *en route* to the precious land of promise. Let us not overlook Joseph Smith *on the way* to Carthage, and Brigham Young *on the vast plains* to the valley home of the Saints. ("Which Road Will You Travel?" *Ensign,* November 1976, 53)

———

Don't take counsel of your fears. Don't say to yourselves, "I'm not wise enough, or I can't apply myself sufficiently well to study this difficult subject or in this difficult field, so I shall choose the easier way." I plead with you to tax your talent, and our Heavenly Father will make you equal to those decisions. ("Life's Greatest Decisions," Church Educational System Fireside Satellite Broadcast, September 7, 2003)

———

In this life, where we have opportunities to strive and to achieve, I bear witness that on occasion we need to make a second effort—and a third effort, and a fourth effort, and as many degrees of effort as may be required to accomplish what we strive to achieve. ("Life's Greatest Decisions," Church

Educational System Fireside Satellite Broadcast, September 7, 2003)

—

Sloth is one of the seven deadly sins, responsible for a great deal of the failing and underachieving we see; but idling away one's time is not enjoying life. ("Constant Truths in Changing Times," BYU Commencement, May 26, 1967)

—

It's not enough to wish, it's not enough to dream, it's not enough to promise, it's not enough to pledge. Literally, we must do. ("A Time to Choose," BYU Devotional, January 16, 1973)

—

It is not enough to want to make [an] effort and to *say* we'll make the effort. We must actually *make* the effort. It's in the *doing*, not just the *thinking*, that we accomplish our goals. If we constantly put our goals off, we will never see them fulfilled. ("A Royal Priesthood," *Ensign*, November 2007, 59)

Enduring to the End

—

We live in a troubled world, a world of many challenges. We are here on this earth to deal with our individual challenges to the best of our ability, to learn from them, and to overcome them. Endure to the end we must, for our goal is eternal life in the presence of our Father in Heaven. He loves us and wants nothing more than for us to succeed in this goal. He will help us and bless us as we call upon Him in our prayers, as we study His words, and as we obey His commandments. Therein is found safety; therein is found peace. ("'Til We Meet Again," *Ensign,* November 2010, 112)

———

You may be tempted to shortcut your preparation. Discouragement, that tool of the devil, can prompt depression. Should this occur, don't quit! ("Eternal Flight," Church Educational System Fireside Satellite Broadcast, February 4, 1996)

———

Each of us is a runner in the race of life. Comforting is the fact that there are many runners. Reassuring is the knowledge that our eternal Scorekeeper is understanding. Challenging is the truth that each must run. But you and I do not run alone. That vast audience of family, friends, and leaders will cheer our courage, will applaud our determination as we rise from our stumblings and pursue our goal. The race of life is not for sprinters running on a level track. The course is marked by pitfalls and checkered with obstacles. . . .

Let us shed any thought of failure. Let us discard any habit that may hinder. Let us seek; let us obtain the prize prepared for all, even exaltation in the celestial kingdom of God. ("The Will Within," *Ensign,* May 1987, 69)

———

In life, as in business, there has always been a need for those persons who could be called finishers. Their ranks are few, their opportunities many, their contributions great.

From the very beginning to the present time, a fundamental question remains to be answered by each who runs the race of life. Shall I falter or shall I finish? On the answer await the blessings of joy and happiness here in mortality and eternal life in the world to come. ("Finishers Wanted," Conference Report, April 1972, 69–70)

———

Lust for power, greed of gold, and disdain for honor have ever appeared as faces of failure in the panorama of life. Captivated by their artificial attraction, many noble souls have stumbled and fallen, thus losing the crown of victory reserved for the finisher of life's great race.

Concerning those who fall short, John Greenleaf Whittier's words seem particularly fitting:

"Of all sad words of tongue or pen, The saddest are these: 'It might have been!'" ("Finishers Wanted," Conference Report, April 1972, 71)

———

We may find that there are times in our lives when we falter, when we become weary or fatigued, or when we suffer a disappointment or a heartache. When that happens, I would hope that we will persevere with even greater effort toward our goal. ("A Royal Priesthood," *Ensign,* November 2007, 50)

ETERNAL LIFE

———

The race of life is not optional—we are on the track and running whether we like it or not. Some see dimly the goal ahead and take costly detours which lead to disappointment and frustration. Others view clearly the prize for running well and remain steadfast in pursuit. This prize, this lofty and desirable goal, is none other than eternal life in the presence of God. ("The Race for Eternal Life," Seminary Day, February 3, 1968)

———

Eternal life in the kingdom of our Father is your goal.

Such a goal is not achieved in one glorious attempt, but rather is the result of a lifetime of righteousness, an accumulation of wise choices, even a constancy of purpose. Like the coveted "A" grade on the report card of a difficult and required college course, the reward of eternal life requires effort. ("Decisions Determine Destiny," LDS Student Association Young Women's Meeting, Logan, Utah, May 16, 1968)

———

The work of the Lord moves forward. The gospel of Jesus Christ blesses countless lives. To Almighty God we acknowledge His watchful care, His welcome guidance, and His heaven-sent gifts, supreme among these the gift of His precious Son and our Redeemer, that we might have the gift of eternal life. ("The Gifts of Christmas," First Presidency Christmas Devotional, December 2, 2001)

EXAMPLE

———

A good example is more effective than good advice and, I might add, more easily and willingly followed. I have never

Example   103

heard anything about the resolutions of the Apostles, but a great deal about their acts. When we are doers of the word and not hearers only, we can, with the Master, say, "Come, follow me." ("Builders of Faith in Children of God," Interfaith Service, Lethbridge, Alberta, Canada, June 10, 1967)

———

Learning of others who trusted God and followed His teachings whispers to our souls, "Be still, and know that I am God" (Psalm 46:10). As they resolutely kept His command-ments and trusted in Him, they were blessed. When we follow their examples, we too will be similarly blessed in our day and in our time. Each one becomes a model to follow. ("Models to Follow," *Ensign,* November 2002, 60)

———

We need not wait for a cataclysmic event, a dramatic oc-currence in the world in which we live, or a special invitation to be an example—even a model to follow. Our opportunities lie before us here and now. But they are perishable. Likely they will be found in our own homes and in the everyday actions of our lives. Our Lord and Master marked the way. . . . He in very deed was a model to follow—even an example of the believers.

Are we? ("An Example of the Believers," *Ensign,* November 1992, 98)

———

We are all aware that we live in a time when there are those who mock virtue, who peddle pornography under the guise of art or culture, who turn a blind eye, a deaf ear, and a calloused heart to the teachings of Jesus and a code of decency. Many of our young people are tugged in the wrong direction and enticed to partake of the sins of the world. Yearningly such individuals seek for the strength of those who have the ability to stand firm for truth. Through righteous living and by extending the helping hand and the understanding heart, you can rescue, you can save. How great will then be your joy. How eternal will be the blessing you will have conferred. ("An Example of the Believers," *Ensign*, November 1992, 98)

———

Youth need fewer critics and more models to follow. Your own personal performance in all aspects of your life, including reading the scriptures regularly and following their teachings, will help you to become such models. ("Three Gates to Open," Church Educational System Satellite Broadcast, January 14, 2001)

———

In the interior of our consciousness, each of us has a private hall of fame reserved exclusively for the real leaders who have influenced the direction of our lives. Relatively few of the many men who exercise authority over us from childhood through adult life meet our test for entry on this roll of honor. That test has very little to do with the outward trappings of power or an abundance of this world's goods. The leaders whom we admit into this private sanctuary of our reflective meditation are usually those who set our hearts afire with devotion to the truth, who make obedience to duty seem the essence of manhood, who transform some ordinary routine occurrence so that it becomes a vista whence we see the person we aspire to be. ("My Personal Hall of Fame," *Ensign*, November 1974, 107–8)

———

In Utah there is a very beautiful river of water—the Provo River. It runs usually beautiful and clear; but one day I noticed that the river was muddy. I determined to find out why. I drove along the highway by the side of the river until I found a little stream that was coming into it. The stream was filled with mud and debris of every kind. Above that particular stream the Provo River was clear, but that one little stream was polluting the entire river.

So it is with the gospel. When we do not do all that we have been commanded to do, we do not present the most beautiful picture to our non-member friends. I feel that each one should so serve that he magnifies his callings and so live that he is an example to the Church and to all. ("Truth, Service, Love," Copenhagen Area Conference, August 5, 1976)

EXCELLENCE

———

As we strive for perfection, we seek excellence. Excellence may leave you sensitive in the face of the jaded; curious in the crowd of uninterested; quiet in groups of static and noise; caring in the company of the unconcerned; exact while all about you is approximation; refined in place of gross; exceptional instead of commonplace. ("Constant Truths in Changing Times," BYU Commencement, May 26, 1967)

———

Be the very best at whatever you pursue as your life's work, your career. If you plan to be an accountant, be the best accountant. If you plan to be a teacher, be the best teacher. Do not settle for mediocrity. I firmly believe that once we have had a view of excellence, we shall never again be content with mediocrity. ("The Way to Eternal Glory," BYU Devotional, October 15, 1991)

———

There are factors within you and within me, even basic principles with which we have been imbued from our creation, which seem to call out and demand of us our best. Those particular yearnings and those cravings and those bits of inspiration seem to be telling you and me, "Seek the best in life. Look for opportunities where you can be of greatest service." (BYU College of Business, March 14, 1973)

———

In the search for our best selves, several questions will guide our thinking: *Am I what I want to be? Am I closer to the Savior today than I was yesterday? Will I be closer yet tomorrow? Do I have the courage to change for the better?* ("Becoming Our Best Selves," *Ensign,* November 1999, 18–19)

FAITH

———

May we choose to build up within ourselves a great power of faith which will be our most effective bulwark against the designs of the Adversary—a real faith, the kind of faith which will sustain us. Every person . . . has read or quoted or heard those famous words from the epistle of James: "If any of you lack wisdom, let him ask of God, that giveth to all men liberally, and upbraideth not; and it shall be given him" (James 1:5).

How many of us have read the next verse: "But let him ask in faith, nothing wavering. For he that wavereth is like a wave of the sea driven with the wind and tossed" (James 1:6). I would urge that we choose to build within ourselves a faith which can be characterized by nothing wavering. If we will do this, our Heavenly Father will sustain us and direct us and guide us. ("The Three R's of Choice," BYU Devotional, November 5, 1963)

———

It was by faith, nothing wavering, that the brother of Jared saw the finger of God touch the stones in response to his plea.

It was by faith, nothing wavering, that Noah erected an ark in obedience to the command from God.

It was by faith, nothing wavering, that Abraham was willing to offer up his beloved Isaac as a sacrifice.

It was by faith, nothing wavering, that Moses led the children of Israel out of Egypt and through the Red Sea.

It was by faith, nothing wavering, that Joshua and his followers brought the walls of Jericho tumbling down.

It was by faith, nothing wavering, that Joseph [Smith] saw God our Eternal Father and Jesus Christ his Son. . . .

There is a golden thread that runs through every account of faith from the beginning of the world to the present time. Abraham, Noah, the brother of Jared, the Prophet Joseph, and countless others wanted to be obedient to the will of God. They had ears that could hear, eyes that could see, and hearts that could know and feel.

They never doubted. They trusted. ("Come unto Me," Conference Report, April 1964, 131, 132)

———

How do we find faith? We do not find faith by reading in a book; we must discover faith for ourselves. . . . It is a good thing to sit down and commune with yourself, to come to an understanding of yourself and to decide in that silent moment what your duty is to your family, to your church, to your country, and to your fellowmen. ("Honor Thy Father and Thy Mother," BYU Fourteen-Stake Fireside, December 3, 1978)

———

It was not raining when Noah was commanded to build an ark. Two Heavenly Personages were not yet seen when Joseph knelt and prayed. There was no visible ram in the thicket when Abraham prepared to sacrifice his son Isaac. First came the test of faith, and then the miracle.

Remember that faith and doubt cannot exist in the same mind at the same time, for one will dispel the other. Cast out doubt. Cultivate faith. Strive always to retain that childlike faith which can move mountains and bring heaven closer to heart and home. ("The Lighthouse of the Lord," General Young Women Meeting, March 22, 1980)

———

Faith has always been a fundamental principle of strength for Latter-day Saints. Without it, we go nowhere. With it, we can accomplish anything in building the kingdom of God. ("Traditions," Dixie College Homecoming, November 2, 1986)

———

I testify to you that our promised blessings are beyond measure. Though the storm clouds may gather, though the rains may pour down upon us, our knowledge of the gospel and our love of our Heavenly Father and of our Savior will comfort and sustain us and bring joy to our hearts as we walk uprightly and keep the commandments. There will be nothing in this world that can defeat us.

My beloved brothers and sisters, fear not. Be of good cheer. The future is as bright as your faith. ("Be of Good Cheer," *Ensign,* May 2009, 92)

———

Many years ago, on an assignment to Tahiti, I was talking to our mission president, President Raymond Baudin, about the Tahitian people. They are known as some of the greatest seafaring people in all the world. Brother Baudin, who speaks French and Tahitian but little English, was trying to describe to me the secret of the success of the Tahitian sea captains. He said, "They are amazing. The weather may be terrible, the vessels may be leaky, there may be no navigational aids except their inner feelings and the stars in the heavens, but they pray and they go." He repeated that phrase three times. There is a lesson in that statement. We need to pray, and then we need to act. Both are important.

The promise from the book of Proverbs gives us courage:

"Trust in the Lord with all thine heart; and lean not unto thine own understanding. In all thy ways acknowledge him, and he shall direct thy paths" (Proverbs 3:5–6).

We need but to turn to the account found in 1 Kings to appreciate anew the principle that when we follow the counsel of the Lord, when we pray and then go, the outcome benefits all. There we read that a most severe drought had gripped the land. Famine followed. Elijah the prophet received from the Lord what to him must have been an amazing instruction: "Get thee to Zarephath . . . : behold, I have commanded a widow woman there to sustain thee." When he had found the widow,

Elijah declared, "Fetch me, I pray thee, a little water in a vessel, that I may drink.

"And as she was going to fetch it, he called to her, and said, Bring me, I pray thee, a morsel of bread in thine hand."

Her response described her desperate situation as she explained that she was preparing a final and scanty meal for her son and for herself, and then they would die.

How implausible to her must have been Elijah's response: "Fear not; go and do as thou hast said: but make me thereof a little cake first, and bring it unto me, and after make for thee and for thy son.

"For thus saith the Lord God of Israel, The barrel of meal shall not waste, neither shall the cruse of oil fail, until the day that the Lord sendeth rain upon the earth.

"And she went and did according to the saying of Elijah: and she, and he, and her house, did eat many days.

"And the barrel of meal wasted not, neither did the cruse of oil fail" (1 Kings 17:9–11, 13–16. See also v. 12). ("They Pray and They Go," *Ensign*, May 2002, 49)

———

Whatever our calling, regardless of our fears or anxieties, let us pray and then go and do, remembering the words of the Master, even the Lord Jesus Christ, who promised, "I am with you alway, even unto the end of the world" (Matthew 28:20).

In the Epistle of James we are counseled, "Be ye doers of the word, and not hearers only, deceiving your own selves" (James 1:22).

Let us . . . be doers of the word, and not hearers only. Let us pray; then let us go and do. ("They Pray and They Go," *Ensign*, May 2002, 51)

Whereas doubt destroys, faith fulfills. It brings one closer to God and to His purposes. Faith implies a certain trust—even a reliance—upon the word of our Creator.

The scriptures are replete with examples of true faith. They tell of Abraham leading his beloved son Isaac to a mountaintop, of Moses stretching forth his hand at the Red Sea, Peter taking his first few tentative steps upon the Sea of Galilee, and Joseph Smith kneeling in a shady grove in New York. The promise of Jesus, in which He said, "If ye have faith as a grain of mustard seed" (Matthew 17:20), takes on added significance when we recognize that faith at this level is complete and all-consuming. ("Each Must Choose," Manchester Area Conference, August 29, 1971)

FAMILY
(SEE ALSO HOME)

Happiness abounds when there is genuine respect one for another. Wives draw closer to their husbands and husbands are more appreciative of their wives; and children are happy, as children are meant to be. Where there is respect in the home children do not find themselves in that dreaded never never land. Never the object of concern, never the recipient of proper parental guidance. ("In Quest of the Abundant Life," Utah State University Baccalaureate, June 2, 1967)

It is our sacred duty to care for our families. Often we see what might be called "parent neglect." Too frequently the emotional, social, and, in some instances, even the material essentials of life are not provided by children to their aged parents. This is displeasing to the Lord. It is difficult to understand how one mother can take care of seven children more easily than seven children can take care of one mother. (Address at Regional Representatives Seminar, April 4, 1986)

When the seas of life are stormy, a wise mariner seeks a port of peace. The family, as we have traditionally known it, is such a refuge of safety. The tremendous increase in the number of single parents has been one of the most profound changes in family composition to have occurred during the past quarter century. All of us are acutely aware of the devastation of divorce and other negative influences in our society that stalk the traditional family.

What is the solution? Where is our answer to be found? "Back to Basics" may well be a formula to give us help. The home is the basis of a righteous life, and no other instrumentality can take its place or fulfill its essential functions. ("The Family Must Endure," International Year of the Family Conference, March 19, 1995)

The family must hold its preeminent place in our way of life because it is the only possible base upon which a society of responsible human beings has ever found it practicable to build for the future and maintain the values they cherish in the present. ("The Family Must Endure," International Year of the Family Conference, March 19, 1995)

———

Some Latter-day Saint families are comprised of mother, father and children, all at home, while others have witnessed the tender departure of one, then another, then another of its members. Sometimes a single individual comprises a family. Whatever its composition, the family continues—for families can be forever. ("Heavenly Homes—Forever Families," Worldwide Leadership Training Satellite Broadcast, February 11, 2006)

———

The family is the ideal place for teaching. It is also a laboratory for learning. Family home evening can bring spiritual growth to each member. . . .

It is in the home where fathers and mothers can teach provident living to their children. Sharing of tasks and helping one another set a pattern for future families as children grow, marry, and leave home. The lessons learned in the home are those that last the longest. ("Your Personal Influence," *Ensign*, May 2004, 20)

———

It is time to choose an oft-forgotten path, the path we might call "The Family Way," so that our children and grandchildren might indeed grow to their full potential. There is a national—even an international—tide running. It carries the unspoken message, "Return to your roots, to your families, to lessons learned, to lives lived, to examples shown, even family values." Often it is just a matter of coming home—coming home to attics not recently examined, to diaries seldom read, to photo albums almost forgotten. . . . What memories do we have of Mother? Father? Grandparents? Family? Friends? ("Becoming Our Best Selves," *Ensign*, November 1999, 19)

FAMILY HISTORY WORK

———

We must plunge into this work and get wet all over. We must prepare for some uphill climbing. This is not an easy task, but the Lord has placed it upon you, and He has placed it upon me.

He loves those children in the spirit world just as much as He loves you and me. He said about them, through the Prophet Joseph Smith, that all that we do for our own salvation must be done for the salvation of our dear ones, because salvation is the same for all. He said something through President Joseph F. Smith which I thought was beautiful: "Through our efforts in their behalf their chains of bondage will fall from them and the darkness surrounding them will clear away, that light may shine upon them, and they shall hear in the spirit world of the work that has been done for them by their children here, and will rejoice with you in the performance of these duties" (in Conference Report, October 1916, 6). (Los Angeles Temple Genealogical Library Dedication, June 20, 1964)

———

Nothing is more important than marrying the right person, at the right time, in the right place, by the right authority; and that authority is one who has the sealing power in the house of God, the temples of God. If this is a beautiful sight to you and to me, think how beautiful it is to those who are waiting and who perhaps have waited for generations of time so that they, too, might have this privilege and this opportunity to have an eternal marriage. (Los Angeles Temple Genealogical Library Dedication, June 20, 1964)

———

In our efforts to save the living, we must not neglect those who have lived and died without the blessings provided by the temples of God. Our renewed efforts are urgently required. This vital work cannot be postponed or neglected.

As we organize our personal and family genealogical efforts, we will be in a position to take full advantage of the computer techniques now available and soon to be expanded and perfected for our benefit and the advancement of the work of the Lord. We pray for temples, but temples cannot function without the genealogical work which is essential to their operation. ("Prophets Speak—The Wise Obey," General Conference Friday Leadership Session, April 3, 1987)

———

Search out your heritage. It is important to know, as far as possible, those who came before us. We discover something about ourselves when we learn about our ancestors. . . .

I owe such a debt of gratitude to . . . noble forebears who loved the gospel and who loved the Lord so deeply that they were willing to sacrifice all they had, including their very lives, for The Church of Jesus Christ of Latter-day Saints. How grateful I am for the temple ordinances which bind us together for all eternity.

I emphasize how essential is the work we do in the temples of the Lord for our kindred dead. ("Constant Truths for Changing Times," *Ensign,* May 2005, 21–22)

———

There are thousands upon thousands, yes, millions upon millions of spirit children of our Heavenly Father who have lived here, who have never heard of the word "Christ," who have died, who have gone back to the spirit world in their state of progression and have been taught the gospel; and now they are waiting the day when you and I will do the research which is necessary to clear the way, that we might likewise go into the house of God and perform that work for them, that they, themselves, cannot perform. Are we willing to accept that challenge? My brothers and sisters, I testify that the Lord will bless you as you do accept and respond to that challenge. (Los Angeles Temple Genealogical Library Dedication, June 20, 1964)

As you begin your genealogical work or as you pursue it, you are going to find yourself running into roadblocks, and you are going to say to yourself, "I've come to the end of my rope. There is nothing I can do." When you come to that point, you get down upon your knees and ask the Lord to open the way, and He will open the way for you. . . . When we do that which we know how to do, when we live as righteously as we know how to live, our Heavenly Father will open the way for the fulfillment of the blessing which we so earnestly and diligently seek. (Los Angeles Temple Genealogical Library Dedication, June 20, 1964)

FAMILY HOME EVENING

We can and should emphasize family home evening. With the world seemingly growing more and more coarse, and with corrupting influences more widespread and common, the stability of homes and families is under increasing attack. Too often that which pollutes is invited into our own homes through means of communication that offer marvelous opportunities to learn and wonderful cultural advantages but which are too frequently permitted to propagate that which is unwholesome and morally destructive. Fathers and mothers are missing golden opportunities to fortify their families against the destructive influences of the day when they do not bring their families together consistently and regularly to build family unity and individual maturity and responsibilities. ("The Perfection of the Saints," Regional Representatives Seminar, April 1, 1988)

FATHER

Beyond the friends of our peer group even our own age, will you make a friend of your father? Really, each of you has three fathers. First, your Heavenly Father. He stands ready to answer the prayer of your heart. Being the father of your spirit, and having created you in His own image, knowing the end from the beginning, His wisdom faileth not and His counsel is ever true. Make a friend of Him.

Second, you have your earthly father. He labors to ensure your happiness. Together with your mother, he prays for your guidance and well being. Make a friend of him.

Third, there is the father of your ward, even the bishop. He has been called of God by prophecy and the laying on of hands, by those who are in authority, to preach the gospel and administer in the ordinances thereof. In short, he is endowed to provide you with counsel and help. Make a friend of him. ("Decisions Determine Destiny," LDS Student Association Young Women's Meeting, Logan, Utah, May 16, 1968)

FELLOWSHIPING

Fellowshiping of the investigator should begin well before baptism. The teachings of the missionaries often need the second witness of a new convert to the Church. It has been my experience that such a witness, borne from the heart of one who has undergone this mighty change himself, brings resolve and commitment. When I served as mission president in eastern Canada, we found that in Toronto, as well as in most of the cities of Ontario and Quebec, there was no dearth of willing helpers to accompany the missionaries and to fellowship the investigators, welcome them to meetings, and introduce them to the ward or branch officers and members. Fellowshiping, friendshiping, and reactivating are ongoing in the daily life of a Latter-day Saint. ("They Will Come," *Ensign,* May 1997, 44–45)

The Church continues to grow, as it has since being organized. . . . It is changing the lives of more and more people every year and is spreading far and wide over the earth as our missionary force seeks out those who are looking for the truths which are found in the gospel of Jesus Christ. We call upon all members of the Church to befriend the new converts, to reach out to them, to surround them with love, and to help them feel at home. ("Welcome to Conference," *Ensign,* November 2009, 5–6)

If we have reverence in the sacrament meeting, we have attention on the focal point—the sacrament—and we enhance fellowshiping to a marvelous extent when the investigators and the new converts can feel that they truly have come to worship. (General Authority Leadership Training, March 27, 1990)

FORGIVENESS

———

I am acquainted with a family which came to America from Germany. The English language was difficult for them. They had but little by way of means, but each was blessed with the will to work and with a love of God.

Their third child was born, lived but two months, and then died. Father was a cabinetmaker and fashioned a beautiful casket for the body of his precious child. The day of the funeral was gloomy, thus reflecting the sadness they felt in their loss. As the family walked to the chapel, with Father carrying the tiny casket, a small number of friends had gathered. However, the chapel door was locked. The busy bishop had forgotten the funeral. Attempts to reach him were futile. Not knowing what to do, the father placed the casket under his arm and, with his family beside him, carried it home, walking in a drenching rain.

If the family were of lesser character, they could have blamed the bishop and harbored ill feelings. When the bishop discovered the tragedy, he visited the family and apologized. With the hurt still evident in his expression, but with tears in his eyes, the father accepted the apology, and the two embraced in a spirit of understanding. No hidden wedge was left to cause further feelings of anger. Love and acceptance prevailed. ("Hidden Wedges," *Ensign*, May 2002, 19)

———

There are some who have difficulty forgiving themselves and who dwell on all of their perceived shortcomings. I quite like the account of a religious leader who went to the side of a woman who lay dying, attempting to comfort her—but to no avail. "I am lost," she said. "I've ruined my life and every life around me. There is no hope for me."

The man noticed a framed picture of a lovely girl on the dresser. "Who is this?" he asked.

The woman brightened. "She is my daughter, the one beautiful thing in my life."

"And would you help her if she were in trouble or had made a mistake? Would you forgive her? Would you still love her?"

"Of course I would!" cried the woman. "I would do anything for her. Why do you ask such a question?"

"Because I want you to know," said the man, "that figuratively speaking, Heavenly Father has a picture of you on His dresser. He loves you and will help you. Call upon Him." ("Hidden Wedges," *Ensign*, May 2002, 19)

———

In the Book of Mormon, Alma describes beautifully the [Lord's mercy] with his words: "The plan of mercy could not be brought about except an atonement should be made; therefore God himself atoneth for the sins of the world, to bring about the plan of mercy, to appease the demands of justice, that God might be a perfect, just God, and a merciful God also" (Alma 42:15).

From the springboard of such knowledge we ask ourselves, *Why, then, do we see on every side those instances where people decline to forgive one another and show forth the cleansing act of mercy and forgiveness? What blocks the way for such healing balm to cleanse human wounds? Is it stubbornness? Could it be pride? Maybe hatred has yet to melt and disappear.* ("Mercy—The Divine Gift," *Ensign,* May 1995, 59)

———

There are those among us who torture themselves through their inability to show mercy and to forgive others some supposed offense or slight, however small it may be. At times the statement is made, "I never can forgive [this person or that person]." Such an attitude is destructive to an individual's well-being. It can canker the soul and ruin one's life. In other instances, an individual can forgive another but cannot forgive himself. Such a situation is even more destructive.

Early in my ministry as a member of the Council of the Twelve, I took to President Hugh B. Brown the experience of a fine person who could not serve in a ward position because he could not show mercy to himself. He could forgive others but not himself; mercy was seemingly beyond his grasp. President Brown suggested that I visit with that individual and counsel him along these lines: "I, the Lord, will forgive whom I will forgive, but of you it is required to forgive all men" (D&C 64:10). Then, from Isaiah and the Doctrine and Covenants: "Though your sins be as scarlet, they shall be as white as snow; though they be red like crimson, they shall be as wool" (Isaiah 1:18). "Behold, he who has repented of his sins, the same is forgiven, and I, the Lord, remember them no more" (D&C 58:42).

With a pensive expression on his face, President Brown added: "Tell that man that he should not persist in remembering that which the Lord has said He is willing to forget." Such counsel will help to cleanse the soul and renew the spirit of any who applies it. ("Mercy—The Divine Gift," *Ensign,* May 1995, 59–60)

FREEDOM

———

The price of freedom has ever been high. Our prayers go out to those whose families feel the absence of loved ones and who experience daily a concern for conflict. We unite in an earnest prayer to Almighty God that a pattern for peace may be found and that good will toward men may be our divinely bestowed blessing.

On a brighter note, the good tidings of the gospel have penetrated political borders which were sealed shut and have sounded in the hearts of those who knew no freedom and waited in darkness for the light of truth. The infamous Berlin Wall is but a memory. Obstacles of steel and stone have crumbled. In many nations, barbed wire fences and closed borders have vanished. ("The Gifts of Christmas," First Presidency Christmas Devotional, December 2, 1990)

FRIENDSHIP

———

We tend to become like those whom we admire. . . . We adopt the mannerisms, the attitudes, even the conduct of those whom we admire—and they are usually our friends. Associate with those who, like you, are planning not for temporary convenience, shallow goals, or narrow ambition, but rather for those things that matter most—even eternal objectives. ("Decisions Determine Destiny," LDS Student Association Young Women's Meeting, Logan, Utah, May 16, 1968)

———

This is a day to develop friendships. I like the phrase, "New friends are silver, but the old are gold." How do you find old friends? You make new friends, don't you? I think we should have a goal for each one of us . . . to make new friends and to ensure that no one goes friendless. ("The Way to Eternal Glory," BYU Devotional, October 15, 1991)

GOALS

———

I plead with you to make a determination right here, right now, not to deviate from the path which will lead to our goal: eternal life with our Father in Heaven. Along that straight and true path there are other goals: missionary service, temple marriage, Church activity, scripture study, prayer, temple work. There are countless worthy goals to reach as we travel through life. Needed is our commitment to reach them. ("The Three Rs of Choice," *Ensign*, November 2010, 68)

———

It is necessary to prepare and to plan so that we don't fritter away our lives. Without a goal, there can be no real success. One of the best definitions of success I have ever found goes something like this: Success is the progressive realization of a worthy ideal. Someone has said the trouble with not having a goal is that you can spend your life running up and down the field and never crossing the goal line. ("In Search of Treasure," *Ensign*, May 2003, 20)

✳

"Be ye therefore perfect" counseled the only perfect man. Such perfection is not achieved simply by wishing or hoping for it to come. It is approached as we establish specific goals in our lives and strive for their successful accomplishment. ("Constant Truths in Changing Times," BYU Commencement, May 26, 1967)

———

Ahead is the open road. Those who walk it successfully ignore irrelevant attractions and refrain from activities which do not contribute to attainment of their purpose. They disregard the billboards designed to divert them into this or that blind alley of ease and pleasure. They stand on their own feet, set their own goals, and win their own victories. ("Yesterday, Today, and Tomorrow," BYU Commencement, April 22, 1999)

GOD THE FATHER

———

The Apostle Paul told the Athenians on Mars Hill that we are "the offspring of God" (Acts 17:29). Since we know that our physical bodies are the offspring of our mortal parents, we must probe for the meaning of Paul's statement. The Lord has declared that "the spirit and the body are the soul of man" (D&C 88:15). It is the spirit which is the offspring of God. The writer of Hebrews refers to Him as "the Father of spirits" (Hebrews 12:9). God Himself is a soul, composed of a spirit and of a body of flesh and bones, as tangible as man's. He is a resurrected, glorified, exalted, omniscient, omnipotent person and is omnipresent in spirit and power and influence, the ruler of the heavens and the earth and all things therein. The spirits of all men are literally His "begotten sons and daughters" (D&C 76:24). ("An Invitation to Exaltation," Satellite Broadcast, March 4, 1984)

———

Can we, in part, appreciate the suffering of God the Eternal Father as His Only Begotten Son in the flesh was placed on a cross and crucified? Is there a father or a mother who could not be moved to complete compassion if he or she heard a son cry out in his own Garden of Gethsemane, "Father, if thou be willing, remove this cup from me: nevertheless not my will, but thine, be done" (Luke 22:42). . . .

As God witnessed the suffering of Jesus, His Only Begotten Son in the flesh, and beheld his agony, there was no voice from heaven to spare the life of Jesus. There was no ram in the thicket to be offered as a substitute sacrifice. "For God so loved the world, that he gave his only begotten Son, that whosoever believeth in him should not perish, but have everlasting life" (John 3:16). ("The Search for Jesus," Conference Report, October 1965, 149)

———

[The] loving God who introduced his crucified and resurrected Son [to the Nephites] was not a God lacking in body, parts, or passions—the God of a man-made philosophy. Rather, God our Father has ears with which to hear our prayers. He has eyes with which to see our actions. He has a mouth with which to speak to us. He has a heart with which to feel compassion and love. He is real. He is living. We are his children made in his image. We look like him and he looks like us. ("I Know That My Redeemer Lives," Conference Report, April 1966, 63)

GRATITUDE

———

Do we remember to give thanks for the blessings we receive? Sincerely giving thanks not only helps us recognize our blessings, but it also unlocks the doors of heaven and helps us feel God's love. ("The Divine Gift of Gratitude," *Ensign,* November 2010, 87)

———

In the book of Matthew in the Bible, we have an account of gratitude . . . as an expression from the Savior. As He traveled in the wilderness for three days, more than 4,000 people followed and traveled with Him. He took compassion on them, for they may not have eaten during the entire three days. His disciples, however, questioned, "Whence should we have so much bread in the wilderness, as to fill so great a multitude?" Like many of us, the disciples saw only what was lacking.

"And Jesus saith unto them, How many loaves have ye? And [the disciples] said, Seven, and a few little fishes.

"And [Jesus] commanded the multitude to sit down on the ground.

"And he took the seven loaves and the fishes, and *gave thanks,* and brake them, and gave to his disciples, and the disciples to the multitude."

Notice that the Savior gave thanks for what they had—and a miracle followed: "And they did all eat, and were filled: and they took up of the broken meat that was left seven baskets full" (see Matthew 15:32–38; emphasis added). ("The Divine Gift of Gratitude," *Ensign,* November 2010, 87–88)

———

We have all experienced times when our focus is on what we lack rather than on our blessings. Said the Greek philosopher Epictetus, "He is a wise man who does not grieve for the things which he has not, but rejoices for those which he has" (*The Discourses of Epictetus; with the Encheiridion and Fragments,* trans. George Long [1888], 429).

Gratitude is a divine principle. The Lord declared through a revelation given to the Prophet Joseph Smith:

"Thou shalt thank the Lord thy God in all things. . . .

"And in nothing doth man offend God, or against none is his wrath kindled, save those who confess not his hand in all things" (D&C 59:7, 21).

In the Book of Mormon we are told to "live in thanksgiving daily for the many mercies and blessings which [God] doth bestow upon you" (Alma 34:38).

Regardless of our circumstances, each of us has much for which to be grateful if we will but pause and contemplate our blessings. ("The Divine Gift of Gratitude," *Ensign,* November 2010, 88)

———

Do material possessions make us happy and grateful? Perhaps momentarily. However, those things which provide deep and lasting happiness and gratitude are the things which money cannot buy: our families, the gospel, good friends, our health, our abilities, the love we receive from those around us. Unfortunately, these are some of the things we allow ourselves to take for granted.

The English author Aldous Huxley wrote, "Most human beings have an almost infinite capacity for taking things for granted" (*Themes and Variations* [1954], 66).

We often take for granted the very people who most deserve our gratitude. Let us not wait until it is too late for us to express that gratitude. Speaking of loved ones he had lost, one man declared his regret this way: "I remember those happy days, and often wish I could speak into the ears of the dead the gratitude which was due them in life, and so ill returned" (William H. Davies, *The Autobiography of a Super-Tramp* [1908], 4).

The loss of loved ones almost inevitably brings some regrets to our hearts. Let's minimize such feelings as much as humanly possible by frequently expressing our love and gratitude to them. We never know how soon it will be too late. ("The Divine Gift of Gratitude," *Ensign,* November 2010, 88–89)

———

The United States Post Office dead letter department receives annually thousands and thousands of children's pre-Christmas letters addressed to Santa Claus asking for things. After it was all over one year, a single, solitary letter thanking Santa Claus was received. Could this be one of the problems of this troubled world; that people think only of getting—not giving? Of receiving—and not even expressing their gratitude for that which they do receive? ("Pathway to Life Eternal," BYU Devotional, February 27, 1968)

———

Think to thank. In these three words you have the finest capsule course for a happy marriage, the formula for enduring friendships, and a pattern for personal happiness. (BYU Commencement, April 26, 2001)

———

We owe an eternal debt of gratitude to all of those, past and present, who have given so much of themselves, that we

might have so much for ourselves. Take things with gratitude rather than for granted. ("Doubt Not—Fear Not," BYU
Commencement, April 24, 2003)

———

This is a wonderful time to be living here on earth. Our
opportunities are limitless. While there are some things wrong
in the world today, there are many things right, such as teachers who teach, ministers who minister, marriages that make it,
parents who sacrifice, and friends who help.

We can lift ourselves, and others as well, when we refuse to remain in the realm of negative thought and cultivate within our
hearts an attitude of gratitude. If ingratitude be numbered among
the serious sins, then gratitude takes its place among the noblest of
virtues. ("An Attitude of Gratitude," *Ensign,* May 1992, 54)

———

✯

Gracias, danke, merci—whatever language is spoken, "thank
you" frequently expressed will cheer your spirit, broaden your
friendships, and lift your lives to a higher pathway as you journey toward perfection. There is a simplicity—even a sincerity—when "thank you" is spoken. ("Think to Thank," *Ensign,*
November 1998, 17–18)

———

As you look at your life thus far, you will learn from past
mistakes, whether they be yours or those of others. You will recognize also that many people have helped you reach this point
in your life. Give thanks to them—your family, your friends,
your teachers, and others. Express gratitude to those profes-
sors who have planted the seeds of learning and curiosity in
your fertile minds and have instilled within you the skills and

knowledge you will need to succeed. ("Guideposts for Life's Journey," University of Utah Commencement, May 4, 2007)

HABITS

———

Avoid the detours which will deprive you of your celestial reward. You can recognize them if you will. They may be labeled, "Just this once won't matter," or, "My parents are so old-fashioned." Bad habits also can be such pitfalls. First we could break them if we would. Later, we would break them if we could. John Dryden said: "Ill habits gather by unseen degrees—As brooks make rivers, rivers run to seas." Good habits, on the other hand, are the soul's muscles. The more you use them the stronger they grow. ("Great Expectations," BYU Devotional, May 11, 1965)

HAPPINESS

———

To measure the goodness of life by its delights and pleasures and safety is to apply a false standard. The abundant life . . . does not make itself content with commercially produced pleasure, the night club idea of what is a good time, mistaking it for joy and happiness.

On the contrary—

OBEDIENCE TO LAW
RESPECT FOR OTHERS

MASTERY OF SELF
JOY IN SERVICE

These constitute the Abundant Life. ("In Quest of the Abundant Life," Utah State University Baccalaureate, June 2, 1967)

———

"Happiness is the object and design of our existence; and will be the end thereof, if we pursue the path that leads to it; and this path is virtue, uprightness, faithfulness, holiness, and keeping all the commandments of God" (*Teachings of the Prophet Joseph Smith* [1976], 255–56).

This description of such a universal goal was provided by the Prophet Joseph Smith. It was relevant then. It is relevant now. With such a clear road map to follow, why then are there so many unhappy people? Frequently, frowns outnumber smiles and despair dampens joy. We live so far below the level of our divine possibilities. Some become confused by materialism, entangled by sin, and lost among the passing parade of humanity. . . .

Happiness does not consist of a glut of luxury, the world's idea of a "good time." Nor must we search for it in faraway places with strange-sounding names. Happiness is found at home. ("Hallmarks of a Happy Home," *Ensign*, November 1988, 69)

———

The happy life is not ushered in at any age to the sound of drums and trumpets. It grows upon us year by year, little by little, until at last we realize that we have it. It is achieved in individuals, not by flights to the Moon or Mars, but by a body of work done so well that we can lift our heads with assurance and look the world in the eye. Of this be sure: You do not find the happy life—you make it. ("Attitudes of Accomplishment," BYU Devotional, May 19, 1970)

HISTORY

———

A review of the past can be helpful—that is, if we learn from the mistakes and follies of those who have gone before. And if we do not repeat them. ("Be All That You Can Be," BYU–Hawaii Commencement, December 14, 2002)

———

The Apostles went before, showing others the way to follow. They were pioneers.

History records, however, that most men did not come unto Christ, nor did they follow the way He taught. Crucified was the Lord, slain were most of the Apostles, rejected was the truth. The bright sunlight of enlightenment slipped away, and the lengthening shadows of a black night enshrouded the earth.

Generations before, Isaiah had prophesied: "Darkness shall cover the earth, and gross darkness the people" (Isaiah 60:2). Amos had foretold of a famine in the land: "Not a famine of bread, nor a thirst for water, but of hearing the words of the Lord" (Amos 8:11). The dark ages of history seemed never to end. Would no heavenly messengers make their appearance?

In due time honest men with yearning hearts, at the peril of their very lives, attempted to establish points of reference, that they might find the true way. The day of the Reformation was dawning, but the path ahead was difficult. Persecutions would be severe, personal sacrifice overwhelming, and the cost beyond calculation. The reformers were pioneers, blazing wilderness trails in a desperate search for those lost points of reference which, they felt, when found would lead mankind back to the truth Jesus taught. . . . Their deeds were heroic, their contributions many, their sacrifices great—but they did not restore the gospel of Jesus Christ.

Of the reformers, one could ask: "Was their sacrifice in vain? Was their struggle futile?" I answer with a reasoned "No." The Holy Bible was now within the grasp of the people. Each person could better find his or her way. Oh, if only all could read and all could understand! But some could read, and others could hear, and all had access to God through prayer. ("They Showed the Way," *Ensign,* May 1997, 51)

———

At times, progressive, eager youth frown on the possibility of learning from the past. Remember that the roads you travel so briskly lead out of dim antiquity, and you study the past chiefly because of its bearing on the living present . . . and its promise for the future. When one fails to learn from the lessons of the past, he is doomed to repeat the same mistakes and suffer their attendant consequences. ("Yesterday, Today, and Tomorrow," Weber State College Baccalaureate, May 31, 1968)

———

You are living in one of the most precious and privileged periods of all human history—a period of change and challenge and infinite promise. You cannot venture into the uncertainties of the future without reference to the certainties of the past. Your challenge is to join the forces of the old and the new—experience and experiment, history and destiny, the world of man and the new world of science. ("Constant Truths in Changing Times," BYU Commencement, May 26, 1967)

HOLY GHOST

When I served in the navy, sonar was in its infant stages. . . . Sonar is the device [in a ship] whereby we are warned of another ship or other obstacle. It has a beep, and the operator becomes accustomed to listening for that beep. When it becomes other than the normal pattern, he knows that danger is at hand, and he can warn the captain, and the course can be changed.

When I went to school, many young men had white sidewall tires on their automobiles. These automobiles were equipped with what we called "whiskers"—a little metal device that was attached to the fender of the car. As the car would pull in against the curb, those "whiskers" would hit the curb, rather than the curb scraping the white sidewall tires, and they would warn the driver that he could not go any closer to the curb without damaging his tires.

If man can invent sonar to warn against disaster, and if he can invent "whiskers" to put on automobile fenders for the protection of white sidewall tires, doesn't it sound reasonable that the Lord would place a warning device within His children, to warn us when we are on a detour, away from His pathway? I bear my testimony that we have a guiding light. It is foolproof if we will but use it. It is known, as you know and as I know, as the Holy Ghost—the still, small voice. ("The Three R's of Choice," BYU Devotional, November 5, 1963)

Be influenced by that still, small voice. Remember that one with authority placed his hands on your head at the time of your confirmation and said, "Receive the Holy Ghost." Open your hearts, even your very souls, to the sound of that special voice which testifies of truth. As the prophet Isaiah promised, "Thine ears shall hear a word . . . saying, This is the way, walk ye in it" (Isaiah 30:21). ("The Lighthouse of the Lord," General Young Women Meeting, March 22, 1980)

———

I hope . . . that we will listen to the whisperings of the Holy Spirit. I promise you that if we have an ear attuned to the Holy Spirit, if there is a desire for righteousness within our heart, and our conduct reflects that desire, we shall be guided by that Holy Spirit. ("A Time to Choose," BYU Devotional, January 16, 1973)

HOME
(SEE ALSO FAMILY)

———

When Jesus walked the dusty pathways of towns and villages which we now reverently call the Holy Land and taught his disciples by beautiful Galilee, he often spoke in parables, in language the people best understood. Frequently he referred to home building in relationship to the lives of those who listened.

He declared: "Every . . . house divided against itself shall not stand" (Matthew 12:25). Later, he cautioned: "Behold, mine house is a house of order, saith the Lord God, and not a house of confusion" (D&C 132:8).

In a revelation given through the Prophet Joseph at Kirtland, Ohio, December 27, 1832, the Master counseled: "Organize yourselves; prepare every needful thing; and establish a house, even a house of prayer, a house of fasting, a house of faith, a house of learning, a house of glory, a house of order, a house of God" (D&C 88:119).

Where could any of us locate a more suitable blueprint whereby he could wisely and properly build a house to personally occupy throughout eternity?

Such a house would meet the building code outlined in Matthew—even a house built "upon a rock"; a house capable of withstanding the rain of adversity, the floods of opposition and the winds of doubt everywhere present in our challenging world. ("Building a House for Eternity," Special Priesthood Session, Logan Temple, May 4, 1967)

———

A home is much more than a house. A house is built of lumber, brick, and stone. A home is made of love, sacrifice, and respect. A house can be a home, and a home can be a heaven when it shelters a family. Like the structure in which it dwells, the family may be large or small. It may be old or young. It may be in excellent condition or it may show signs of wear, of neglect, of deterioration. ("Heavenly Homes—Forever Families," Satellite Broadcast, January 12, 1986)

———

All of us remember the home of our childhood. Interestingly, our thoughts do not dwell on whether the house was large or small, the neighborhood fashionable or downtrodden. Rather, we delight in the experiences we shared as a family. The home is the laboratory of our lives, and what we learn there largely determines what we do when we leave there. ("Hallmarks of a Happy Home," *Ensign*, November 1988, 69)

———

Slowly but surely we face the truth: We are responsible for the home we build. We must build wisely, for eternity is not a short voyage. There will be calm and wind, sunlight and shadows, joy and sorrow. But if we really try, our home can be a bit of heaven here on earth. The thoughts we think, the deeds we do, the lives we live influence not only the success of our earthly journey; they mark the way to our eternal goals. ("Hallmarks of a Happy Home," *Ensign*, November 1988, 69)

———

Let us make of our homes sanctuaries of righteousness, places of prayer, and abodes of love, that we might merit the blessings that can come only from our Heavenly Father. We need His guidance in our daily lives. ("To Learn, to Do, to Be," *Ensign*, May 1992, 47)

———

When we are tired or ill or discouraged, how sweet the comfort of being able to turn homeward. We are blessed to belong and to have a place in the family circle.

At times we may become bored or irritated with home and family and familiar surroundings. Such may seem less than glamorous, with a sense of sameness, and other places may sometimes seem more exciting. But when we have sampled much and have wandered far and have seen how fleeting and sometimes superficial a lot of the world is, our gratitude grows for the privilege of being part of something we can count on— home and family and the loyalty of loved ones. We come to know what it means to be bound together by duty, by respect, by belonging. We learn that nothing can fully take the place of the blessed relationship of family life. ("A Sanctuary from the

World," Worldwide Leadership Training Satellite Broadcast, February 9, 2008)

HOME TEACHING

———

Is every ordained teacher given the assignment to home teach? What an opportunity to prepare for a mission. What a privilege to learn the discipline of duty. A boy will automatically turn from concern for self when he is assigned to "watch over" others. ("The Aaronic Priesthood Pathway," *Ensign,* November 1984, 42)

———

Recently our grandchildren received their report cards. They displayed them with satisfaction to their parents and to us. . . . I would like all of the priesthood to mark their own grade on the report card of home teaching. . . . *Yes* or *No* answers are sufficient.

1. Are you assigned as a home teacher?
2. Do home teachers visit your home at least once per month?
3. Do home teachers prepare and present a gospel message?
4. Do home teachers inquire concerning each member of the family—even those members who may be away at school or serving on missions?
5. What lesson did the home teachers bring to your home last month?
6. Did the home teachers join with your family in prayer during their visit?

7. Did you go home teaching last month?

("Duty Calls," *Ensign*, May 1996, 45)

———

Most of you are home teachers. You are the eyes and ears of the bishops in seeking out the poor and the afflicted. While doing their duty, vigilant home teachers have observed unemployed fathers anxious to obtain work; distraught mothers seeing their tiny broods suffer; children crying from hunger, inadequately clothed to protect them from the cold of winter. In one instance, all of the family members were sleeping on the floor because they had no beds. Without delay, needed help was provided. ("Be Thou an Example," *Ensign*, November 1996, 47)

———

The home teaching program is a response to modern revelation commissioning those ordained to the priesthood to "teach, expound, exhort, baptize, and watch over the church, . . . and visit the house of each member, and exhort them to pray vocally and in secret and attend to all family duties, . . . to watch over the church always, and be with and strengthen them; and see that there is no iniquity in the church, neither hardness with each other, neither lying, backbiting, nor evil speaking" (D&C 20:42, 47, 53–54). . . .

From the Book of Mormon, Alma "consecrated all their priests and all their teachers; and none were consecrated except they were just men. Therefore they did watch over their people, and did nourish them with things pertaining to righteousness" (Mosiah 23:17–18).

In performing our home teaching responsibilities, we are wise if we learn and understand the challenges of the members of each family. A home teaching visit is also more likely to be successful if an appointment is made in advance. ("Home Teaching—A Divine Service," *Ensign,* November 1997, 46–47)

———

As years come and then go and life's challenges become more difficult, the visits of home teachers to those who have absented themselves from Church activity can be the key which will eventually open the doors to their return. ("Home Teaching—A Divine Service," *Ensign,* November 1997, 48)

———

Home teaching is more than a mechanical visit once per month, that the statistical report of the ward will be pleasing. Ours is the responsibility to teach, to inspire, to motivate, to bring to activity and to eventual exaltation the sons and daughters of God. ("Prophets Speak—The Wise Obey," General Conference Friday Leadership Session, April 3, 1987)

———

Are Aaronic Priesthood men and young men fully utilized in home teaching? They should be paired with those who are strong in spirit, meaning high priests and elders. As they prepare to go into the homes, they should have prayer. The "junior companion," or Aaronic Priesthood holder, should take part in the instruction or teaching to be given in each home.

When the leadership of the stakes and wards get firmly behind this effort, the homes will be visited, the gospel will be taught and precious souls will be saved. ("The Perfection of the Saints," Regional Representatives Seminar, April 1, 1988)

HOPE

———

My brothers and sisters, today, as we look at the world around us, we are faced with problems which are serious and of great concern to us. The world seems to have slipped from the moorings of safety and drifted from the harbor of peace.

Permissiveness, immorality, pornography, dishonesty, and a host of other ills cause many to be tossed about on a sea of sin and crushed on the jagged reefs of lost opportunities, forfeited blessings, and shattered dreams.

My counsel for all of us is to look to the lighthouse of the Lord. There is no fog so dense, no night so dark, no gale so strong, no mariner so lost but what its beacon light can rescue. It beckons through the storms of life. The lighthouse of the Lord sends forth signals readily recognized and never failing.

I love the words found in Psalms: "The Lord is my rock, and my fortress, and my deliverer; my God, my strength, in whom I will trust; . . . I will call upon the Lord . . . so [I shall] be saved from mine enemies" (Psalm 18:2, 3).

The Lord loves us, my brothers and sisters, and will bless us as we call upon Him. ("A Word at Closing," *Ensign*, May 2010, 113)

———

The Apostle Paul, in his second epistle to the Corinthians, urges that we turn from the narrow confinement of the letter of the law and seek the open vista of opportunity which the Spirit provides. I love and cherish Paul's statement: "The letter killeth, but the spirit giveth life" (2 Corinthians 3:6).

In a day of danger or a time of trial, such knowledge, such hope, such understanding bring comfort to the troubled mind and grieving heart. The entire message of the New Testament breathes a spirit of awakening to the human soul. Shadows of despair are dispelled by rays of hope, sorrow yields to joy, and the feeling of being lost in the crowd of life vanishes with the certain knowledge that our Heavenly Father is mindful of each of us.

The Savior provided assurance of this truth when He taught that even a sparrow shall not fall to the ground unnoticed by our Father. He then concluded the beautiful thought by saying, "Fear ye not therefore, ye are of more value than many sparrows" (Matthew 10:29–31). ("The Spirit Giveth Life," *Ensign,* May 1985, 68)

———

We live in a complex world with daily challenges. There is a tendency to feel detached—even isolated—from the Giver of every good gift. We worry that we walk alone.

From the bed of pain, from the pillow wet with the tears of loneliness, we are lifted heavenward by that divine assurance and precious promise, "I will not fail thee, nor forsake thee" (Joshua 1:5).

Such comfort is priceless as we journey along the pathway of mortality, with its many forks and turnings. Rarely is the assurance communicated by a flashing sign or a loud voice. Rather, the language of the Spirit is gentle, quiet, uplifting to the heart and soothing to the soul. ("The Spirit Giveth Life," *Ensign,* May 1985, 68)

Human Relations

———

Perhaps never in history has the need for cooperation, understanding, and goodwill among all people—nations and

individuals alike—been so urgent as today. It is not only fitting—it is imperative—that we emphasize the ideal of brotherhood and the responsibility true brotherhood confers upon us
all. ("Conference Is Here," *Ensign*, May 1990, 5)

———

When we deal in generalities, we will seldom have a success;
but when we deal in specifics, we will rarely have a failure. ("A
Better Way," Training Meeting, April 4, 2002)

———

Let us learn respect for others if we are to realize the abundant life. Man, by nature, is tempted to seek only his own glory
and not the glory of his neighbor or the glory of his God. None
of us lives alone—in our city, our nation, or our world. There
is no dividing line between our prosperity and our neighbor's
wretchedness.

Before we can love and respect our neighbor, we must
place him in proper perspective. One man said, "I looked at
my brother with the microscope of criticism and I said, 'How
coarse my brother is.' I looked at my brother with the telescope
of scorn and I said, 'How small my brother is.' Then I looked
into the mirror of truth and I said, 'How like me my brother
is.'"

Respect for others implies a concern and a love for our
fellow men. ("In Quest of the Abundant Life," Utah State
University Baccalaureate, June 2, 1967)

———

Frequently we are too quick to criticize, too prone to judge,
and too ready to abandon an opportunity to help, to lift,
and, yes, even to save. Some point the accusing finger at the

wayward or unfortunate and in derision say, "Oh, she will never change. She has always been a bad one." A few see beyond the outward appearance and recognize the true worth of a human soul. When they do, miracles occur. The downtrodden, the discouraged, the helpless become "no more strangers and foreigners, but fellowcitizens with the saints, and of the household of God" (Ephesians 2:19). True love can alter human lives and change human nature. ("An Example of the Believers," *Ensign,* November 1992, 97)

———

I would encourage members of the Church wherever they may be to show kindness and respect for all people everywhere. The world in which we live is filled with diversity. We can and should demonstrate respect toward those whose beliefs differ from ours. ("Looking Back and Moving Forward," *Ensign,* May 2008, 90)

———

We are a global church, brothers and sisters. Our membership is found throughout the world. May we be good citizens of the nations in which we live and good neighbors in our communities, reaching out to those of other faiths, as well as to our own. May we be men and women of honesty and integrity in everything we do. ("Until We Meet Again," *Ensign,* November 2008, 106)

———

What a different world this would be if men's hearts all over the world would turn to the principles of true religion and exemplify them in their lives and in their actions. Where religion finds its finest expression there is no conflict, really.

And if there is anything this world needs, it is the peace that comes of understanding, of worship of one's God, and of loyalty to principles of religious life. (BYU International Law and Religion Symposium Luncheon, October 7, 2009)

INSPIRATION

As you approach the Crisis of the Crossroads of Life, as each Latter-day Saint must do, you will perhaps recall a particular passage of scripture, a relevant illustration, a testimony of truth heard and felt. . . . As such a thought floods through your memory, that still, small voice will whisper—"Remember, remember, remember to be true!" ("Decisions Determine Destiny," LDS Student Association Young Women's Meeting, Logan, Utah, May 16, 1968)

Lessons from the past, challenges of the future display dramatically the need for God's help today. Earnestly seek it and you shall surely find it. ("Yesterday, Today, and Tomorrow," Weber State College Baccalaureate, May 31, 1968)

We have been provided divine attributes to guide our journey. We enter mortality not to float with the moving currents of life, but with the power to think, to reason, and to achieve. We left our heavenly home and came to earth in the purity and innocence of childhood.

Our Heavenly Father did not launch us on our eternal

voyage without providing the means whereby we could receive from Him guidance to ensure our safe return. Yes, I speak of prayer. I speak, too, of the whisperings from that still, small voice within each of us; and I do not overlook the holy scriptures, written by mariners who successfully sailed the seas we too must cross. ("An Invitation to Exaltation," Satellite Broadcast, March 4, 1984)

———

If you want to see the light of heaven, if you want to feel the inspiration of Almighty God, if you want to have that feeling within your bosom that your Heavenly Father is guiding you to the left or guiding you to the right, follow the instruction from the passage, "Stand ye in holy places, and be not moved" (D&C 87:8), and then the spirit of our Heavenly Father will be yours. ("Timeless Truths for a Changing World," BYU Women's Conference, May 4, 2001)

———

In the performance of our responsibilities, I have learned that when we heed a silent prompting and act upon it without delay, our Heavenly Father will guide our footsteps and bless our lives and the lives of others. I know of no experience more sweet or feeling more precious than to heed a prompting only to discover that the Lord has answered another person's prayer through you. ("Peace, Be Still," *Ensign,* November 2002, 55)

———

The sweetest spirit and feeling in all of mortality is when we have an opportunity to be on the Lord's errand and to know that He has guided our footsteps. ("Guideposts for Life's Journey," BYU Devotional, November 13, 2007)

INTEGRITY

As we view the world around us, it's possible to feel at times that no one is really honest or virtuous or honorable anymore. We see those who seemingly get ahead in life as a result of deceit, through false promises or by cheating others. In the glow of unearned good repute, people are apt to fall prey to self-delusion and think that they can get away with anything. Others who want too badly for all men to speak well of them come to care more about outside opinions than their own actions.

Being true to oneself is anything but easy if the moral standards of one's associates conflict with his or her own. The herd instinct is strong in the human animal, and the phrase "Everybody else is doing it" has an insidious attraction. To resist what "everybody else" is doing is to risk being ostracized by one's peers, and it's normal to dread rejection. Nothing takes more strength than swimming against the current. ("Three Bridges to Cross," Dixie State College Commencement, May 6, 2011)

———

Perhaps the surest test of an individual's integrity is his or her refusal to do or say anything to damage his or her self-respect. The cornerstone of one's value system should be the question, "What will I think of myself if I do this?"("Three Bridges to Cross," Dixie State College Commencement, May 6, 2011)

———

What is the point of . . . fame and glory if, in the end, we can't look ourselves in the eye, knowing that we have been honest and true? ("Three Bridges to Cross," Dixie State College Commencement, May 6, 2011)

———

True to yourself, fair with your neighbor, you will not find it difficult to be faithful to your God. ("Yesterday, Today, and Tomorrow," Weber State College Baccalaureate, May 31, 1968)

———

When we speak of the demon of **dishonesty**, we can find it in a variety of locations. One such place is in school. Let us avoid cheating, falsifying, taking advantage of others, or anything like unto it. Let integrity be our standard. ("Peace, Be Still," *Ensign,* November 2002, 53)

———

Be honest with yourself; be honest with others; be honest with God. Then you will acquire what the eminent English statesman William H. Gladstone described as the world's greatest need: "A living faith in a personal God." And in this personal God, our Heavenly Father, we place our trust. As the psalmist wrote ever so long ago: "It is better to trust in the Lord than to put confidence in man. It is better to trust in the Lord than to put confidence in princes" (Psalm 118:8–9). ("Learning the ABC's at Dixie," Dixie College D-Day, April 15, 1972)

JESUS CHRIST
(SEE ALSO ATONEMENT)

———

Jesus, throughout His ministry, blessed the sick, restored sight to the blind, made the deaf to hear and the halt and maimed to walk. He taught forgiveness by forgiving. He taught compassion by being compassionate. He taught devotion by giving of Himself. Jesus taught by example. . . .

The challenge today is not necessarily that we should go forth upon the battlefield and lay down our lives, but rather that we should let our lives reflect our love of God and our fellowman by the obedience we render His commandments and the service we give mankind.

Jesus instructed us, "If ye love me, keep my commandments" (John 14:15). "He that hath my commandments, and keepeth them, he it is that loveth me: and he that loveth me shall be loved of my Father, and I will love him, and will manifest myself to him" (John 14:21).

The oft-repeated statement is yet ever true: *Actions speak louder than words.* And the actions whereby we demonstrate that we truly do love God and our neighbor as ourselves will rarely be such as to attract the gaze and admiration of the world. Usually our love will be shown in our day-by-day associations with one another. ("We Should Love As Jesus Loves," Deseret Sunday School Union Conference, April 4, 1965)

Born in a stable, cradled in a manger, [the Savior] came forth from Heaven to live on earth as mortal man and to establish the kingdom of God. During His earthly ministry, He taught men the higher law. His glorious gospel reshaped the thinking of the world. He blessed the sick; He caused the lame to walk, the blind to see, the deaf to hear. He even raised the dead to life.

What was the reaction to His message of mercy, His words of wisdom, His lessons of life? There were a precious few who appreciated Him. They bathed His feet. They learned His word. They followed His example.

Then there were the many who denied Him. When asked by

Pilate, "What shall I do then with Jesus which is called Christ?" (Matthew 27:22), they cried, "Crucify him" (Luke 23:21). They mocked Him. They gave Him vinegar to drink. They reviled Him. They smote Him with a reed. They did spit upon Him. They crucified Him. ("The Search for Jesus," Centennial Service, Lethbridge, Alberta, Canada, June 11, 1967)

———

Before we can successfully undertake a personal search for Jesus, we must first prepare time for Him in our lives and room for Him in our hearts. In these busy days there are many who have time for golf, time for shopping, time for work, time for play, but no time for Christ.

Lovely homes dot the land and provide rooms for eating, rooms for sleeping, playrooms, sewing rooms, television rooms, but no room for Christ.

Do we get a pang of conscience as we recall His own words: "Foxes have holes, and birds of the air have nests, but the Son of man hath not where to lay his head" (Matthew 8:20). Or do we flush with embarrassment when we remember, "And she brought forth her firstborn son, and wrapped him in swaddling clothes, and laid him in a manger; because there was no room for them in the inn" (Luke 2:7). No room. No room. No room. Ever has it been. ("The Search for Jesus," Centennial Service, Lethbridge, Alberta, Canada, June 11, 1967)

———

We may never open gates of cities or doors of palaces, but we will find true happiness and lasting joy when there enters our heart and soul a knowledge and understanding of our Savior's sacrifice. He may come "to us as One unknown, without a name, as of old, by the lake-side, He came to those men who knew Him not. He speaks to us the same word: 'Follow thou me!' and sets us to the tasks which He has to fulfil for our time. He commands. And to those who obey Him, whether they be wise or simple, He will reveal Himself in the toils, the conflicts, the sufferings which they shall pass through in His fellowship, and . . . they shall learn in their own experience who He is" (Albert Schweitzer, *The Quest of the Historical Jesus* [1948], 403).

May each of us be successful in a personal search for the Man of Galilee, even the Son of God, and may our lives reflect our gratitude for His ministry and His sacrifice. ("The Search for Jesus," Centennial Service, Lethbridge, Alberta, Canada, June 11, 1967)

———

Two thousand years ago the Son of Man was born. . . . Sixty-three years had passed since Roman legions under Pompey had conquered Palestine and taken Jerusalem. The helmets, broadswords, and eagles of the Roman legionary were everywhere to be seen. The oppressive yoke of the Caesars was universally felt.

Deep in the depths of human hearts there dwelt a longing, even a yearning, for the advent of the promised Messiah. When will he come? This was the unanswered question on the lips of the righteous.

Generations had lived and died since the Prophet Isaiah had declared: "Behold, a virgin shall conceive, and bear a son" (Isaiah 7:14). "The government shall be upon his shoulder: and his name shall be called Wonderful, Counsellor, The mighty God, The everlasting Father, The Prince of Peace" (Isaiah 9:6).

With such a promise ringing in his ears, can you and I appreciate the supreme joy and overwhelming exultation that coursed through one called Philip when he heard the Savior of the world speak unto him those immortal words, that divine injunction, "Follow me"? The dawn of promise had dispelled the night of despair. The King of kings, the Lord of lords had come.

Such knowledge could not be hidden, nor could Philip of Bethsaida keep to himself such glad tidings. "Philip findeth Nathanael, and saith unto him, We have found him, of whom Moses in the law, and the prophets, did write, Jesus of Nazareth, the son of Joseph.

"And Nathanael said unto him, Can there any good thing come out of Nazareth? Philip saith unto him, Come and see" (John 1:46).

Shall we, too, join Nathanael? Come and see.

Could Nazareth be so honored? Nazareth, the most disregarded valley in a despised province of a conquered land?

Nazareth, just 80 miles from Jerusalem, was situated on the main trade route that ran from Damascus through the Galilean cities to the Mediterranean Coast at Acre. This, however, was not to be the village's claim to fame. Nor was its glory to be found in the beauty of its environs. Nazareth was the scene of more lasting events and profound consequence than routes of trade or landscapes of beauty.

To a city of Galilee, called Nazareth, came the Angel Gabriel, sent from God. To a virgin whose name was Mary, he declared, "Fear not, Mary: for thou hast found favor with God.

"And, behold, thou shalt conceive in thy womb, and bring forth a son, and shalt call his name Jesus.

"He . . . shall be called the Son of . . . God" (Luke 1:30–32). ("Can There Any Good Thing Come Out of Nazareth?" Conference Report, April 1968, 123–24)

———

Down through the generations of time come his excellent example, his welcome words, his divine deeds.

They inspire patience to endure affliction, strength to bear grief, courage to face death, and confidence to meet life. In this world of chaos, of trial, of uncertainty, never has our need for such divine guidance been more desperate.

Lessons from Nazareth, Capernaum, Jerusalem, and Galilee transcend the barriers of distance, the passage of time, the limits of understanding, and bring to troubled hearts a light and a way. ("Can There Any Good Thing Come Out of Nazareth?" Conference Report, April 1968, 125)

———

[Jesus] demonstrated genuine love of God by living the perfect life, by honoring the sacred mission that was His. Never was He haughty. Never was He puffed up with pride. Never was He disloyal. Ever was He humble. Ever was He sincere. Ever was He true.

Though He was led up of the Spirit into the wilderness to be tempted by that master of deceit, even the devil; though He was physically weakened from fasting forty days and forty nights and was an hungered; yet when the evil one proffered Jesus the most alluring and tempting proposals, He gave to us a divine example of true love of God by refusing to deviate from what He knew was right (see Matthew 4:1–11). ("Those Who Love Jesus," *Ensign*, November 1985, 33)

———

Of him who delivered each of us from endless death, I testify that He is a teacher of truth—but He is more than a teacher. He is the exemplar of the perfect life—but He is more than an exemplar. He is the great physician—but He is more than a physician. He who rescued the lost battalion of mankind is the literal Savior of the world, the Son of God, the Prince of Peace, the Holy One of Israel, even the risen Lord, who declared, "I am the first and the last; I am he who liveth, I am he who was slain; I am your advocate with the Father" (D&C 110:4).

As His witness, I testify to you that He lives. ("Building a House for Eternity," San Diego Temple Workers Devotional, November 18, 2001)

———

Our Lord and Savior, Jesus Christ, is our Exemplar and our strength. He is the light that shineth in darkness. He is the Good Shepherd. Though engaged in His majestic ministry, He embraced the opportunity to lift burdens, provide hope, mend bodies, and restore life. ("Meeting Life's Challenges," *Ensign*, November 1993, 71)

———

From time to time the question has been posed, "If Jesus appeared to you today, what questions would you ask of Him?"

My answer has always been, "I would not utter a word. I would listen to Him." ("Christ at Bethesda's Pool," *Ensign*, November 1996, 17)

———

In times past, great throngs journeyed in the crusades of Christianity, feeling that, if only the Holy Land could be secured from the infidel, then Christ would be found in their lives. How mistaken they were. Thousands upon thousands perished. Many others committed heinous crimes in the very name of Christianity. *Jesus will not be found by crusades of men.*

Still others searched for Jesus in councils of debate. Such was the historic Council of Nicea in 325 A.D. There, with the help of the Roman Emperor, the delegates did away in Christendom with the concept of a personal God and a personal Son—the two separate and distinct Glorified Beings of the scriptures. The Creed of Nicea, the "incomprehensible mystery" of which its originators seemed so proud precisely because it could not be understood, substituted for the personal God of love and for Jesus of the New Testament an immaterial abstraction. The result was a maze of confusion and a compoundment of error. *Jesus will not be found in councils of debate.* Men of the world have modified his miracles, doubted his divinity, and rejected his resurrection.

The formula for finding Jesus has always been and ever will be the same—*the earnest and sincere prayer of a humble and pure heart.* ("The Search for Jesus," Conference Report, October 1965, 142–43)

We turn backward in time that we might go forward with hope. Back, back beyond the silent generation, the beat generation, the lost generation. Back, back beyond the Space Age, the Computer Age, and Industrial Age. Back, back to Him who walked the dusty paths of villages we now reverently call the Holy Land, to Him who caused the blind to see, the deaf to hear, the lame to walk, and the dead to live. To Him who tenderly and lovingly assured us, "I am the way, the truth and the life" (John 14:6).

His constant truths prevail in these changing times. He speaks to [us] . . . as He spoke to the multitudes who thronged about Him those many years ago.

Do you remember His words? Do you recall His actions? Do you reflect His teachings in your life? His words and those of His Apostles stand forth as rays of hope penetrating the dullness of despair. ("Constant Truths in Changing Times," BYU Commencement, May 26, 1967)

———

Against the doubting in today's world concerning Christ's divinity, we seek a point of reference, an unimpeachable source, even a testimony of eyewitnesses. Stephen, from biblical times, doomed to the cruel death of a martyr, looked up to heaven and cried, "I see the heavens opened, and the Son of man standing on the right hand of God" (Acts 7:56).

Who can help but be convinced by the stirring testimony of Paul to the Corinthians? He declared "that Christ died for our sins according to the scriptures; and that he was buried, and that he rose again the third day according to the scriptures: and . . . was seen of Cephas, then of the twelve: . . . And," said Paul, "last of all he was seen of me" (1 Corinthians 15:3–8).

In our dispensation, this same testimony was spoken boldly by the Prophet Joseph Smith, as he and Sidney Rigdon testified, "And now, after the many testimonies which have been given of him, this is the testimony, last of all, which we give of him: That he lives!" (D&C 76:22).

This is the knowledge that sustains. This is the truth that comforts. This is the assurance that guides those who are bowed down with grief—out of the shadows and into the light. ("I Know That My Redeemer Lives!" *Ensign*, May 2007, 23–24)

———

We need not visit the Holy Land to feel Him close to us. We need not walk by the shores of Galilee or among the Judean hills to walk where Jesus walked.

In a very real sense, all can walk where Jesus walked when, with His words on our lips, His spirit in our hearts, and His teachings in our lives, we journey through mortality.

I would hope that we would walk as He walked—with confidence in the future, with an abiding faith in His Father, and a genuine love for others. ("The Paths Jesus Walked," *Ensign*, May 1974, 48)

JOSEPH SMITH

To get to the true meaning of the birth of the Prophet [Joseph Smith], we need to go back beyond the year of our Lord 1805. We need to go back a long way into history and read what another great prophet said—that prophet, Joseph, who was sold into Egypt and who literally saved his brothers. . . . Said Joseph: "A seer shall the Lord my God raise up, who shall be a choice seer unto the fruit of my loins" (2 Nephi 3:6).

"And his name shall be called after me; and it shall be after the name of his father. And he shall be like unto me; for the thing, which the Lord shall bring forth by his hand, by the power of the Lord shall bring my people unto salvation" (2 Nephi 3:15).

Joseph Smith, Jr., was called after the name of Joseph who was sold into Egypt. He was also called Joseph after his own father, Joseph Smith, Sr., literally fulfilling that prophecy which had been spoken many hundreds of years before his birth. (Twenty-First Annual Joseph Smith Memorial Sermon, December 11, 1963)

Our Heavenly Father inspired Christopher Columbus in his discovery of America. Our Heavenly Father inspired the leaders of the renaissance period. Our Heavenly Father inspired men and caused that they would dream dreams and see visions and discover marvelous instruments and inventions which would enable them to set forth upon the oceans and to be led to the place where our Father in Heaven would have them led. Our Heavenly Father inspired the man who invented movable type, that His holy word, as found in the Bible, could be printed and disseminated widely to the people. Our Heavenly Father inspired the leaders of . . . the United States of America, that they might together, under His direction, having been raised up by God for the purpose, establish the Constitution of this country and . . . Bill of Rights, that . . . by the year of our Lord 1805 [there would be] a climate where our Heavenly Father could send into this period of mortality a choice spirit who would be known as Joseph Smith, Jr. His life's mission would alter the course of all future events. Thus came Joseph into the world. (Twenty-First Annual Joseph Smith Memorial Sermon, December 11, 1963)

———

Following the visits of the angel Moroni to young Joseph and his acquisition of the plates, Joseph commenced the difficult assignment of translation. One can but imagine the dedication, the devotion, and the labor required to translate in fewer than 90 days this record of over 500 pages covering a period of 2,600 years. I love the words Oliver Cowdery used to describe the time he spent assisting Joseph with the translation of the Book of Mormon: "These were days never to be forgotten—to sit under the sound of a voice dictated by the inspiration of heaven, awakened the utmost gratitude of this bosom!" (Joseph Smith—History 1:71, footnote). ("The Prophet Joseph Smith: Teacher by Example," *Ensign,* November 2005, 68)

———

I think one of the sweetest lessons taught by the Prophet Joseph, and yet one of the saddest, occurred close to the time of his death. He had seen in vision the Saints leaving Nauvoo and going to the Rocky Mountains. He was anxious that his people be led away from their tormentors and into this promised land which the Lord had shown him. He no doubt longed to be with them. However, he had been issued an arrest warrant on trumped up charges. Despite many appeals to Governor

Ford, the charges were not dismissed. Joseph left his home, his wife, his family, and his people and gave himself up to the civil authorities, knowing he would probably never return. . . .

In Carthage Jail he was incarcerated with his brother Hyrum and others. On June 27, 1844, Joseph, Hyrum, John Taylor, and Willard Richards were together there when an angry mob stormed the jail, ran up the stairway, and began firing through the door of the room they occupied. Hyrum was killed, and John Taylor was wounded. Joseph Smith's last great act here upon the earth was one of selflessness. He crossed the room, most likely "thinking that it would save the lives of his brethren in the room if he could get out, . . . and sprang into the window where two balls pierced him from the door, and one entered his right breast from without" (*History of the Church* [1932–1952], 6:618). He gave his life; Willard Richards and John Taylor were spared. "Greater love hath no man than this, that a man lay down his life for his friends" (John 15:13). The Prophet Joseph Smith taught us **love**—by example. ("The Prophet Joseph Smith: Teacher by Example," *Ensign,* November 2005, 68–69)

I love the words of President Brigham Young, who said, "I feel like shouting Hallelujah, all the time, when I think that I ever knew Joseph Smith, the Prophet whom the Lord raised up and ordained, and to whom He gave keys and power to build up the kingdom of God on earth" (*Teachings of Presidents of the Church: Brigham Young* [1997], 343).

To this fitting tribute to our beloved Joseph, I add my own testimony that I know he was God's prophet, chosen to restore the gospel of Jesus Christ in these latter days. ("The Prophet Joseph Smith: Teacher by Example," *Ensign,* November 2005, 69–70)

———

Through Joseph Smith, the gospel—which had been lost during centuries of apostasy—was restored, the priesthood and its keys were received, the doctrines of salvation were revealed, the gospel and temple ordinances—along with the sealing power—were returned and, in 1830, the Church of Jesus Christ was re-established on the earth.

Though reviled and persecuted, the Prophet Joseph never wavered in his testimony of Jesus Christ. His peers watched him lead with dignity and grace, endure hardships, and time and again rise to new challenges until his divine mission was completed. Today that heritage he established still shines for all the world to see. The teachings he translated and his legacy of love for his fellow man continue in the millions of hearts touched by the message he declared so long ago.

Few in this dispensation have paid so dearly for an irrevocable testimony of Jesus Christ as did the Prophet Joseph Smith. On June 18, 1844, he gave what was to be his last sermon. He very likely knew that he would not again address his people. His concluding remarks were these: "God has tried you. You are a good people; . . . I love you with all my heart. Greater love hath no man than that he should lay down his life for his friends. You have stood by me in the hour of trouble, and I am willing to sacrifice my life for your preservation. May the Lord God of Israel bless you forever and ever." His words sank deep into the hearts of the people. It was the last time, in the flesh, that they were to listen to . . . his voice, or to feel . . . his inspiration (from *Historical Record,* edited and published by Andrew Jenson [1889], 555).

Ultimately, the Prophet Joseph was slain by evil men who assumed the church would collapse after his death. George Q. Cannon, who served as a member of the Quorum of the Twelve Apostles and as a counselor to several Church presidents, wrote: "The enemies of truth were sure that they had now destroyed the work. And yet it lives, greater and stronger after the lapse of years. It is indestructible, for it is the work of God. And knowing that it is the eternal work of God, we know that Joseph Smith who established it was a prophet holy and pure" (*Life of Joseph Smith the Prophet* [1999], 527). . . .

We do not worship the Prophet Joseph; however he left behind a legacy that enables [his] followers today on every continent to proclaim him as a prophet of God. May we, each of us, strive to continue the Prophet Joseph's vision for this work and to magnify his legacy through our works and testimonies to others, that they may know him as we do and that they may experience the peace and joy of the gospel he restored.

When the Savior returns to the earth in glory, the Prophet Joseph will come forth with the righteous as a resurrected being and will continue to minister under the Savior's direction. As our beloved hymn affirms, "Millions shall know 'Brother Joseph' again." Of this truth I testify. ("The Prophet Joseph Smith," 200th Birthday Commemoration, December 23, 2005)

———

No description of models for us to follow would be complete without including Joseph Smith, the first prophet of this dispensation. When but fourteen years of age, this courageous young man entered a grove of trees, which later would be called sacred, and received an answer to his sincere prayer.

There followed for Joseph unrelenting persecution as he related to others the account of the glorious vision he received in that grove. Yet, although he was ridiculed and scorned, he stood firm. Said he, "I had seen a vision; I knew it, and I knew that God knew it, and I could not deny it, neither dared I do it" (Joseph Smith—History 1:25).

Step by step, facing opposition at nearly every turn and yet always guided by the hand of the Lord, Joseph organized The Church of Jesus Christ of Latter-day Saints. He proved courageous in all that he did.

Toward the end of his life, as he was led away with his brother Hyrum to Carthage Jail, he bravely faced what he undoubtedly knew lay ahead for him, and he sealed his testimony with his blood.

As we face life's tests, may we ever emulate that undaunted courage epitomized by the Prophet Joseph Smith. ("Models to Follow," *Ensign,* November 2002, 62)

———

"I was born in the year of our Lord 1805 on the 23rd day of December in the town of Sharon, Windsor County, state of Vermont." Thus spoke the first prophet of this great dispensation, the dispensation of the fulness of times. His testimony has been translated into Portuguese, Spanish, Chinese, Russian, German, French, Polish, and almost every language of the civilized world. When it has been read by honest men and honest women, it has changed thinking and they have changed lives. This is the value of the simple testimony of the boy prophet, Joseph Smith. ("The Prophet Joseph Smith—Teacher by Example," General Authority Family Home Evening, June 28, 1993)

———

Volumes have been written concerning the life and accomplishments of Joseph Smith, but for our purposes . . . perhaps a highlight or two will suffice: He was visited by the angel Moroni. He translated, from the precious plates to which he was directed, the Book of Mormon, with its new witness of Christ to all the world. He was the instrument in the hands of the Lord through whom came mighty revelations pertaining to the establishment of The Church of Jesus Christ of Latter-day Saints. In the course of his ministry he was visited by John the Baptist, Moses, Elijah, Peter, James, and John, that the

Restoration of all things might be accomplished. He endured persecution; he suffered grievously, as did his followers. He trusted in God. He was true to his prophetic calling. He commenced a marvelous missionary effort to the entire world, which today brings light and truth to the souls of mankind. At length, Joseph Smith died the martyr's death, as did his brother Hyrum.

Joseph Smith was a pioneer indeed. ("They Showed the Way," *Ensign,* May 1997, 51–52)

JUDGING

I'd like to share with you a few thoughts concerning how we view each other. . . . Are we making judgments when we don't have all the facts? What do we see when we look at others? What judgments do we make about them?

Said the Savior: "Judge not" (Matthew 7:1). He continued, "Why beholdest thou the mote that is in thy brother's eye, but considerest not the beam that is in thine own eye?" (Matthew 7:3).

None of us is perfect. I know of no one who would profess to be so. And yet for some reason, despite our own imperfections, we have a tendency to point out those of others. We make judgments concerning their actions or inactions.

There is really no way we can know the heart, the intentions, or the circumstances of someone who might say or do something we find reason to criticize. Thus, the commandment: "Judge not" (Matthew 7:1). ("Charity Never Faileth," *Ensign,* November 2010, 122)

———

Appearances can be so deceiving, such a poor measure of a person. Admonished the Savior, "Judge not according to the appearance" (John 7:24).

A member of a women's organization once complained when a certain woman was selected to represent the organization. She had never met the woman, but she had seen a photograph of her and didn't like what she saw, considering her to be overweight. She commented, "Of the thousands of women in this organization, surely a better representative could have been chosen."

True, the woman who was chosen was not "model slim." But those who knew her and knew her qualities saw in her far more than was reflected in the photograph. The photograph *did* show that she had a friendly smile and a look of confidence. What the photograph *didn't* show was that she was a loyal and compassionate friend, a woman of intelligence who loved the Lord and who loved and served His children. It didn't show that she volunteered in the community and was a considerate and concerned neighbor. In short, the photograph did not reflect who she really was.

I ask: If attitudes, deeds, and spiritual inclinations were reflected in *physical features,* would the countenance of the woman who complained be as lovely as that of the woman she criticized? ("Charity Never Faileth," *Ensign,* November 2010, 122–23)

———

Each of you is unique. You are different from each other in many ways. There are those of you who are married. Some of you stay at home with your children, while others of you work outside your homes. Some of you are empty nesters. There are those of you who are married but do not have children. There are those who are divorced, those who are widowed. Many of you are single women. Some of you have college degrees; some of you do not. There are those who can afford the latest fashions and those who are lucky to have one appropriate Sunday outfit. Such differences are almost endless. Do these differences tempt us to judge one another?

Mother Teresa, a Catholic nun who worked among the poor in India most of her life, spoke this profound truth: "If you judge people, you have no time to love them." The Savior has admonished, "This is my commandment, That ye love one another, as I have loved you" (John 15:12). I ask: *can we love one another, as the Savior has commanded, if we judge each other?* And I answer—with Mother Teresa: no, we cannot.

The Apostle James taught, "If any . . . among you seem to be religious, and bridleth not his tongue, but deceiveth his own heart, this man's [or woman's] religion is vain" (James 1:26). ("Charity Never Faileth," *Ensign,* November 2010, 124)

———

I believe there are many times when refraining from judgment—or gossip or criticism, which are certainly akin to judgment—takes an act of courage.

Unfortunately, there are those who feel it necessary to criticize and to belittle others. You have, no doubt, been with such people, as you will be in the future. . . . We are not left to wonder what our behavior should be in such situations. . . . [The Savior] admonished, "Cease to find fault one with another" (D&C 88:124). It will take real courage, when you are surrounded by your peers and feeling the pressure to participate in such criticisms and judgments, to refrain from joining in.

. . . I plead with you to have the courage to refrain from judging and criticizing those around you, as well as the courage to make certain everyone is included and feels loved and valued. ("May You Have Courage," *Ensign,* May 2009, 124–25)

LAW

———

The laws of the land . . . do not restrict our conduct so much as they guarantee our freedom, provide us protection and safeguard all that is dear to us.

In our time when otherwise honorable men bend the law, twist the law, and wink at violations of the law, when crime goes unpunished, legally imposed sentences go unserved, and irresponsible and illegal conduct soars beyond previously recorded heights, there is a very real need to return to the basic justice which the laws provide when honest men sustain them. ("In Quest of the Abundant Life," Utah State University Baccalaureate, June 2, 1967)

LEADERSHIP

———

The expression, "Knowledge is Power," is often attributed to Sir Francis Bacon, but it had its origin long before his time, in the saying of Solomon that "A wise man is strong; yea, a man of knowledge increaseth strength" (Proverbs 24:5).

Do you . . . have a knowledge of your particular assignment? Do you know what is expected of you? Do you know the Handbook? Do you really know those who serve under your direction, that you might provide guidance and counsel for them? But above and beyond this knowledge, do you know the gospel? "And this is life eternal, that they might know thee the only true God, and Jesus Christ, whom thou hast sent" (John 17:3).

Such knowledge will dispel that hidden and insidious enemy who lurks within and limits your capacity, destroys your initiative, and strangles your effectiveness. This enemy of whom I speak is fear: a fear to wholeheartedly accept your calling; a fear to provide direction to others; a fear to lead, to motivate, to inspire. (June Conference, June 18, 1966)

———

"Until willingness overflows obligation, men fight as conscripts rather than following the flag as patriots. Duty is never worthily performed until it is done by one who would gladly do more if he could" (Harry Emerson Fosdick). The Lord counseled, "Wherefore, be not weary in well-doing, for ye are laying the foundation of a great work. And out of small things proceedeth that which is great. Behold, the Lord requireth the heart and a willing mind; and the willing and obedient shall eat the good of the land of Zion in these last days" (D&C 64:33–34).

. . . Faithful service enables us to work as a team, which teamwork eliminates the weakness of a man standing alone and substitutes, therefore, the strength of men standing together.

Our task is larger than ourselves, our influence more lasting than our lives. We need the help of Almighty God. For the boys we lead are created in His own image. ("Builders of Boys," 47th Annual Scouters Convention, February 14, 1966)

———

We cannot be careless in our reach. Lives of others depend on us. The power to lead is indeed the power to mislead; and the power to mislead is the power to destroy. ("Be All That You Can Be," BYU–Hawaii Commencement, December 14, 2002)

———

Any of us in the western part of the United States and Canada can, on occasion, see sheepherders driving their flocks to summer pasture or returning from the mountains as winter may approach. Usually the sheepherder is slouched over in the saddle, trailing his flock, with a host of anxious dogs yapping at the heels of the sheep and driving them onward in a determined course. How different is this scene from one which I viewed in Munich, Germany, where a true shepherd, with staff in hand, walked in front of his flock. The sheep recognized him as their leader, and indeed their shepherd, and followed him willingly wheresoever he would lead them. (June Conference, June 28, 1969)

———

✸ As leaders, may we remember that the mantle of leadership is not the cloak of comfort, but the robe of responsibility. ("Builders of Faith in Children of God," Interfaith Service, Lethbridge, Alberta, Canada, June 10, 1967)

———

Some attempt to build a bridge with inferior materials, inadequate planning, and improper tools. The finished product may appear substantial, attractive, and be ready for use in a minimum of time. But then come the storms and the stresses of life and the telltale sign: "Danger! Bridge washed out!" You cannot risk such an occurrence in your bridge-building. Your responsibility is too great, your influence too lasting, your opportunity too perishable. You must build wisely, skillfully, and, with meticulous care, follow your blueprint. ("Building Bridges," Address to YWMIA Executives, June 24, 1967)

———

You cannot perform all of the needed work by yourself. Executive capacity is a quality to be cultivated. The renowned business leader J.C. Penney advises: "My definition of an executive's job is brief and to the point. It is simply this: Getting things done through other people." Cooperativeness is not so much learning how to get along with others as taking the kinks out of yourself, so that others can get along with you. ("Building Bridges," Address to YWMIA Executives, June 24, 1967)

———

We live in troubled times. Those for whom we have responsibility look to us for guidance and example. They know that the dropout of today is going to be the shutout in tomorrow's economy. ("Duty—Honor—Country," National Boy Scouts of America Duty to God Breakfast, May 29, 2003)

———

As priesthood and auxiliary leaders, we are entitled to the Lord's assistance in magnifying our callings and fulfilling our responsibilities. Seek His help, and when the inspiration comes to you, move on that inspiration concerning where to go, whom to see, what to say, and how to say it. We can think a thought to death, but only when we move upon the thought do we bless human lives.

May we be true shepherds of those for whom we have responsibility. . . . The Lord Himself said to Ezekiel the prophet, "Woe be to the shepherds of Israel that . . . feed not the flock" (Ezekiel 34:2–3).

Ours is the responsibility to care for the flock, for the precious sheep, these tender lambs, are everywhere to be found—at home in our own families, in the homes of our extended families, and waiting for us in our Church callings. Jesus is our Exemplar. Said He, "I am the good shepherd, and know my sheep" (John 10:14). We have a shepherding responsibility. ("Heavenly Homes, Forever Families," *Ensign,* June 2006, 101–2)

———

Increasingly we hear from leaders in business, professions, and government that it is easy to find people who can do what they are told but difficult to find people who know what to do without being told. ("Be All That You Can Be," BYU–Hawaii Commencement, December 14, 2002)

———

The calling of the early Apostles reflected the influence of the Lord. When He sought a man of faith, He did not select him from the throng of the self-righteous who were found regularly in the synagogue. Rather, He called him from among the fishermen of Capernaum. Peter, Andrew, James, and John heard the call, "Follow me, and I will make you fishers of men" (Matthew 4:19). They followed. Simon, man of doubt, became Peter, Apostle of faith.

When the Savior was to choose a missionary of zeal and power, He found him not among His advocates but amidst His adversaries. Saul of Tarsus—the persecutor—became Paul the proselyter. The Redeemer chose imperfect men to teach the way to perfection. He did so then; he does so now.

He calls you and me to serve Him here below and sets us to the task He would have us fulfill. The commitment is total. There is no conflict of conscience.

As we follow that Man of Galilee—even the Lord Jesus Christ—our personal influence will be felt for good wherever we are, whatever our callings. ("Your Personal Influence," *Ensign*, May 2004, 20)

———

The shifting sands of popular opinion, the power of the peer group, in all too many instances become an irresistible magnet drawing downward to destruction the precious sons and daughters of God. You become the stable force, the port of safety in the storm-tossed seas, the watchman on the tower, even the guide at the crossroads. (MIA June Conference, June 25, 1971)

———

In many businesses throughout the countries of the world, where a successful owner of a business wants to train his son to follow in his father's footsteps, he will insure that the son has experience in each phase of the company's operations. Once he has experience in one department, then he is moved to another department and yet to another department. Then, when he becomes the manager of the business, he is not an amateur or a novice, but he has an awareness of his responsibility. We all know the story of the ruling monarch who sent his son out to live among the peasants of the land so that he would learn how to rule his people with mercy and so that he would see the government from the people's standpoint.

. . . We are part of a kingdom. We have the responsibility to preside and to prepare ourselves for eventual godhood. It's important, therefore, that we understand the needs of the people—to be prepared in such leadership. Since the Church is our Father's business, . . . we have the responsibility to prepare ourselves to govern in humility, but with ability. And our Heavenly Father will hold us accountable for our performance. We must magnify our callings. ("What Can We Do?" Amsterdam Area Conference, August 7, 1976)

———

Young men are entitled to wise leadership. They are entitled to leadership that leads by example. Do we have clean hands and pure hearts, brethren? Do we put first the kingdom of God and His righteousness? Do we have the capacity to serve the Lord with all of our heart, mind, might, and strength (see D&C 4:2)? Do we have the wisdom to be our brother's keeper (see Genesis 4:9)? This is our responsibility. And Lucifer, that evil one, would attempt to cause us to fail. He would cause us to lose sight of our objective. He would cause us to become discouraged.

Brethren, let us not come to discouragement. Let us accept our responsibility unwaveringly. Let us fill our duty and perform our assignment as though the entire kingdom of God depended upon us alone. ("What Can We Do?" Amsterdam Area Conference, August 7, 1976)

LOVE

———

As Jesus, our Lord and Savior, ministered among men, He was constantly beset by groups such as the Sadducees or the Pharisees who would direct leading questions to Him in an effort to confound Him. Such was the inquiring lawyer who stepped forward and boldly asked: "Master, which is the great commandment in the law?"(Matthew 22:36). I suppose Jesus must have been weary by this time, having answered query after query, and perhaps we would be critical of the impetuous lawyer; yet I am grateful that this cardinal question was asked.

Matthew records that Jesus said unto him, "Thou shalt love the Lord thy God with all thy heart, and with all thy soul, and with all thy mind. This is the first and great commandment. And the second is like unto it, Thou shalt love thy neighbor as thyself" (Matthew 22:37–39). And Mark concludes the account with the Savior's statement, "There is none other command greater than these" (Mark 12:31).

Not one could find fault with the Master's answer. His very actions gave credence to His words of instruction. He demonstrated genuine love of God by living the perfect life, by honoring the sacred mission that was His. ("We Should Love As Jesus Loves," Deseret Sunday School Union Conference, April 5, 1965)

———

Years after the law of Moses was given, there came the meridian of time, when a great endowment emerged—a power stronger than weapons, a wealth more lasting than the coins of Caesar; for the King of kings and Lord of lords introduced into the principles of law the concept of love. ("In Quest of the Abundant Life," Utah State University Baccalaureate, June 2, 1987)

———

President George Albert Smith said, "It does not pay to scold. I believe you can get people to do anything (if you can get them to do it at all) by loving them into doing it." . . .

Our brothers can be lifted to God through the faith we help to build within them. Do our human relations reflect the spirit of love? Are we concerned with the salvation of others or simply the satisfaction of self? . . .

Do you hear the echo of the ancient prophet's voice, "He that loveth silver shall not be satisfied with silver; nor he that loveth abundance with increase" (Ecclesiastes 5:10)? Could we not counter, "He that loveth his fellow men can lead them to

God." "Love one another, as I have loved you" (John 15:12). ("Builders of Faith in Children of God," Interfaith Service, Lethbridge, Alberta, Canada, June 10, 1967)

———

On the journey along the pathway of life, there are casualties. Indifference, carelessness, selfishness, and sin all take their costly toll in human lives. There are those who, for unexplained reasons, march to the sound of a different drummer, later to learn they have followed the Pied Piper of sorrow and suffering. Fractured families and shattered homes need the binding band—even the healing balm—of love. ("Three Hallmarks of a Happy Family," Interfaith Conference on the American Family, September 13, 2003)

———

Love is the catalyst that causes change. Love is the balm that brings healing to the soul. But love doesn't grow like weeds or fall like rain. Love has its price. "God so loved the world, that he gave his only begotten Son, that whosoever believeth in him should not perish, but have everlasting life" (John 3:16). That Son, even the Lord Jesus Christ, gave His life that we might have eternal life, so great was His love for His Father and for us. ("A Doorway Called Love," *Ensign,* November 1987, 66)

———

[The] opportunity of serving in the Church will enable you to demonstrate a love of God and a love of your neighbor. . . . There is no finer way to demonstrate love of God than by serving Him in the positions to which we may be called. Occasionally, the reward for that service will be prompt, and we'll see the light in the eyes of the person whom we have helped. Other times, however, the Lord will let us wait a little while and let our reward come another way. Many of you will be in the process of helping less active people. Never give up, but forever press on in your efforts to help them. The best way to help a person to become fully active in the Church is to love him into that activity. (BYU Fourteen-Stake Fireside, October 11, 1981)

———

Of all the blessings which I have had in my life, the greatest blessing I can share with you is that feeling which the Lord provides when you know that He, the Lord, has answered the prayer of another person through you. As you love the Lord, as you love your neighbor, you will discover that our Heavenly Father will answer the prayers of others through your ministry. (BYU Fourteen-Stake Fireside, October 11, 1981)

———

We do not live alone—in our city, our nation, or our world. There is no dividing line between our prosperity and our neighbor's wretchedness. "Love thy neighbor" (3 Nephi 12:43) is more than a divine truth. It is a pattern for perfection. This truth inspires the familiar charge, "Go forth to serve." Try as some may, we cannot escape the influence our lives have upon the lives of others. Ours is the opportunity to build, to lift, to inspire, and indeed to lead. ("Be All That You Can Be," BYU–Hawaii Commencement, December 14, 2002)

———

The New Testament teaches that it is impossible to take a right attitude toward Christ without taking an unselfish attitude toward men. "Inasmuch as ye have done it unto one of the least of these my brethren, ye have done it unto me"

(Matthew 25:40). We may think as we please, but there is no question about what the Bible teaches. In the New Testament there is no road to the heart of God that does not lead through the heart of man. ("Be All That You Can Be," BYU–Hawaii Commencement, December 14, 2002)

———

You cannot serve your neighbor without demonstrating your love for God. Service is a product of love. So long as we love, we serve. ("The Spirit of Relief Society," Relief Society Sesquicentennial Conference, March 14, 1992)

———

[The Lord] speaks, and when men obey they receive the blessings. When they do not obey, they receive not the blessings. You remember the lawyer who came to the Savior and asked Him what the great commandment in the law was. And the Savior answered him that one should love his Lord, even his God, with all of his might, mind, and strength. And He indicated that this was the first and great commandment, and the second was like unto it: Thou shalt love thy neighbor as thyself (see Matthew 22:36–39).

Could I ask the question, "Who is my neighbor?" . . . As we follow the example of the Lord, . . . we shall have no difficulty identifying who our neighbor really is. You remember the experience of the woman at the well, a confessed sinner . . . in the process of repentance. She was a neighbor to Jesus (see John 4:6–30). You remember the man who had the experience at the time of the trial and crucifixion of Jesus, the man who so aroused the ire of the servants of the Lord that a servant did smite off his ear. The Lord restored that ear. He, too, was a neighbor to Jesus (see Mark 14:47; John 18:10). You remember the thief upon the cross, and that beautiful assurance given him by the Master, even of hope beyond the grave. He, too, was a neighbor of Jesus.

When I think of the word *neighbor,* when I let my mind reflect upon what we ought to be doing for one another, and the spirit in which we should be doing it, I think of the parable of the Good Samaritan. Here was a man desperately in need. The priest with all of his vestments passed him by and did not help him. Then came the Levite who likewise did not help him. Then came the Samaritan who rendered the necessary aid. And then came the question from the Master: Who was the neighbor to the man in need? This is our example. ("Who Is My Neighbor?" Amsterdam Area Conference, August 7, 1976)

✳ MAN ✳

God made a computer once, constructing it with infinite care and precision exceeding that of the efforts of all the scientists combined. Using clay for the main structure, He installed within it a system for the continuous intake of information of all kinds and descriptions, by sight, hearing, and feeling; a circulatory system to keep all channels constantly clean and serviceable; a digestive system to preserve its strength and vigor; and a nervous system to keep all parts in constant communication and coordination. It far surpassed the finest modern computer and was equally dead. It was equipped to memorize and calculate and work out the most complex equation, but there was something lacking.

Then God "breathed into his nostrils the breath of life; and man became a living soul" (Genesis 2:7).

This is why man has powers no modern computer possesses or ever will possess. God gave man life and with it the power to think and reason and decide and love. ("In Quest of the Abundant Life," *Ensign*, March 1988, 5)

———

Each of us should remember that he or she is a son or daughter of God, endowed with faith, gifted with courage, and guided by prayer. Our eternal destiny is before us. The Apostle Paul speaks to us today as he spoke to Timothy long years ago: "Neglect not the gift that is in thee" (1 Timothy 4:14). "O Timothy, keep that which is committed to thy trust" (1 Timothy 6:20).

At times many of us let that enemy of achievement—even the culprit "self-defeat"—dwarf our aspirations, smother our dreams, cloud our vision, and impair our lives. The enemy's voice whispers in our ears, "You can't do it." "You're too young." "You're too old." "You're nobody." This is when we remember that we are created in the image of God. Reflection on this truth provides a profound sense of strength and power. ("Choose You This Day," *Ensign*, November 2004, 68)

———

A wise man, a noble ruler, King David, king of all Israel, once asked a question of the Lord—and this same question has been asked time and time again down through the centuries of time. He said, as recorded in the eighth Psalm, "When I consider thy heavens, the work of thy fingers, the moon and the stars, which thou hast ordained; What is man, that thou art mindful of him?" (Psalm 8:3–4).

"What is man, that thou art mindful of him?" The Lord Himself chose to give an answer to King David when He made a declaration which rings down through the years: "Remember the worth of souls is great in the sight of God" (D&C 18:10). (MIA June Conference, June 12, 1964)

Marriage

———

I have thought a lot lately about . . . young men who are of an age to marry but who have not yet felt to do so. I see lovely young ladies who desire to be married and to raise families, and yet their opportunities are limited because so many young men are postponing marriage.

This is not a new situation. Much has been said concerning this matter by past Presidents of the Church. I share with you just one or two examples of their counsel.

Said President Harold B. Lee, "We are not doing our duty as holders of the priesthood when we go beyond the marriageable age and withhold ourselves from an honorable marriage to these lovely women" ("President Harold B. Lee's General Priesthood Address," *Ensign,* January 1974, 100).

President Gordon B. Hinckley said this: "My heart reaches out to . . . our single sisters, who long for marriage and cannot seem to find it. . . . I have far less sympathy for the young men, who under the customs of our society have the prerogative to take the initiative in these matters but in so many cases fail to do so" ("What God Hath Joined Together," *Ensign,* May 1991, 71).

I realize there are many reasons why you may be hesitating to take that step of getting married. If you are concerned about providing financially for a wife and family, may I assure you that there is no shame in a couple having to scrimp and save. It is generally during these challenging times that you will grow closer together as you learn to sacrifice and to make difficult decisions. Perhaps you are afraid of making the wrong choice. To this I say that you need to exercise faith. Find someone with whom you can be compatible. Realize that you will not be able to anticipate every challenge which may arise, but be assured that almost anything can be worked out if you are resourceful and if you are committed to making your marriage work.

Perhaps you are having a little too much fun being single, taking extravagant vacations, buying expensive cars and toys, and just generally enjoying the carefree life with your friends. I've encountered groups of you running around together, and I admit that I've wondered why you aren't out with the young ladies.

. . . There is a point at which it's time to think seriously about marriage and to seek a companion with whom you want to spend eternity. If you choose wisely and if you are committed to the success of your marriage, there is nothing in this life which will bring you greater happiness.

When you marry, brethren, you will wish to marry in the house of the Lord. For you who hold the priesthood, there should be no other option. Be careful lest you destroy your eligibility to be so married. You can keep your courtship within proper bounds while still having a wonderful time. ("Priesthood Power," *Ensign,* May 2011, 67–68)

———

Choose a companion carefully and prayerfully; and when you are married, be fiercely loyal one to another. Priceless advice comes from a small framed plaque I once saw in the home of an uncle and aunt. It read: "Choose your love; love your choice." There is great wisdom in those few words. Commitment in marriage is absolutely essential. ("Priesthood Power," *Ensign,* May 2011, 68)

———

If any of you are having difficulty in your marriage, I urge you to do all that you can to make whatever repairs are necessary, that you might be as happy as you were when your marriage started out. We who are married in the house of the Lord do so for time and for all eternity, and then we must put forth the necessary effort to make it so. I realize that there are situations where marriages cannot be saved, but I feel strongly that for the most part they can be and should be. Do not let your marriage get to the point where it is in jeopardy. ("Priesthood Power," *Ensign,* May 2011, 69)

———

Those who marry in the hope of forming a permanent partnership require certain skills and attitudes of mind. They must be skillful in adapting to each other, they need capacity to work out mutual problems, they need willingness to give and take in the search for harmony; and they need unselfishness of the highest sort—thought for their partners taking the place of desire for themselves. ("In Quest of the Abundant Life," *Ensign,* March 1988, 4)

———

It is essential that you become well acquainted with the person whom you plan to marry, that you can make certain that you are looking down the same pathway, with the same objectives in mind. It is ever so significant that you do this.

I should like to dispel one rumor that is very hard to put to rest. I know of no mission president in all the world who has ever told a missionary that he had the responsibility to marry within six months after his mission. I think that rumor was commenced by a returned missionary, and if not by a returned missionary, by the girlfriend of a returned missionary.

In making the momentous decision concerning whom you will marry—and in making other decisions throughout your life—you have a formula, a guide, to assist you. It is found in the ninth section of the Doctrine and Covenants, verses 8–9: "You must study it out in your mind; then you must ask me if it be right, and if it is right I will cause that your bosom shall burn within you; therefore, you shall feel that it is right.

"But if it be not right you shall have no such feelings, but you shall have a stupor of thought." ("Life's Greatest Decisions," Church Educational System Fireside Satellite Broadcast, September 7, 2003)

———

Be patient, be tender, be loving, be considerate, be understanding, be your best self as you sustain your husband, remembering that children often outgrow their need for affection, but husbands never do. ("The Spirit of Relief Society," Relief Society Sesquicentennial Conference, March 14, 1992)

———

Our most cherished friend is our partner in marriage. This old world would be so much better off today if kindness and deference were daily a reflection of our gratitude for wife, for husband. ("An Attitude of Gratitude," *Ensign,* May 1992, 60)

———

Brethren, let's treat our wives with dignity and with respect. They're our eternal companions. Sisters, honor your husbands. They need to hear a good word. They need a friendly smile. They need a warm expression of true love. ("Abundantly Blessed," *Ensign,* May 2008, 112)

MEDIA

Scarcely can we see a television program now that doesn't have something suggestive in it. Movies are made just enough off key so that ratings will appeal to that which many in the American public clamor for. I have seen a trend from the G movies to the PG movie, and then from the PG-13 movie to the R movie. Today when we go to a video shop, we will find that the majority of the videos available for rental are in the R category.

I was rather complimented [one] evening when I went into a video shop. I was checking a particular video, and the proprietor said, "Oh, Brother Monson, you wouldn't want that one. You don't have your glasses on." I couldn't see what the rating was, so he said, "I wouldn't let you take that one." When I borrowed his glasses and read the rating, I concurred. "Good heavens," I said, "I wouldn't want that one." I thought, "Isn't it nice that others want us to live to our highest standards." (All-Church Coordinating Council, November 15, 1988)

Don't be afraid to walk out of a movie, turn off a television set, or change a radio station if what's being presented does not meet your Heavenly Father's standards. In short, if you have any question about whether a particular movie, book, or other form of entertainment is appropriate, don't see it, don't read it, don't participate. ("Preparation Brings Blessings," *Ensign,* May 2010, 65–66)

We live in perilous times; the signs are all around us. We are acutely aware of the negative influences in our society that stalk traditional families. At times television and movies portray worldly and immoral heroes and heroines and attempt to hold up as role models some actors and actresses whose lives are anything but exemplary. Why should we follow a blind guide? Radios blare forth much denigrating music with blatant lyrics, dangerous invitations, and descriptions of almost every type of evil imaginable.

We, as members of The Church of Jesus Christ of Latter-day Saints, must stand up to the dangers which surround us and our families. ("Constant Truths for Changing Times," *Ensign,* May 2005, 19)

MEDITATION

Everywhere, people are in a hurry. Jet-powered planes speed their precious human cargo across broad continents and vast oceans. Appointments must be kept, tourist attractions beckon, and friends and family await the arrival of a particular flight. Modern freeways with multiple lanes carry millions of automobiles, occupied by millions of people, in a seemingly endless stream from dawn to dusk, east to west, north to south.

Does this pulsating, mobile ribbon of humanity ever come to a halt? Is the helter-skelter pace of life at times punctuated with moments of meditation—even thoughts of timeless truths? ("An Invitation to Exaltation," *Ensign,* July 1984, 69)

President David O. McKay would frequently suggest the need for us to turn from the hectic day-to-day schedule filled with letters to answer, calls to be made, people to see, meetings to attend, and take time to meditate, to ponder, and to reflect on the eternal truths and the sources of the joy and happiness which comprise each person's quest.

When we do, the mundane, the mechanical, the repetitious patterns of our lives yield to the spiritual qualities, and we acquire a much-needed dimension which inspires our daily living. When I follow this counsel, thoughts of family, experiences with friends, and treasured memories of special days and quiet nights course through my mind and bring a sweet repose to my being. ("Gifts," *Ensign,* May 1993, 59)

Missionary Work

The holy scriptures contain no proclamation more relevant, no responsibility more binding, no instruction more direct than the injunction given by the resurrected Lord as He appeared in Galilee to the eleven disciples. Said He: "All power is given unto me in heaven and in earth.

"Go ye therefore, and teach all nations, baptizing them in the name of the Father, and of the Son, and of the Holy Ghost:

"Teaching them to observe all things whatsoever I have commanded you: and lo, I am with you alway, even unto the end of the world" (Matthew 28:18–20).

This divine command, coupled with its glorious promise, is our watchword today as in the meridian of time. Missionary work is an identifying feature of The Church of Jesus Christ of Latter-day Saints. It has always been so; it shall ever be. As the Prophet Joseph Smith declared: "After all that has been said, the greatest and most important duty is to preach the Gospel" (*History of the Church* [1932–1952], 2:478). ("Messengers of Glory," Conference Report, October 1969, 92)

At best, [full-time] missionary work necessitates drastic adjustment to one's pattern of living. No other labor requires longer hours or greater devotion, nor such sacrifice and fervent prayer. As a result, dedicated missionary service returns a dividend of eternal joy which extends throughout life and into eternity.

Today our challenge is to be more profitable servants in the Lord's vineyard.

May I suggest, particularly to you bearers of the Aaronic Priesthood, a formula that will ensure your success:

First: Search the scriptures with diligence!
Second: Plan your life with purpose!
Third: Teach the truth with testimony!
Fourth: Serve the Lord with love.

("Messengers of Glory," Conference Report, October 1969, 93)

The scriptures testify of God and contain the words of eternal life. They become the burden of your message—even the tools of your trade. Your confidence will be directly related to your knowledge of God's word. Oh, I am sure you have heard of some missionaries who were lazy, less than effective, and anxious for their missions to conclude. A careful examination of such instances will reveal that the actual culprit is not laziness, nor disinterest, but is the foe known as *fear*. Our Father chastised such: "With some I am not well pleased, for they will not open their mouths, but they hide the talent which I have given unto them, because of the fear of man" (D&C 60:2).

Had not this same loving Heavenly Father provided a prescription to overcome this malady, His words perhaps would appear overly harsh. In a revelation given through Joseph

Smith the Prophet, January 2, 1831, the Lord declared: "If ye are prepared ye shall not fear" (D&C 38:30). This is the key. ("Messengers of Glory," Conference Report, October 1969, 93–94)

———

The executives in the world of corporate business have found that maximum success is most often achieved if full effort is exerted in those areas of greatest potential yield. Various markets are thoroughly surveyed and screened in an effort to determine their potential. Then manpower requirements are assembled, trained, and wisely motivated. Thus, adequate and proper preparation, coupled with intelligent effort, bring about the accomplishment of desired objectives.

This same approach is applicable to our Father's business. Too often when we speak of missionary work we think only of faraway places with strange-sounding names and thereby overlook the opportunities to be found in own backyards. (Priesthood Missionary Conference, October 1, 1965)

———

Preparation for a mission begins early. It is a wise parent who encourages [a] young [son] to commence even in boyhood his personal missionary fund. As the fund grows, so does [his] desire to serve. He may well be encouraged as the years go by to study a foreign language, that if necessary his language skills could be utilized. Didn't the Lord say, "Teach all nations" (Matthew 28:19)?

Then comes that glorious day when the bishop invites [the young man] into his office. Worthiness is ascertained; a missionary recommendation is completed. There follow those anxious moments of wonderment and the unspoken question, "I wonder where I will be called?"

During no other [time] does the entire family so anxiously watch and wait for the mailman and the letter which contains the return address: 47 East South Temple, Salt Lake City, Utah. The letter arrives, the suspense is overwhelming, the call is read. Often the assigned field of labor is a faraway place with a strange sounding name. . . . More frequently, the assignment may be closer to home. The response of the prepared missionary is the same: *"I will serve."* ("Messengers of Glory," Conference Report, October 1969, 94)

———

I have found the following characteristics present in almost every successful proselyting situation:

1. The presence of Latter-day Saints who love the gospel so much that they live it.
2. The presence of Latter-day Saints who love and live the gospel to the point that they willingly share it.
3. Adequate houses of worship where the program of the Church can be carried out in full operation.
4. A missionary attitude, which begins with stake and ward leaders and permeates the membership of the stake. This attitude is reflected in the welcome extended to the missionaries. . . . It is shown in the manner in which the membership participates in sharing the gospel . . . and, of course, includes the friendly fellowshiping of investigators and new converts to the Church.

(Priesthood Missionary Conference, October 1, 1965)

———

Obey the counsel of the Apostle Peter, who urged: "Be ready always to give an answer to every man that asketh you a reason of the hope that is in you" (1 Peter 3:15). Lift up your voices and testify to the true nature of the Godhead. Declare your witness concerning the Book of Mormon. Convey the glorious and beautiful truths contained in the plan of salvation. Regarding your testimony, remember, that which you willingly share you keep, while that which you selfishly keep you lose. Have the courage and the kindness, as did Jesus, to teach the Nicodemuses whom you may meet that baptism is essential to salvation. Teach and testify. There is no better combination. ("Messengers of Glory," Conference Report, October 1969, 95)

———

The perfect Shepherd of souls, the missionary who redeemed mankind, gave us His divine assurance: "If it so be that you should labor all your days in crying repentance unto this people, and bring, save it be one soul unto me, how great shall be your joy with him in the kingdom of my Father!

"And now, if your joy will be great with one soul that you have brought unto me into the kingdom of my Father, how great will be your joy if you should bring many souls unto me!" (D&C 18:15–16). ("Messengers of Glory," Conference Report, October 1969, 97)

———

No mission achieves its optimum success without enlisting the help of the membership of the Church in the proselyting program, working together with the missionaries. ("A Better Way," Training Meeting, April 4, 2002)

———

Every worthy, able young man should prepare to serve a mission. Missionary service is a priesthood duty—an obligation the Lord expects of us who have been given so very much. Young men, I admonish you to prepare for service as a missionary. Keep yourselves clean and pure and worthy to represent the Lord. Maintain your health and strength. Study the scriptures. Where such is available, participate in seminary or institute. Familiarize yourself with the missionary handbook *Preach My Gospel*. ("As We Meet Together Again," *Ensign*, November 2010, 5–6)

The priesthood represents a mighty army of righteousness—even a royal army. We are led by a prophet of God. In supreme command is our Lord and Savior, Jesus Christ. Our marching orders are clear. They are concise. Matthew describes our challenge in these words from the Master: "Go ye therefore, and teach all nations, baptizing them in the name of the Father, and of the Son, and of the Holy Ghost:

"Teaching them to observe all things whatsoever I have commanded you: and lo, I am with you alway, even unto the end of the world" (Matthew 28:19–20). Did those early disciples listen to this divine command? Mark records, "And they went forth, and preached every where, the Lord working with them" (Mark 16:20).

The command to go has not been rescinded. Rather, it has been reemphasized. . . .

[Those] who hold the Aaronic Priesthood and honor it have been reserved for this special period in history. The harvest truly is great. Let there be no mistake about it; the opportunity of a lifetime is yours. The blessings of eternity await you. . . .

Preparation for a mission is not a spur-of-the-moment matter. It began before you can remember. Every class in Primary, Sunday School, seminary—each priesthood assignment—had a larger application. Silently, almost imperceptibly, a life was molded, a career commenced, a man made. ("The Army of the Lord," *Ensign*, May 1979, 35–36)

Some time ago, as the General Authorities met together on an upper floor of the temple, President [Spencer W.] Kimball stood and instructed us, saying: "Brethren, of late I have been concerned and troubled by the fact that we do not have sufficient missionaries proclaiming the message of the Restoration. I hear some parents say, 'We're letting our son make up his own mind regarding a mission,' or 'We hope our son fills a mission because it would be such a growing experience for him.'" He continued: "I have heard some young men say, 'I think I might serve a mission if I really want to go.'" President Kimball raised his voice, stood on tiptoe—as he is prone to do when anxious to communicate with power a special thought—and said: "It doesn't really matter whether Mother or Father thinks it might be nice for a son to serve a mission. It doesn't really matter whether or not John, Bill, and Bob want to go—they *must* go!" President Kimball then proceeded to point out the missionary obligation each of us has to repay the sacrifice and service of those missionaries who left home and family and brought the gospel to our parents or grandparents in lands near and far. ("The Aaronic Priesthood Pathway," *Ensign,* November 1984, 41)

For many years I had the opportunity of serving on the Church Missionary Committee, and I have held in my hands the missionary recommendation forms of many. . . . I can honestly testify that the Lord knows where He wants his missionaries to serve. I have had this made abundantly clear to me almost every week when those assignments were being made. No one judges but the Lord. ("Traditions," Dixie College Homecoming, November 2, 1986)

———

The seeds of testimony frequently do not immediately take root and flower. Bread cast upon the water returns, at times, only after many days. But it does return. ("Stand in Your Appointed Place," *Ensign,* May 2003, 57)

———

Some missionaries are gifted with the power of expression, while others have a superior knowledge of the gospel. Some, however, are late bloomers who day by day become more proficient and successful. Avoid the temptation of ladder climbing in the mission leadership ranks. It matters little whether you are a district or zone leader or assistant to the president. The important thing is that each one does his very best in the work to which he has been called. Why, I had some missionaries who were so adept at training new missionaries that I couldn't spare them for other leadership assignments. ("Who Honors God, God Honors," *Ensign,* November 1995, 49–50)

———

[Our] missionaries go forward with faith. They know their duty. They understand that they are a vital link between the persons they will meet as missionaries and the teaching and in the testifying they will experience as they bring others to the truth of the gospel.

They yearn for more persons to teach. They pray for the essential help each member can give to the conversion process.

The decision to change one's life and come unto Christ is, perhaps, the most important decision of mortality. Such a dramatic change is taking place daily throughout the world. ("They Will Come," *Ensign,* May 1997, 44)

Most of those who embrace the message of the missionaries have had other exposures to The Church of Jesus Christ of Latter-day Saints—perhaps hearing the magnificent Tabernacle Choir perform, . . . or just in knowing another person who is a member and for whom respect exists. We, as members, should be at our best. Our lives should reflect the teachings of the gospel, and our hearts and voices ever be ready to share the truth. ("They Will Come," *Ensign,* May 1997, 44)

To reach, to teach, to touch the precious souls whom our Father has prepared for His message is a monumental task. Success is rarely simple. Generally it is preceded by tears, trials, trust, and testimony. ("Tears, Trials, Trust, Testimony," *Ensign,* May 1987, 43)

We are a missionary minded people. We have a divine mandate to proclaim the message of the Restoration. . . . That energetic missionary from the Book of Mormon, even Alma, provides for us a blueprint for missionary conduct: "This is my glory, that perhaps I may be an instrument in the hands of God to bring some soul to repentance; and this is my joy" (Alma 29:9).

I add my personal witness: Our missionaries are not salesmen with wares to peddle; rather, they are servants of the Most High God, with testimonies to bear, truths to teach, and souls to save.

Each missionary who goes forth in response to a sacred call becomes a servant of the Lord whose work this truly is. ("Missionary Memories," *Ensign,* November 1987, 42)

In many respects, a mission is a family calling. The letters which a missionary sends to Mother and Father are packed with power—spiritual power. They are filled with faith—abiding faith. I've always maintained that such letters seem to pass through a heavenly post office before being delivered to home and family. Mother treasures every word. Father fills with pride. The letters are read over and over again—and are never discarded.

I trust parents will remember that their letters to a missionary son or daughter bring home and heaven close to him or to her and provide a renewal of commitment to the sacred calling of missionary. God will inspire you as you take pen in hand to express to one you love the feelings of your soul and the love of your heart. ("Missionary Memories," *Ensign,* November 1987, 43)

I commend the many couples who now go forth to serve. Leaving the comforts of home, the companionship of family, they walk hand in hand as eternal companions, but also hand in hand with God as His representatives to a faith-starved world. ("Missionary Memories," *Ensign,* November 1987, 43)

I trust that all young men . . . are preparing now to serve a full-time mission in the service of the Lord. . . . Prepare to serve worthily, with an eye single to the glory of God and His purposes. You will never know the full influence of your testimony and your service, but you will return with gladness for having had the privilege of responding to a sacred call to serve the Master. You will be forever loved by those to whom you bring the light of truth. Your teachings will be found in their service. Your examples will be guides to follow. Your faith will prompt courage to meet life's challenges. ("Called to Serve," *Ensign,* November 1991, 48)

———

Most of you young men will one day receive a call to serve a mission. How I pray that your response will be as was Samuel's: "Here am I. . . . Speak, Lord; for thy servant heareth" (1 Samuel 3:8–9). Then will heavenly help be yours. Every missionary strives to be the missionary his mother thinks he is, the missionary his father hopes he is—even the missionary the Lord knows he can become. ("The Priesthood in Action," *Ensign,* November 1992, 47)

———

[The Lord] sends forth His word through the many thousands of missionaries serving far and wide proclaiming His gospel of good tidings and salutation of peace. Vexing questions, such as "Where did I come from? What is the purpose of my being? Where do I go after death?" are answered by His special servants. Frustration flees, doubt disappears, and uncertainty wanes when truth is taught in boldness, yet in a spirit of humility by those who have been called to serve the Prince of Peace—even the Lord Jesus Christ. ("The Gifts of Christmas," *Ensign,* December 2003, 4)

———

Serving throughout the world is a great missionary force, going about doing good as did the Savior. Missionaries teach truth. They dispel darkness. They spread joy. They bring precious souls to Christ.

On that special day when a mission call is received, parents,

brothers and sisters, and grandparents gather around the prospective missionary and note his nervousness as he carefully
opens the letter of call. There is a pause, and then he an-
nounces where the prophet of the Lord has assigned him to
serve. Feelings are very near to the surface. Tears come easily,
and the family rejoices in the bond of love and the goodness of
God.

The full-time missionaries and all others engaged in the
work of the Lord have answered His call. We are on His errand.
We shall succeed in the solemn charge given by Mormon to
declare the Lord's word among the people. Wrote Mormon:
"Behold, I am a disciple of Jesus Christ, the Son of God. I have
been called of him to declare his word among his people,
that they might have everlasting life" (3 Nephi 5:13). ("Today
Determines Tomorrow," *Ensign*, November 1998, 50)

———

Let there be no mistake—there is a need for every one of
us to be a missionary. Our Lord and Savior has endowed you
and me with certain abilities and characteristics. He has made
it possible for some missionaries to appeal to certain men, others to appeal to another group. Every holder of the priesthood
of God is needed in this great missionary cause. The Apostle
Peter described you and me in the second chapter of 1 Peter,
the ninth verse. "Ye are a chosen generation, a royal priesthood, an holy nation, a peculiar people that ye should show
forth the praises of him who hath called you out of darkness
into his marvelous light." ("A Royal Priesthood," Paris Area
Conference, July 31, 1976)

———

There are millions of people yet to hear the message of the
Restoration, and we must not say no in their behalf. We cannot

judge whom the Lord may prepare to hear His message. Some we may least expect are ones who are best prepared to accept the gospel. What is needed by you and me? A vision of our opportunity. And then a desire to really be a neighbor. ("Who Is My Neighbor?" Amsterdam Area Conference, August 7, 1976)

MORTALITY

How grateful we should be that a wise Creator fashioned an earth and placed us here, with a veil of forgetfulness of our previous existence, so that we might experience a time of testing, an opportunity to prove ourselves, and qualify for all that God has prepared for us to receive.

Clearly, the primary purposes of our existence upon the earth are to obtain a body of flesh and bones and to gain experience that could only come through separation from our heavenly parents. In a thousand ways, we are privileged to choose for ourselves. Here we learn from the hard taskmaster of experience. We discern between good and evil. We differentiate as to the bitter and the sweet. ("An Invitation to Exaltation," *Ensign*, July 1984, 70)

When we contemplate the wonderful world in which we live and then realize the tumultuous times which beset us, joyful are we to know Jesus, our leader, ever is near. We live in a world of waste. Too often our natural resources are squandered. We live in a world of want. Some enjoy the lap of luxury, yet others stare starvation in the face. Food, shelter, clothing, and love are not found by all. Unrelieved suffering, unnecessary illness, and premature death stalk too many. We live in a world of wars. Some are political in nature, while others are economic by definition. The greatest battle of all, however, is for the souls of mankind. ("Duty Calls," *Ensign,* May 1996, 43)

MOTHER

———

"Mother," more than any other word, is held in universal esteem by all peoples everywhere. It brings forth from the soul the most tender of hidden emotions, prompts more good deeds, kindles memories' fires as they burn low, and reminds all to strive to be better.

"Mother," or its abbreviated version, "Mama," is the first word tiny lips form. What joy fills mother's heart when first she hears this expression from her child. "Mother" becomes the most frequently spoken word, as well. As little ones grow, they call mother to their side to share each new discovery, each accomplishment, each disappointment, each concern. And mother always obliges.

Years pass, and children become more independent. They move away from mother's protective care; but they are ever influenced by mother's teachings, mother's example, and mother's love. Some appear by their actions to have forgotten this influence. Wild and wasteful pathways are pursued, evil deeds done, and honor sacrificed for the sham of worldly gain. However far from the home hearth the wanderer travels, the word "mother" mentally and emotionally brings him homeward once again. And mother, as always, stands ready to forgive. ("Honor Thy Mother," Mother's Day Pamphlet, 1981)

———

What a pity that many need a special day called "Mother's Day" to be reminded of a divinely designated responsibility to remember and to honor. Good intentions remain just that—good intentions—as so-called busy individuals salve their consciences with expressions such as, "I'll look in on Mother next week"; "Next month I'm going to visit Mother"; or "I've been too busy to give Mother a call." Days pass; weeks become months; months turn to years, and mother is not called, not seen, not remembered. Rarely does she complain. Rather, she outwardly justifies the neglect, but inwardly her heart yearns for the friendly voice, the familiar laughter, the gentle embrace and tender kiss. ("Honor Thy Mother," Mother's Day Pamphlet, 1981)

———

As we journey along the pathway of life, may we pause to remember Mother—our own mothers, and the mothers of all men everywhere. God, our Father, remembers mothers. We, His children, can do no less. ("Honor Thy Mother," Mother's Day Pamphlet, 1981)

———

Reflect upon the helplessness of a newborn child. No better example can be found for total dependency. Needed is nourishment for the body and love for the soul. Mother provides both. She who, with her hand in the hand of God, descended into "the valley of the shadow of death" (Psalm 23:4), that you and I might come forth to life, is not in her maternal mission abandoned by God. Precious children are welcomed by eager families. ("An Invitation to Exaltation," *Ensign,* July 1984, 70)

———

Oh, I recognize that there are times when Mother's nerves are frayed, her patience exhausted, and her energies consumed; when she says, "My children don't appreciate a single thing I do." I think they do appreciate you. One of the questions after a study of magnets at the Olympus Junior High was: "What begins with 'M' and picks things up?" The obvious answer was "magnet." However, more than a third of the kids answered, "Mother."

There is no scene more touching or beautiful than a mother kneeling with her child, teaching the little one to pray. Then, arising from their knees, the child is tucked tenderly in bed and receives a good night kiss. Mother gently closes the door and says, "Good night, Sleep tight, Wake up bright, In the morning light, To do what's right, With all your might—I love you."

I think it significant that usually the first word a child utters is "Mama." Historians of battlefields of war state that frequently the last word spoken by a fallen combatant before dying is the word "Mother" or "Mama."

Love of mother and her teachings has prompted more bad men to be good and good men to be better than any other motivational force. ("Timeless Truths for a Changing World," BYU Women's Conference, May 4, 2001)

———

Being a mother has never been an easy role. Some of the oldest writings in the world admonish us not to forsake the law of our mother, instruct us that a foolish son is the heaviness of his mother, and warn us not to ignore our mother when she is old (see Proverbs 1:8; 10:1; 23:22).

The scriptures also remind us that what we learn from our mothers comprises our very core values, as with the 2,000 stripling sons and warriors of Helaman, who "had been taught by their mothers, that if they did not doubt, God would deliver them" (Alma 56:47). And He did! ("If Ye Are Prepared Ye Shall Not Fear," *Ensign,* November 2004, 116)

MOTIVATION

We can learn much from the words of an American businessman, Robert Woodruff. From his vast study and experience, he summarized the principles of success in motivating others. He referred to his formula as "A Capsule Course in Human Relations":

> The five most important words are these: "I
> am proud of you."
> The four most important words are: "What is
> your opinion?"
> The three most important words are: "If you
> please."
> The two most important words are: "Thank you."
> The least important word is: "I."

(Primary General Conference, April 8, 1966)

Effective communication is essential to effective motivation. The leader must first educate himself, develop enthusiasm, and perfect himself in the skill he desires to teach (communicate). He must then project his feeling on the subject until it is shared by the follower. This is the process of most effective motivation. ("How to Communicate Effectively," General Authority Training Meeting, December 1967)

MUSIC

In New Zealand a tragic drowning claimed the lives of two instructors at the Church College at Temple View. The young widows and their children were overcome by grief and heartache. Many well-wishing and sympathetic friends offered words of consolation, but the remorse remained. There came a soft knock at the door; a group of Maori Saints entered the room. Not a word was spoken, but song came forth from their lips and hearts. The bereaved families received a sustaining influence that accompanied them through the lonely and long journey homeward and even today turns tears of sorrow to warm smiles of gratitude. ". . . the song of the righteous is a prayer unto me [saith the Lord], and it shall be answered with a blessing upon their heads" (D&C 25:12). ("God's Gifts to Polynesia's People," Conference Report, October 1966, 9)

Music can help you draw closer to your Heavenly Father. It can be used to educate, edify, inspire, and unite. However, music can, by its tempo, beat, intensity, and lyrics, dull your spiritual sensitivity. You cannot afford to fill your minds with unworthy music. ("Preparation Brings Blessings," *Ensign,* May 2010, 66)

OBEDIENCE

To a generation steeped in the tradition of animal sacrifice, Samuel boldly declared, "To obey is better than sacrifice, and to hearken than the fat of rams" (1 Samuel 15:22). Prophets, ancient and modern, have known the strength that comes through obedience. Think of Nephi: "I will go and do the things which the Lord hath commanded" (1 Nephi 3:7). Or Alma's beautiful description of the strength possessed by the sons of Mosiah: "They had waxed strong in the knowledge of the truth; for they were men of a sound understanding and they had searched the scriptures diligently, that they might know the word of God.

"But this is not all; they had given themselves to much prayer, and fasting; therefore they had the spirit of prophecy, and the spirit of revelation, and when they taught, they taught with power and authority of God" (Alma 17:2–3).

President David O. McKay, in his opening message to the membership of the Church at a general conference in April 1957, stated very simply and yet so powerfully, "Keep the commandments of God." His successors have urged the same compliance.

Such was the burden of our Savior's message, when He declared, "For all who will have a blessing at my hands shall abide the law which was appointed for that blessing, and the conditions thereof, as were instituted from before the foundation of the world" (D&C 132:5). ("Strength Through Obedience," *Ensign,* July 1996, 2)

———

The strength that we earnestly seek today to meet the challenges of a complex and changing world can be ours when, with fortitude and resolute courage, we stand and declare with Joshua, "As for me and my house, we will serve the Lord" (Joshua 24:15). ("Strength Through Obedience," *Ensign,* July 1996, 5)

———

All of us love the beautiful account of Abraham and Isaac found in the Holy Bible. How exceedingly difficult it must have been for Abraham, in obedience to God's command, to take his beloved Isaac into the land of Moriah, there to present him as a burnt offering. Can you imagine the heaviness of his heart as he gathered the wood for the fire and journeyed to the appointed place? Surely pain must have racked his body and tortured his mind as he bound Isaac and laid him on the altar upon the wood and stretched forth his hand and took the knife to slay his son. How glorious was the pronouncement, and with what wondered welcome did it come, "Lay not thine hand upon the lad, neither do thou any thing unto him; for now I know that thou fearest God, seeing thou has not withheld thy son, thine only son from me" (Genesis 22:12). ("The Search for Jesus," *Ensign*, December 1990, 4)

———

Ofttimes the wisdom of God appears as foolishness to men, but the greatest single lesson we can learn in mortality is that, when God speaks and a man obeys, man will always be right. ("The Call of Duty," *Ensign*, May 1986, 37)

———

It takes a spirit of obedience if we want to qualify for blessings today. It isn't enough simply to say, "Tomorrow I am going to do better." The Lord expects us to do better today. . . . I would hope that every one of us would have a tradition of obedience in his life, in her life, because all of the blessings of God are predicated upon obedience to the commandments. As we live the commandments, we shall find the answers to our prayers and receive direction in our lives. We will have to put the Lord to the test by following His command, by living the principle, and then we shall receive the reward. ("Traditions," Dixie College Homecoming, November 2, 1986)

How might you and I demonstrate our love for God and love for our fellowmen? Through obedience to God's commands and the counsel of his servants. We have the privilege to obey the law of tithing, to obey the code of morality, to obey in each facet of our lives the word of our Heavenly Father. ("A Time to Choose," BYU Devotional, January 16, 1973)

I have been thinking . . . [of a] garden created by our Heavenly Father. It was established eastward in Eden. The holy records indicate the garden was prepared beautifully by its Creator. There were abundant rivers, there were fowls of the air, and there were the beasts of the field. And there were those things which were upon the ground and within the waters. . . .

I believe that we are all aware of what took place in that garden. We are aware that there was a tree of knowledge of good and evil, and there was a tree of life, and that man had decisions even then. We are aware that Adam did fall. And then there came to him in that garden the voice of the Lord walking through the garden. And one of the most significant questions ever to be asked of man was asked on that day. He asked Adam a fundamental question: "Where art thou?" (Genesis 3:9). We remember that Adam did hide himself because of his nakedness.

Pause now. Let each of us ask himself that same question. If our Heavenly Father should say to you or say to me, "Adam, where art thou?" how would you and I answer? What are our thoughts? What are our actions? What are our habits? How strong is our testimony in defense of the truth? In short, how do we stand before God? Do we stand naked before Him? Or do we stand clothed in the spirit of obedience to His command-ments? Each person must answer.

How do you and I stand on the fundamental principle of tithing? Is each one of us a full tithepayer in the kingdom of God? Remember His promise to us, that he who is tithed shall not be burned at His coming.

How do you and I stand with respect to keeping the Word of Wisdom? Great promises have been given to those who live the Word of Wisdom. How do we stand with respect to keep-ing the Sabbath day holy? What is our attitude with respect to personal prayer? ("Significant Questions," Helsinki Area Conference, August 2, 1976)

OPPORTUNITY

———

Sometimes we let our thoughts of tomorrow take up too much of today. Daydreaming of the past and longing for the future may provide comfort but will not take the place of living in the present. This is the day of our opportunity, and we must grasp it. ("In Search of Treasure," *Ensign,* May 2003, 20)

———

No space of regret will make amends for your life's op-portunities misused. I bear testimony that regardless of how long you live, your mortal life will be far too short for its vast means of usefulness. I bear testimony that as you lift your eyes heavenward to the star of Christ, as you incorporate within your lives the gospel of Jesus Christ, that light which will come from our Lord will guide you to your opportunity. ("True

Shepherds After the Way of the Lord," Address to Seminaries and Institutes, July 15, 1970)

OPTIMISM
(SEE ALSO ATTITUDE)

———

Should you become discouraged or feel burdened down, remember that others have passed this same way; they have endured and then have achieved. When we have done all that we are able to do, we can then rely on God's promised help. ("Life's Greatest Decisions," Church Educational System Fireside Satellite Broadcast, September 7, 2003)

———

Don't let old gloomy depression get you, even if we lose a game or two. We are going to win more than we lose, and so it is in life. Stay on the Lord's side of the line. Stay close to the teachings of the Presidents of the Church. (Address at Brigham Young University, February 15, 1994)

———

It would be easy to become discouraged and cynical about the future—or even fearful of what might come—if we allowed ourselves to dwell only on that which is wrong in the world and in our lives. Today, however, I'd like us to turn our thoughts and our attitudes away from the troubles around us and to focus instead on our blessings as members of the Church. The Apostle Paul declared, "God hath not given us the spirit of fear;

but of power, and of love, and of a sound mind" (2 Timothy
1:7). ("'Be of Good Cheer,'" *Ensign,* May 2009, 89)

———

None of us makes it through this life without problems
and challenges—and sometimes tragedies and misfortunes.
After all, in large part we are here to learn and grow from such
events in our lives. We know that there are times when we will
suffer, when we will grieve, and when we will be saddened.
However, we are told, "Adam fell that men might be; and men
are, that they might have joy" (2 Nephi 2:25).

How might we have joy in our lives, despite all that we may
face? Again from the scriptures: "Wherefore, be of good cheer,
and do not fear, for I the Lord am with you, and will stand by
you" (D&C 68:6).

The history of the Church in this, the dispensation of the
fulness of times, is replete with the experiences of those who
have struggled and yet who have remained steadfast and of
good cheer as they have made the gospel of Jesus Christ the
center of their lives. This attitude is what will pull us through
whatever comes our way. It will not remove our troubles from us
but rather will enable us to face our challenges, to meet them
head on, and to emerge victorious. ("'Be of Good Cheer,'"
Ensign, May 2009, 89)

PARENTHOOD

———

As parents, we should remember that our lives may be the
book from the family library which the children most treasure.
Are our examples worthy of emulation? Do we live in such a way

that a son or a daughter may say, "I want to follow my dad," or "I want to be like my mother"? Unlike the book on the library shelf, the covers of which shield the contents, our lives cannot be closed. Parents, we truly are an open book. ("Hallmarks of a Happy Home," *Ensign,* November 1988, 70)

———

Should a parent need added inspiration to commence his God-given teaching task, let him remember that the most powerful combination of emotions in the world is not called out by any grand cosmic event nor found in novels or history books—but merely by a parent gazing down upon a sleeping child. "Created in the image of God," that glorious biblical passage, acquires new and vibrant meaning as a parent repeats this experience. Home becomes a haven called heaven, and loving parents teach their children "to pray, and to walk uprightly before the Lord" (D&C 68:28). Never does such an inspired parent fit the description, "only a teacher." ("Only a Teacher," Conference Report, April 1970, 97–98)

———

I know that you and I have given our parents "fits," as it were, as they have attempted to rear us. When we consider some of the things we have done as children, some of the things that we contemplate doing as teenagers, some of the things we do as young adults, I think it is a wonder at times that our parents retain their sanity. In fact, one woman said to her neighbor, "You know, I believe that insanity is hereditary—we get it from our children." ("Great Expectations," BYU Devotional, May 11, 1965)

———

Just a few short generations ago, one could not have imagined the world in which we now live and the problems it presents. We are surrounded by immorality, pornography, violence, drugs, and a host of other ills which afflict modern-day society. Ours is the challenge, even the responsibility, not only to keep ourselves "unspotted from the world" (James 1:27), but also to guide our children and others for whom we have responsibility safely through the stormy seas of sin surrounding all of us, that we might one day return to live with our Heavenly Father.

The training of our own families requires our presence, our time, our best efforts. To be effective in our training, we must be stalwart in our examples to our family members and available for private time with each member, as well as time for counseling and guidance. ("Heavenly Homes, Forever Families," *Ensign,* June 2006, 99–100)

———

I would say to each mother, each father—be a good listener. Communication is so vital today in our fast-paced world. Take time to listen. And to you children, talk to your mother and to your father. It may be difficult to realize, but your parents have lived through many of the same challenges which you face today. Often they see the big picture more clearly than you can. They pray for you each day and are entitled to the inspiration of our Heavenly Father in providing you counsel and advice.

Mothers, share household duties. It is often easier to do everything yourself than to persuade your children to help, but it is so essential for them to learn the importance of doing their share.

Fathers, I would counsel you to demonstrate love and kindness to your wife. Be patient with your children. Don't indulge them to excess, for they must learn to make their own way in the world.

I would encourage you to be available to your children. I have heard it said that no man, as death approaches, has ever declared that he wished he had spent more time at the office. ("Constant Truths for Changing Times," *Ensign,* May 2005, 20)

———

To you who are parents, I say, show love to your children. You know you love them, but make certain they know it as well. They are so precious. Let them know. Call upon our Heavenly Father for help as you care for their needs each day and as you deal with the challenges which inevitably come with parenthood. You need more than your own wisdom in rearing them. ("Abundantly Blessed," *Ensign,* May 2008, 112)

———

If you have children who are grown and gone, in all likelihood you have occasionally felt pangs of loss and the recognition that you didn't appreciate that time of life as much as you should have. Of course, there is no going back, but only forward. Rather than dwelling on the past, we should make the most of today, of the here and now, doing all we can to provide pleasant memories for the future.

If you are still in the process of raising children, be aware that the tiny fingerprints that show up on almost every newly cleaned surface, the toys scattered about the house, the piles and piles of laundry to be tackled, will disappear all too soon and that you will—to your surprise—miss them profoundly.

Stresses in our lives come regardless of our circumstances. We must deal with them the best we can. But we should not let them get in the way of what is most important—and what is most important almost always involves the people around us.

Often we assume that they *must* know how much we love them. But we should never assume; we should let them know. . . . We will never regret the kind words spoken or the affection shown. Rather, our regrets will come if such things are omitted from our relationships with those who mean the most to us. ("Finding Joy in the Journey," *Ensign,* November 2008, 85–86)

PATIENCE

If any of us feels his challenges are beyond his capacity to meet them, let him or her read of Job. By so doing, there comes the feeling, "If Job could endure and overcome, so will I."

Job was a "perfect and upright" man who "feared God, and eschewed evil" (Job 1:1). Pious in his conduct, prosperous in his fortune, Job was to face a test which could have destroyed anyone. Shorn of his possessions, scorned by his friends, afflicted by his suffering, shattered by the loss of his family, he was urged to "curse God, and die" (Job 2:9). He resisted this temptation and declared from the depths of his noble soul, "Behold, my witness is in heaven, and my record is on high" (Job 16:19). "I know that my redeemer liveth" (Job 19:25).

Job became a model of unlimited patience. To this day we refer to those who are long-suffering as having the patience of Job. He provides an example for us to follow. ("Models to Follow," *Ensign,* November 2002, 60)

Life is full of difficulties, some minor and others of a more serious nature. There seems to be an unending supply of challenges for one and all. Our problem is that we often expect instantaneous solutions to such challenges, forgetting that frequently the heavenly virtue of patience is required.

The counsel heard in our youth is still applicable today and should be heeded. "Hold your horses," "Keep your shirt on," "Slow down," "Don't be in such a hurry," "Follow the rules," "Be careful" are more than trite expressions. They describe sincere counsel and speak the wisdom of experience. . . .

In sickness, with its attendant pain, patience is required. If the only perfect man who ever lived—even Jesus of Nazareth—was called upon to endure great suffering, how can we, who are less than perfect, expect to be free of such challenges?

Who can count the vast throngs of the lonely, the aged, the helpless—those who feel abandoned by the caravan of life as it moves relentlessly onward and then disappears beyond the sight of those who ponder, who wonder, and who sometimes question as they are left alone with their thoughts. Patience can be a helpful companion during such stressful times. ("Patience—A Heavenly Virtue," *Ensign*, November 1995, 59)

———

I believe that I can learn patience by better studying the life of our Lord and Savior. Can you imagine the disappointment which He must have felt, knowing that He had the keys to eternal life, knowing that He had the way for you and for me to gain entrance into the celestial kingdom of God, as He took His gospel to those people in the meridian of time and saw them reject Him and reject His message? Yet He demonstrated patience. He accepted His responsibility in life, even to the cross, the Garden of Gethsemane preceding it. I would hope to learn patience from the Lord. ("A Time to Choose," BYU Devotional, January 16, 1973)

PATRIARCHAL BLESSINGS

Centuries [ago], a righteous and loving father by the name of Lehi took his beloved family into a desert wasteland. He journeyed in response to the voice of the Lord, but the Lord did not decree that such a "flight" be undertaken without heavenly help. The words of Nephi describe the gift provided on the morning of the historic trek:

"And it came to pass that as my father arose in the morning, and went forth to the tent door, to his great astonishment he beheld upon the ground a round ball of curious workmanship; and it was of fine brass. And within the ball were two spindles; and the one pointed the way whither we should go into the wilderness" (1 Nephi 16:10).

War and man-made means of destruction could not confuse or destroy this curious compass. Neither could the sudden desert sandstorms render useless its guiding powers. The prophet Alma explained that this "Liahona," as it was called, was a compass prepared by the Lord. It worked for them according to their faith and pointed the way they should go (see Alma 37:38–40).

The same Lord who provided a Liahona for Lehi provides for you and for me today a rare and valuable gift to give direction to our lives, to mark the hazards to our safety, and to chart the way, even safe passage—not to a promised land, but to our heavenly home. The gift to which I refer is known as your patriarchal blessing. Every worthy member of the Church is entitled to receive such a precious and priceless personal treasure. ("Your Patriarchal Blessing: A Liahona of Light," *Ensign,* November 1986, 65)

———

A patriarchal blessing is a revelation to the recipient, even a white line down the middle of the road, to protect, inspire, and motivate activity and righteousness. A patriarchal blessing literally contains chapters from your book of eternal possibilities. I say eternal, for just as life is eternal, so is a patriarchal blessing. What may not come to fulfillment in this life may occur in the next. We do not govern God's timetable. "For my thoughts are not your thoughts, neither are your ways my ways, saith the Lord.

"For as the heavens are higher than the earth, so are my ways higher than your ways, and my thoughts than your thoughts" (Isaiah 55:8–9).

Your patriarchal blessing is yours and yours alone. It may be brief or lengthy, simple or profound. Length and language do not a patriarchal blessing make. It is the Spirit that conveys the true meaning. Your blessing is not to be folded neatly and tucked away. It is not to be framed or published. Rather, it is to be read. It is to be loved. It is to be followed. Your patriarchal blessing will see you through the darkest night. It will guide you through life's dangers. . . . Your patriarchal blessing is to you a personal Liahona to chart your course and guide your way. . . .

Patience may be required as we watch, wait, and work for a promised blessing to be fulfilled. ("Your Patriarchal Blessing: A Liahona of Light," *Ensign*, November 1986, 66)

———

A blessing you can qualify to receive is your patriarchal blessing. Your parents and your bishop will know when the time is right for you to receive it. . . . To you it will be as a lighthouse on a hill, warning of dangers, and directing you to the tranquility of safe harbors. It is a prophetic utterance from the lips of one called and ordained to provide you such a blessing. ("Your Celestial Journey," *Ensign*, May 1999, 98)

——

Help in maintaining the proper perspective in these permissive times can come to you from many sources. One valuable resource is your patriarchal blessing. Read it frequently. Study it carefully. Be guided by its cautions. Live to merit its promises. If you have not yet received your patriarchal blessing, plan for the time when you will receive it, and then cherish it. ("May You Have Courage," *Ensign,* May 2009, 125–26)

PEACE

——

In a world where peace is such a universal quest, we sometimes wonder why violence walks our streets, accounts of murder and senseless killings fill the columns of our newspapers, and family quarrels and disputes mar the sanctity of the home and smother the tranquility of so many lives.

Perhaps we stray from the path which leads to peace and find it necessary to pause, to ponder, and to reflect on the teachings of the Prince of Peace and determine to incorporate them in our thoughts and actions and to live a higher law, walk a more elevated road, and be a better disciple of Christ.

The ravages of hunger in Somalia, the brutality of hate in Bosnia, and the ethnic struggles across the globe remind us that the peace we seek will not come without effort and determination. Anger, hatred, and contention are foes not easily subdued. These enemies inevitably leave in their destructive wake tears of sorrow, the pain of conflict, and the shattered hopes of what could have been. Their sphere of influence is not restricted to the battlefields of war but can be observed altogether too frequently in the home, around the hearth, and within the heart. So soon do many forget and so late do they remember the counsel of the Lord: "There shall be no disputations among you, . . .

"For verily, verily I say unto you, he that hath the spirit of contention is not of me, but is of the devil, who is the father of contention, and he stirreth up the hearts of men to contend with anger, one with another.

"Behold, this is not my doctrine, to stir up the hearts of men with anger, one against another; but this is my doctrine, that such things should be done away" (3 Nephi 11:28–30). ("The Path to Peace," *Ensign,* May 1994, 60)

———

World peace, though a lofty goal, is but an outgrowth of the personal peace each individual seeks to attain. I speak not of the peace promoted by man, but peace as promised of God. I speak of peace in our homes, peace in our hearts, even peace in our lives. Peace after the way of man is perishable. Peace after the manner of God will prevail. ("The Path to Peace," *Ensign,* May 1994, 61)

PIONEERS

———

[The pioneer] trek of 1847, organized and led by Brigham Young, is described by historians as one of the great epics of United States history. Mormon pioneers by the hundreds suffered and died from disease, exposure, or starvation. There were some who, lacking wagons and teams, literally walked the 1,300 miles across the plains and through the mountains, pushing and pulling handcarts. In these groups, one in six perished.

For many the journey didn't begin at Nauvoo, Kirtland, Far West, or New York, but rather in distant England, Scotland, Scandinavia, and Germany. Tiny children could not fully comprehend nor understand the dynamic faith that motivated their parents to leave behind family, friends, comfort, and security. A little one might inquiringly ask, "Mommy, why are we leaving home? Where are we going?"

"Come along, precious one; we're going to Zion, the City of our God."

Between the safety of home and the promise of Zion stood the angry and treacherous waters of the mighty Atlantic. Who can recount the fear that gripped the human heart during those perilous crossings? Prompted by the silent whisperings of the Spirit, sustained by a simple, yet abiding faith, they trusted in their God and set sail on their journey. Europe was behind, America ahead. . . .

Tombstones of sage and rock marked tiny graves the entire route from Nauvoo to Salt Lake City. Such was the price some pioneers paid. Their bodies are buried in peace, but their names live on evermore.

Tired oxen lumbered, wagon wheels creaked, brave men toiled, war drums sounded, and coyotes howled. Our faith-inspired and storm-driven ancestors pressed on. They, too, had their cloud by day and pillar of fire by night. . . .

These pioneers remembered the words of the Lord: "My people must be tried in all things, that they may be prepared to receive the glory that I have for them, even the glory of Zion" (D&C 136:31).

As the long, painful struggle approached its welcomed end, a jubilant spirit filled each heart. Tired feet and weary bodies somehow found new strength.

Time-marked pages of a dusty pioneer journal speak movingly to us: "We bowed ourselves down in humble prayer to Almighty God with hearts full of thanksgiving to Him, and dedicated this land unto Him for the dwelling place of His people" (author unknown). ("Come, Follow Me," Conference Report, April 1967, 55–56)

The first winter the pioneers experienced in the Salt Lake Valley was mild, but by the spring of 1848 provisions became scarce. Heavy spring snow and rain descended. The homes which had been constructed with flat sod roofs leaked profusely. It was not uncommon to see women going about their household duties holding umbrellas over their heads.

Rationing was imposed. Each person was limited to about one-half pound of flour per day. They also ate thistle tops, bark, and roots.

We really have few ways today to comprehend the difficulty, the sacrifice, the hunger and deprivation which were required to build the roads, the culture, the schools, the very basis of today's civilization, in the Salt Lake Valley in the State of Utah. But we should never forget it. . . . Let us not only remember the past and its required sacrifice, let us also remember that we are responsible to build a legacy for the generations which follow us. Good character, craftsmanship, spirituality: these are among the precious things we can leave as our addition to the heritage of sacrifice and hard work that was left to us by those who pioneered before. ("The Legacy Continues," Days of '47 Video, May 1994)

I wonder how we would have felt if we lived in Nauvoo with our beautiful brick home with all of the comforts of life. I wonder how we would have felt looking at the beautiful grass never needing to be watered because of the abundant rain fall. The flowers would grow so beautifully with a minimum of weeds with an opportunity to have all of the best of both worlds—the world of business and opportunity as well as the world of The

Church of Jesus Christ of Latter-day Saints—and then to hear the call to move westward to leave our homes, to leave our families in some cases, to leave behind the beautiful greenery and put our vision westward to the valleys of the great Salt Lake, where one tree greeted us upon our arrival as pioneers. Yet, where would we have been today were it not for the courage of Latter-day Saints to expand the frontiers of the Church? (BYU College of Business, March 14, 1973)

Each of us has a heritage—whether from pioneer forebears, later converts, or others who helped to shape our lives. This heritage provides a foundation built of sacrifice and faith. Ours is the privilege and responsibility to build on such firm and stable footings. ("In Search of Treasure," *Ensign,* May 2003, 19)

PLAN OF SALVATION

"Created in the image of God." You cannot sincerely hold this conviction without experiencing a profound new sense of strength and power. As Latter-day Saints we know that we lived before we came to earth, that mortality is a probationary period wherein we might prove ourselves obedient to God's command and therefore worthy of celestial glory. Thus we learn who we are. Now what does God expect us to become? ("Timeless Truths for a Changing World," BYU Women's Conference, May 4, 2001)

Sacred writ and prophetic revelations provide us knowledge of who we are, from whence we came, and where we shall go when we depart mortality. *Baptism, confirmation, priesthood, mission, marriage,* and *family* are more than mere words. To you and to me they are God-given directions for our safe flight. ("Eternal Flight," Church Educational System Fireside Satellite Broadcast, February 4, 1996)

POLITICS

The themes of the aspirants to political office from both parties will emphasize the same popular topics—topics which they hope will get them elected. Family togetherness, reduction in crime and a return to basic values will be prominently featured, along with cutting the national debt and a downsizing of government at all levels. Ours, as an electorate, will be the responsibility to separate fact from fiction, reality from rhetoric, and truth from error. ("Eternal Flight," Church Educational System Fireside Satellite Broadcast, February 4, 1996)

PORNOGRAPHY

[Concerning pornography], at first we scarcely realize we have been infected. We laugh and make light-hearted comment concerning the off-color story or the clever cartoon. With evangelical zeal we protect the so-called rights of those who would contaminate with smut and destroy all that is precious and sacred. The beetle of pornography is doing his deadly task—undercutting our will, destroying our immunity, and stifling that upward reach within each of us. ("Pornography—the Deadly Carrier," *Ensign*, November 1979, 66)

———

I am concerned that there is a great war going on for the souls of mankind. We have all known that, but I think we are witnessing it with greater clarity and force than ever before. Professionally, I come from the printing and publishing industry, where I have seen examples of the deterioration of the printed product. In Los Angeles some of the largest lithographers have as their number one priority the printing of pornography. I am sickened to see some of the finest printing machinery in the world spewing forth millions of copies of pornography to corrupt the souls of men.

In contrast, I like the bold attitude of one lithographer whose sign in the window said, "We are lithographers, not pornographers." Nonetheless, today there is an avalanche of printed pornography, beautifully done as far as the quality of printing is concerned, but totally degrading as far as its content is concerned. We who are on the Lord's side of the ledger have to compete ever more diligently to offset that which is on the devil's side of the ledger. (All-Church Coordinating Council, November 15, 1988)

———

Some publishers and printers prostitute their presses by printing millions of pieces of pornography each day. No expense is spared to produce a product certain to be viewed, then viewed again. One of the most accessible sources of pornography today is the Internet, where one can turn on a computer and instantly have at his fingertips countless sites featuring pornography. . . . Tainted as well is the movie producer, the television programmer, or the entertainer who promotes pornography. Long gone are the restraints of yesteryear. So-called realism is the quest, with the result that today we are surrounded by this filth.

Avoid any semblance of pornography. It will desensitize the spirit and erode the conscience. We are told in the Doctrine and Covenants: "That which doth not edify is not of God, and is darkness" (D&C 50:23). Such is pornography. ("True to the Faith," *Ensign*, May 2006, 18–19)

Now, a word of caution to all—both young and old, both male and female. We live at a time when the adversary is using every means possible to ensnare us in his web of deceit, trying desperately to take us down with him. There are many pathways along which he entices us to go—pathways that can lead to our destruction. Advances in many areas that can be used for good can also be used to speed us along those heinous pathways.

I feel to mention one in particular, and that is the Internet. On one hand, it provides nearly limitless opportunities for acquiring useful and important information. Through it we can communicate with others around the world. The Church itself has a wonderful Web site, filled with valuable and uplifting information and priceless resources.

On the other hand, however—and extremely alarming—are the reports of the number of individuals who are utilizing the Internet for evil and degrading purposes, the viewing of pornography being the most prevalent of these purposes. My brothers and sisters, involvement in such will literally destroy the spirit. Be strong. Be clean. Avoid such degrading and destructive types of content at all costs—wherever they may be! I sound this warning to everyone, everywhere. I add—particularly to the young people—that this includes pornographic images transmitted via cell phones.

My beloved friends, under no circumstances allow yourselves to become trapped in the viewing of pornography, one of the most effective of Satan's enticements. And if you have allowed yourself to become involved in this behavior, cease now. Seek the help you need to overcome and to change the direction of your life. Take the steps necessary to get back on the strait and narrow, and then stay there. ("Until We Meet Again," *Ensign,* May 2009, 113)

PRAYER

———

Unfortunately, prosperity, abundance, honor, and praise lead some men to the false security of haughty self-assurance and the abandonment of the inclination to pray. Conversely, trial, tribulation, sickness, and death crumble the castles of men's pride and bring them to their knees to petition for power from on high. ("The Prayer of Faith," *Ensign,* May 1978, 21)

———

Be seeking God in personal and family prayer, we and our loved ones will develop the fulfillment of what the great English statesman William H. Gladstone described as the world's greatest need: "A living faith in a personal God." Who can evaluate the real worth of such a blessing? Such a faith will light the pathway for any honest seeker of divine truth. Wives will draw closer to their husbands and husbands will all the more appreciate their wives; and children will be happy children, as children are meant to be. Children in the homes blessed by prayer will not find themselves in that dreaded *Never, Never Land:* Never the object of concern; never the recipient of proper parental guidance. . . . Our children will grow physically from childhood to adulthood, and mentally from ignorance to knowledge, emotionally from insecurity to stability and spiritually to an abiding faith in God. ("America Needs You," *Church of the Air,* October 4, 1964)

———

We live in troubled times. Doctors' offices throughout the land are filled with individuals who are beset with emotional problems as well as physical distress. Our divorce courts are doing a land office business because people have unsolved problems. Personnel workers and grievance committees in modern industry work long hours in an effort to assist people with their problems.

One personnel officer assigned to handle petty grievances concluded an unusually hectic day by placing facetiously a little sign on his desk for those with unsolved problems to read. It read, "Have you tried prayer?"

What that personnel director did not know when he placed such a sign upon his desk was that he was providing counsel and direction which would solve more problems, alleviate more suffering, prevent more transgression, and bring about greater peace and contentment in the human soul than could be obtained in any other way.

A prominent American judge was asked what we as citizens of the countries of the world could do to reduce crime and disobedience to law and to bring peace and contentment into our lives and into our nations. He carefully replied, "I would suggest a return to the old-fashioned practice of family prayer."

As a people, aren't we grateful that family prayer is not an out-of-date practice with us? There is no more beautiful sight in all this world than to see a family praying together. The oft-repeated phrase is ever true, "The family that prays together stays together."

The Lord directed that we have family prayer when He said, "Pray in your families unto the Father, always in my name, that your wives and your children may be blessed" (3 Nephi 18:21). . . .

As we offer unto the Lord our family and our personal prayers, let us do so with faith and trust in Him. Let us remember the injunction of Paul to the Hebrews: "For he that cometh to God must believe that he is, and that he is a rewarder of them that diligently seek him" (Hebrews 11:6). ("Come unto Me," Conference Report, April 1964, 129–30)

———

Men and women of integrity, character, and purpose have ever recognized a power higher than themselves and have sought through prayer to be guided by such power. Such has it ever been. So shall it ever be. ("The Prayer of Faith," *Ensign,* May 1978, 20)

———

Every [person] needs a sacred grove to which he can retire to meditate and to pray for guidance. Mine [when I was a bishop] was our old ward chapel. I could not begin to count the occasions when on a dark night at a late hour I would make my way to the stand of this building where I was blessed, confirmed, ordained, taught, and eventually called to preside. The chapel was dimly lighted by the street light in front; not a sound would be heard, no intruder to disturb. With my hand on the pulpit I would kneel and share with Him above my thoughts, my concerns, my problems. ("Bishop—Center Stage in Welfare," *Ensign,* November 1980, 90)

———

When we are weighed in the balances we will not be found wanting if we make personal prayer a pattern for our lives. When we remember that each of us is literally a spirit son or daughter of God, we will not find it difficult to approach our Father in Heaven. ("Pathway to Life Eternal," BYU Devotional, February 27, 1968)

———

A boy, born in the year of our Lord one thousand eight hundred and five, on the twenty-third of December, in the town of Sharon, Windsor County, State of Vermont, paused to pray that bright day in the grove near Palmyra. Who can calculate the far-reaching effects of that one prayer by that one boy? Do you pause to pray? ("Pathway to Life Eternal," BYU Devotional, February 27, 1968)

———

Oh, do not pray for tasks equal to your powers. Pray for powers equal to your tasks. Then the doing of your work shall be no miracle, but you shall be the miracle.

Your Heavenly Father will not leave you to struggle along, but stands ever ready to help. Most often such assistance comes quietly, at other times with dramatic impact. ("Pathway to Life Eternal," BYU Devotional, February 27, 1968)

———

Will you join me as we look in on a typical Latter-day Saint family offering prayers unto the Lord? Father, mother, and each of the children kneel, bow their heads and close their eyes. A sweet spirit of love, unity, and peace fills the home. As father hears his tiny son pray unto God that his dad will do the right things and be obedient to the Lord's bidding, do you think that such a father would find it difficult to honor the prayer of his precious son? As a teenage daughter hears her sweet mother plead unto God that her daughter will be inspired in the selection of her companions, that she will prepare herself for a temple marriage, don't you believe that such a daughter will seek to honor this humble, pleading petition of her mother whom she so dearly loves? When father, mother, and each of the children earnestly pray that the fine sons in the family will live worthy, that they may in due time receive a call to serve as ambassadors of the Lord in the mission fields of the Church, don't we begin to see how such sons grow to young manhood with an overwhelming desire to serve as missionaries? ("Heavenly Homes—Forever Families," Satellite Broadcast, January 12, 1986)

———

As we offer unto God our family prayers and our personal prayers, let us do so with faith and trust in Him. If any of us has been slow to hearken to the counsel to pray always, there is no finer hour to begin than now. Those who feel that prayer might denote a physical weakness should remember that a man never stands taller than when he is upon his knees. ("Heavenly Homes—Forever Families," Satellite Broadcast, January 12, 1986)

———

Each of you is a [child] of God, created in His image. Yours is a celestial journey. Heavenly Father wants you to check in with Him through sincere and fervent prayer. Remember, you are never alone. Never forget that you are loved. Never doubt that someone surely cares for you. . . .

Pray fervently. ("A Time to Choose," *Ensign*, May 1995, 98)

———

Prayer is the passport to spiritual power. ("Hallmarks of a Happy Home," *Ensign*, November 1988, 70)

———

As we pray, let us really communicate with our Father in Heaven. It is easy to let our prayers become repetitious, expressing words with little or no thought behind them. . . . Let us pray with sincerity and meaning, offering our thanks and asking for those things we feel we need. Let us listen for His answers, that we may recognize them when they come. As we do, we will be strengthened and blessed. We will come to know Him and His desires for our lives. By knowing Him, by trusting His will, our foundations of faith will be strengthened. ("How Firm a Foundation," *Ensign*, November 2006, 67)

———

Let us not neglect our family prayers. Such is an effective deterrent to sin, and thence a most beneficent provider of joy and happiness. . . . By providing an example of prayer to our children, we will also be helping them to begin their own deep foundations of faith and testimonies which they will need throughout their lives. ("How Firm a Foundation," *Ensign*, November 2006, 67)

———

He who knows each of His children will answer our fervent and heartfelt prayer as we seek help in guiding them. Such prayer will solve more problems, alleviate more suffering, prevent more transgression, and bring about greater peace and contentment in the human soul than any other way.

Besides needing such guidance for our own families, we

have been called to positions where we have responsibility for others. As a bishop or counselor, as a priesthood quorum leader or an auxiliary leader, you have the opportunity to make a difference in the lives of others. There may be those who come from part-member or less-active families; some may have turned from their parents, disregarding their pleadings and counsel. We could well be the instrument in the Lord's hands to make a difference in the life of one in such a situation. Without the guidance of our Heavenly Father, however, we cannot do all that we have been called to do. Such help comes through prayer. ("Heavenly Homes, Forever Families," *Ensign,* June 2006, 100)

———

In the frantic pace of life today, provide place for prayer. Our task is larger than ourselves. We need God's divine help. I testify that His help is but a prayer away. (MIA June Conference, June 25, 1971)

———

When the burdens of life become heavy, when trials test one's faith, when pain, sorrow, and despair cause the light of hope to flicker and burn low, communication with our Heavenly Father provides peace. ("Finishers Wanted," Conference Report, April 1972, 72)

———

To those within the sound of my voice who are struggling with challenges and difficulties large and small, prayer is the provider of spiritual strength; it is the passport to peace. Prayer is the means by which we approach our Father in Heaven, who loves us. Speak to Him in prayer and then listen for the answer. Miracles are wrought through prayer. ("Be Your Best Self," *Ensign,* May 2009, 68)

PREPARATION

Preparation for life's opportunities and responsibilities has never been more vital. We live in a changing society. Intense competition is a part of life. The role of husband, father, grandfather, provider, and protector is vastly different from what it was a generation ago. Preparation is not a matter of *perhaps* or *maybe*. It is a mandate. The old phrase "Ignorance is bliss" is forever gone. Preparation precedes performance. ("Duty Calls," *Ensign*, May 1996, 43)

Paul described life as a race. He said, "Know ye not that they which run in a race run all, but one receiveth the prize? So run, that ye may obtain" (1 Corinthians 9:24).

. . . The race of life is so important, the prize so valued, that great emphasis must necessarily be placed on adequate and thorough preparation.

When we contemplate the eternal nature of our choices, preparation is a vital factor in our lives. The day will come when we will look upon our period of preparation and be grateful that we properly applied ourselves. ("Great Expectations," BYU Devotional, May 11, 1965)

Concerning your preparation, let me share with you this time-honored advice, which has never been more applicable than it is right now: it is not the number of hours you put in, but what you put in the hours that counts.

Have discipline in your preparations. Have checkpoints where you can determine if you're on course. . . . You can't get the jobs of tomorrow until you have the skills of today. Business in the new economy, where the only guarantee is change, brings us to serious preparation. ("Three Gates Only You Can Open," *New Era,* August 2008, 4)

Priesthood
(see also Aaronic Priesthood)

———

Priesthood is the central power in the Church and the authority through which the Church is administered. ("Correlation Brings Blessings," General Relief Society Conference, September 28, 1966)

———

Long years ago and distant miles away, in the conquered country of Palestine, a marvelous miracle occurred. The setting was bleak, the time one of tumult. In these, the days of Herod, king of Judea, there lived a priest named Zacharias and his wife, Elisabeth. "They were . . . righteous before God" (Luke 1:6). However, long years of yearning had returned no reward—Zacharias and Elisabeth remained childless.

Then came that day of days ever to be remembered. There appeared to Zacharias the angel Gabriel, who proclaimed: "Fear not, Zacharias: for thy prayer is heard; and thy wife Elisabeth shall bear thee a son, and thou shalt call his name John.

"He shall be great in the sight of the Lord" (Luke 1:13–15).

Elisabeth did conceive. In due time a son was born, and according to the angel's instruction he was named John.

As with the master, Jesus Christ, so with the servant, John—precious little is recorded of their years of youth. A single sentence contains all that we know of John's history for a space of thirty years—the entire period which elapsed between his birth and his walk into the wilderness to commence his public ministry: "The child grew, and waxed strong in spirit, and was in the deserts till the day of his showing unto Israel" (Luke 1:80).

His dress was that of the old prophets—a garment woven of camel's hair. His food was such as the desert afforded—locusts and wild honey. His message was brief. He preached faith, repentance, baptism by immersion, and the bestowal of the Holy Ghost by an authority greater than that possessed by himself.

"I am not the Christ," he told his band of faithful disciples (John 1:20). "But . . . I am sent before him" (John 3:28). "I indeed baptize you with water . . . but one mightier than I cometh . . . : he shall baptize you with the Holy Ghost, and with fire" (Luke 3:16).

Then there transpired the climactic scene of John's mission—the baptism of Christ. Jesus came down from Galilee expressly "to be baptized" by John. Humbled of heart and contrite in spirit, John pleaded, "I have need to be baptized of thee, and comest thou to me?" The Master's reply, "It becometh us to fulfill all righteousness" (Matthew 3:13–15). . . .

"And Jesus, when he was baptized, went up straightway out of the water: and, lo, the heavens were opened unto him, and he saw the Spirit of God descending like a dove, and lighting upon him:

And lo a voice from heaven, saying, This is my beloved Son, in whom I am well pleased" (Matthew 3:16–17).

John's testimony that Jesus was the Redeemer of the world was declared boldly. Without fear, and with courage, John taught: "Behold the Lamb of God, which taketh away the sin of the world" (John 1:29).

Of John, the Savior later testified, "Among them that are

born of women there hath not risen a greater than John the Baptist" (Matthew 11:11).

John's public ministry moved toward its close. He had, at the beginning of it, condemned the hypocrisy and worldliness of the Pharisees and Sadducees; and he now had occasion to denounce the lust of a king. The result is well known. A king's weakness and a woman's fury combined to bring about the death of John.

The tomb in which his body was placed could not contain that body. Nor could the act of murder still that voice. To the world we declare that at Harmony, Pennsylvania, on May 15, 1829, an angel, "who announced himself as John, the same that is called John the Baptist in the New Testament," came as a resurrected personage to Joseph Smith and Oliver Cowdery. "The angelic visitant averred that he was acting under the direction of Peter, James, and John, the ancient Apostles, who held the keys of the higher Priesthood, which was called the Priesthood of Melchizedek" (D&C 13, section heading). The Aaronic Priesthood was restored to the earth. ("Preparing the Way," *Ensign,* May 1980, 7–8)

———

The greatest safeguard we have in the Church is a strong, firm, committed, dedicated, and testifying Melchizedek Priesthood base. ("The Need to Add Men to the Melchizedek Priesthood," Regional Representatives Seminar, April 6, 1984)

———

All who hold the priesthood have opportunities for service to our Heavenly Father and to His children here on earth. It is contrary to the spirit of service to live selfishly within ourselves and disregard the needs of others. The Lord will guide us and make us equal to the challenges before us. Remember His promise and counsel: "The power and authority of the higher, or Melchizedek Priesthood, is to hold the keys of all the spiritual blessings of the church—

"To have the privilege of receiving the mysteries of the kingdom of heaven, to have the heavens opened unto them, to commune with the general assembly and church of the Firstborn, and to enjoy the communion and presence of God the Father, and Jesus the mediator of the new covenant" (D&C 107:18–19). ("The Priesthood—A Sacred Trust," *Ensign,* May 1994, 50)

As bearers of the priesthood, all of us united as one can qualify for the guiding influence of our Heavenly Father as we pursue our respective callings. We are engaged in the work of the Lord Jesus Christ. We, like those of olden times, have answered His call. We are on His errand. We shall succeed in the solemn charge given by Mormon to declare the Lord's word among His people. He wrote: "Behold, I am a disciple of Jesus Christ, the Son of God. I have been called of him to declare his word among his people, that they might have everlasting life" (3 Nephi 5:13).

May we ever remember the truth, "Who honors God, God honors." ("Who Honors God, God Honors," *Ensign,* November 1995, 50)

Brethren, the world is in need of your help. There are feet to steady, hands to grasp, minds to encourage, hearts to inspire, and souls to save. The blessings of eternity await you. Yours is the privilege to be not spectators but participants on the stage of priesthood service. ("To the Rescue," *Ensign,* May 2001, 48)

———

As bearers of the priesthood, we have been placed on earth in troubled times. We live in a complex world with currents of conflict everywhere to be found. Political machinations ruin the stability of nations, despots grasp for power, and segments of society seem forever downtrodden, deprived of opportunity and left with a feeling of failure.

We who have been ordained to the priesthood of God can make a difference. When we qualify for the help of the Lord, we can build boys, we can mend men, we can accomplish miracles in His holy service. Our opportunities are without limit.

Though the task looms large, we are strengthened by the truth: "The greatest force in this world today is the power of God as it works through man." If we are on the Lord's errand, we are entitled to the Lord's help. That divine help, however, is predicated upon our worthiness. To sail safely the seas of mortality, to perform a human rescue mission, we need the guidance of that eternal mariner—even the great Jehovah. We reach out, we reach up, to obtain heavenly help. ("You Make a Difference," *Ensign,* May 1988, 41)

———

As priesthood leaders, we soon discover that some of our work, though not recorded on any written report, is of vital significance. The visits to the homes of quorum members, blessing the sick, helping a member with a project, or comforting grieving hearts when a loved one passes on are all sacred privileges of priesthood service. True, they may not be recorded on a written report; but more important, they find lodgement in the soul and bring joy to the heart. They are also known of the Lord. ("Called to Serve," *Ensign,* November 1991, 48)

———

Come all ye sons of God who have received the priesthood; let us consider our callings, let us reflect on our responsibilities, let us determine our duty, and let us follow Jesus Christ, our Lord.

While we may differ in age, in custom, or in nationality, we hold membership in the same church and are united as one in our priesthood callings. ("That We May Touch Heaven," *Ensign,* November 1990, 45)

———

To you who are or have been presidents of your quorums, may I suggest that your duty does not end when your term of office concludes. That relationship with your quorum members, your duty to them, continues throughout your life. ("True to Our Priesthood Trust," *Ensign,* November 2006, 57)

———

Ours is the responsibility to so conduct our lives that when the call comes to provide a priesthood blessing or to assist in any way, we are worthy to do so. We have been told that truly we cannot escape the effect of our personal influence. We must be certain that our influence is positive and uplifting.

Are our hands clean? Are our hearts pure? ("True to Our Priesthood Trust," *Ensign,* November 2006, 58)

———

We become alarmed when we see how many are confirmed members of the Church and then receive perhaps the Aaronic Priesthood, and then we lose too many as deacons. We lose others as they become teachers. We lose others as they become priests or don't become priests. Our biggest loss, I think, is from the Aaronic Priesthood into the Melchizedek Priesthood.

What can we do to ensure activity for all the priesthood bearers of the Church?

. . . I believe that projects are needed for priesthood quorums, where together they remove the weakness of men serving alone and provide the strength of brothers serving together in a common project of helping others. (General Authority Training Meeting, March 29, 2007)

———

The priesthood is a gift which brings with it not only special blessings but also solemn responsibilities. It is our responsibility to conduct our lives so that we are ever worthy of the priesthood we bear. We live in a time when we are surrounded by much that is intended to entice us into paths which may lead to our destruction. To avoid such paths requires determination and courage. ("The Priesthood—A Sacred Gift," *Ensign,* May 2007, 57)

———

Wherever we go, our priesthood goes with us. Are we standing in "holy places"? . . .

My brethren of the priesthood—from the youngest to the oldest—are you living your life in accordance with that which the Lord requires? Are you worthy to bear the priesthood of God? If you are not, make the decision here and now, muster the courage it will take, and institute whatever changes are necessary so that your life is what it should be. ("The Priesthood—A Sacred Gift," *Ensign,* May 2007, 57–58)

———

Let us ever remember that the priesthood of God which we bear is a sacred gift which brings to us and to those we serve the blessings of heaven. May we, in whatever place we may be, honor and protect that priesthood. May we ever be on the Lord's errand, that we might ever be entitled to the Lord's help. ("The Priesthood—A Sacred Gift," *Ensign,* May 2007, 60)

———

I hope with all my heart and soul that every young man who receives the priesthood will honor that priesthood and be true to the trust which is conveyed when it is conferred. May each of us who holds the priesthood of God know what he believes. . . . There will be occasions in each of our lives when we will be called upon to explain or to defend our beliefs. When the time for performance arrives, the time for preparation is past.

Most of you young men will have the opportunity to share your testimonies when you serve as missionaries throughout the world. Prepare now for that wonderful privilege. ("Our Sacred Priesthood Trust," *Ensign,* May 2006, 54)

———

The oath and covenant of the priesthood pertains to all of us. To those who hold the Melchizedek Priesthood, it is a declaration of our requirement to be faithful and obedient to the laws of God and to magnify the callings which come to us. To those who hold the Aaronic Priesthood, it is a pronouncement concerning future duty and responsibility, that they may prepare themselves here and now. ("The Sacred Call of Service," *Ensign,* May 2005, 54)

———

Each man and each boy who holds the priesthood of God must be worthy of that great privilege and responsibility. Each must strive to learn his duty and then to do it to the best of his ability. As we do so, we provide the means by which our Heavenly Father and His Son, Jesus Christ, can accomplish Their work here upon the earth. It is we who are Their representatives here. ("Be Your Best Self," *Ensign,* May 2009, 67)

———

Holders of the priesthood may not necessarily be eloquent in their speech. They may not hold advanced degrees in difficult fields of study. They may very well be men of humble means. But God is no respecter of persons, and He will sustain His servants in righteousness as they avoid the evils of our day and live lives of virtue and purity. ("Be Your Best Self," *Ensign,* May 2009, 69)

———

We are surrounded by so much that is designed to divert our attention from those things which are virtuous and good and to tempt us with that which would cause us to be unworthy to exercise the priesthood we bear. I speak not just to the young men of the Aaronic Priesthood but to those of all ages. Temptations come in various forms throughout our lives.

Brethren, are we qualified at all times to perform the sacred duties associated with the priesthood we bear? Young men—you who are priests—are you clean in body and spirit as you sit at the sacrament table on Sunday and bless the emblems of the sacrament? Young men who are teachers, are you worthy to prepare the sacrament? Deacons, as you pass the sacrament to the members of the Church, do you do so knowing that you are spiritually qualified to do so? Does each of you fully understand the importance of *all* the sacred duties you perform? ("Examples of Righteousness," *Ensign,* May 2008, 65)

Great promises await us if we are true and faithful to the oath and covenant of this precious priesthood which we hold. May we be worthy sons of our Heavenly Father. May we ever be exemplary in our homes and faithful in keeping all of the commandments, that we may harbor no animosity toward any man but rather be peacemakers, ever remembering the Savior's admonition, "By this shall all men know that ye are my disciples, if ye have love one to another" (John 13:35). ("School Thy Feelings, O My Brother," *Ensign,* November 2009, 69)

PRIORITIES

Our beloved Savior beckons us to follow Him. The choice is ours. You will recall the rich, young ruler who asked the Savior what he should do to have eternal life and, when told to sell his possessions and give to the poor, "went away sorrowful: for he had great possessions" (see Matthew 19:16–22). He preferred the comforts of earth to the treasures of heaven. He would not purchase the things of eternity by abandoning those of time. He made, as Dante calls it, "the great refusal." And so he vanishes from the gospel history, nor do the evangelists know anything of him further. His riches and many possessions had become his God. ("Timeless Truths for a Changing World," BYU Women's Conference, May 4, 2001)

While we reach outward, we have the responsibility to *press onward.* Whatever part you choose to play on the world stage, keep in mind that life is like a candid camera; it does not wait for you to pose. Learning how to direct our resources wisely is a high priority. We don't have to keep up with the change. We have to keep ahead of it. ("Be All That You Can Be," BYU–Hawaii Commencement, December 14, 2002)

———

If you do something that turns out not quite as you had planned, you can almost always put it right, get over it, learn from it. But once you've missed out on something, it's gone. Oh, there will be regrets. There will be the brilliant professor whose class you never took, the relative with whom you never became close, the friend you didn't call, the thanks you didn't express, the dress you didn't buy, the soccer game you missed. Try to keep the list as short as possible.

Send that note to the friend you've been neglecting; give your child a compliment and a hug; say "I love you" more; always express your thanks. Never let a problem to be solved become more important than a person to be loved. Friends move away, children grow up, loved ones pass on. It's so easy to take others for granted, until that day when they're gone from our lives and we are left with feelings of "what if" and "if only." . . .

Let us relish life as we live it, find joy in the journey and share our love with friends and family. One day, each of us will run out of tomorrows. Let us not put off what is most important. ("Joy in the Journey," BYU Women's Conference, May 2, 2008)

PROCRASTINATION

———

Have we been guilty of declaring, "I've been thinking about making some course corrections in my life. I plan to take the first step—tomorrow"? With such thinking, tomorrow is for-ever. Such tomorrows rarely come unless we do something about them today. ("Now Is the Time," *Ensign,* November 2001, 60)

———

I know of a university student who was so busy with the joys of student life that preparation for an exam was postponed. The night before, she realized the hour was late and the preparation was not done. She rationalized, "Now what is more important—my health, which requires that I must sleep, or the drudgery of study?" Well, you can probably guess the outcome. Sleep won, study failed, and the test was a personal disaster. Work we must. ("Pathways to Perfection," *Ensign,* May 2002, 101)

———

There is no tomorrow to remember if we don't do some-thing today, and to live most fully today, we must do that which is of greatest importance. Let us not procrastinate those things which matter most.

I recently read the account of a man who, just after the passing of his wife, opened her dresser drawer and found there an item of clothing she had purchased when they visited the Eastern part of the United States nine years earlier. She had not worn it but was saving it for a special occasion. Now, of course, that occasion would never come.

In relating the experience to a friend, the husband said, "Don't save something only for a special occasion. Every day in your life is a special occasion." ("In Search of Treasure," *Ensign,* May 2003, 21)

———

Two centuries ago, Edward Young said that procrastination is the thief of time. Actually, procrastination is much more. It is the thief of our self-respect. It nags at us and spoils our fun. It deprives us of the fullest realization of our ambitions and hopes. Knowing this, we jar ourselves back to reality with the sure knowledge that, "This is my day of opportunity. I will not waste it."

Our attitude, then, is to make the most of our God-given talents. To study, to learn, to achieve, to excel, to prepare for our life's opportunities. ("Learning the ABC's at BYU," BYU Devotional, February 8, 1966)

———

Two twins stand before us, about whom we must make a choice. They are: "Do it now" and "Put it off." Remember, decision is of little account unless it is followed by action, and there is no recipe for getting things done so good as the one to start doing them. ("Constant Truths in Changing Times," BYU Commencement, May 26, 1967)

Progress

———

Through modern science, man has been permitted to fly through space at great speeds and to silently and without effort cruise sixty days under water in nuclear-powered ships. Now that man can fly like a bird and swim like a fish, if only he could learn to walk on earth like a man. ("In Quest of the Abundant Life," Utah State University Baccalaureate, June 2, 1967)

———

It took man five thousand years to go from the sailboat to the steamboat; a hundred years from the steamboat to the airplane. There were only forty years from the Air Age to the Atomic Age and only twelve years from the Atomic Age to the Space Age.

In the Space Age, the flow of knowledge is as relentless and in a real sense as uncompromising as the spring flow of the rushing waters of the Snake River. It imposes on us the stiff, and in many ways new, requirement that we not merely adjust to, but that we anticipate the future. ("The Race for Eternal Life," Seminary Day, February 3, 1968)

———

The world is advancing—our challenge is to advance with it. To do so, we had better take time to be informed, or time will leave us behind. ("Yesterday, Today, and Tomorrow," Weber State College Baccalaureate, May 31, 1968)

———

Machines are not creative or imaginative, nor even responsible. They are simply tools, and tools do not work and serve mankind until skilled hands take them up. Because our tools are growing in complexity and in potential usefulness, we must grow in order to use them both profitably and wisely. Let us not be frightened. Rather, let us be challenged. Only the human mind has the capacity for creativity, imagination, insight, vision, and responsibility. ("Be All That You Can Be," BYU–Hawaii Commencement, December 14, 2002)

———

To meet the combined demands of the accumulated past and of the accumulating future, all of us need:

- To act—not just react.
- To innovate—not just imitate.
- To program—not just protest.
- To perform—not just proclaim.
- To solve—not just resolve.
- To accelerate—not just vacillate.

("Spectrum-on-the-Road," Bountiful, Utah, March 14, 1968)

PROPHETS
(SEE ALSO JOSEPH SMITH)

Follow the prophets of God. When you follow the prophets, you will be in safe territory. I know that the Lord inspires His prophets, His seers, and His revelators. ("Life's Greatest Decisions," Church Educational System Fireside Satellite Broadcast, September 7, 2003)

Is the voice of the Lord heard today? How does it come to man? Can your search for truth be guided by His voice? Can mine? Today, as always when the true Church of Christ is on the earth, there stands at its head a prophet. And just as the voice of the Lord came to Jeremiah, Ezekiel, and Isaiah, it has likewise come to latter-day prophets. ("In Search of Truth," Conference Report, October 1964, 18)

REACTIVATION

Amidst the storms of life, danger lurks; and men, like boats, find themselves stranded and facing destruction. Who will man the lifeboats, leaving behind the comforts of home and family, and go to the rescue? ("To the Rescue," *Ensign*, May 2001, 48)

I firmly believe that the Church today is stronger than it has ever been. Activity levels of our youth testify that this is a generation of faith and devotion to truth. Yet there are some who drop by the wayside, who find other interests that persuade them to neglect their Church duties. We must not lose such precious souls.

There are growing numbers among the prospective elders who are not found in Church meetings nor filling Church assignments. This situation can and must be remedied. The task is ours. Responsibility needs to be assigned and effort put forth without delay. ("Stand in Your Appointed Place," *Ensign*, May 2003, 54)

Over the years as I have visited many stakes throughout the world, there have been those stakes where ward and stake leaders, out of necessity or in response to duty, stopped wringing their hands, rolled up their sleeves, and, with the Lord's help, went to work and brought precious men to qualify for the Melchizedek Priesthood and, with their wives and children, to enter the holy temple for their endowments and sealings. . . .

In each of these [stakes], there were four elements which led them to success:

1. The reactivation opportunity was pursued at the ward level.

2. The bishop of the ward was involved.

3. Qualified and inspired teachers were provided.

4. Attention was given to each individual.

("Stand in Your Appointed Place," *Ensign*, May 2003, 55–56)

———

There are tens of thousands of priesthood holders scattered among you who, through indifference, hurt feelings, shyness, or weakness, cannot bless to the fullest extent their wives and children—without considering the lives of others they could lift and bless. Ours is the solemn duty to bring about a change, to take such an individual by the hand and help him arise and be well spiritually. As we do so, sweet wives will call our names blessed, and grateful children will marvel at the change in Daddy as lives are altered and souls are saved. ("The Priesthood—A Sacred Trust," *Ensign*, May 1994, 52)

———

High-powered sales techniques are not the answer in priesthood leadership; rather, devotion to duty, continuous effort, abundant love, and personal spirituality combine to touch the heart, prompt the change, and bring to the table of the Lord His hungry children who have wandered in the wilderness of the world but who now have returned "home." ("The Priesthood—A Sacred Trust," *Ensign*, May 1994, 52)

———

Beyond the new convert to the Church are some who have drifted from that pathway which upward leads and, for one reason or another, have become less active for months, even years. Perhaps they were not fellowshiped; maybe friends departed from their lives. Whatever the reason, the fact remains:

We need them, and they need us. Missionaries can effectively visit the homes where these individuals reside. When they approach, those within the shelter of home may come to remember the glorious feelings which came over them when they first heard the principles of the gospel taught to them. The missionaries can teach such individuals and witness the changes which come into their lives as they return to activity.

They need friends with testimonies. They need to know that we truly care for the one. ("They Will Come," *Ensign*, May 1997, 46)

———

Let me share with you two typical comments from those who were once blind but who now walk in light and truth, thanks to faithful home teachers and a program . . . planned and instituted to motivate brethren long inactive.

From a family in central Utah: "Before our newly found church activity, we thought we were living average, normal lives. We had our problems, our ups and downs. But there was one thing missing in our home and that was a togetherness that only the priesthood can bring. Now we have that blessing, and our love for one another is greater than we ever dreamed it could be. We are truly happy."

From another family: "We thank our Heavenly Father every night for our bishopric and our home teachers who have helped us to achieve blessings that seemed so far away, so impossible to obtain. We now have a peace of mind beyond description." ("The Precious Gift of Sight," Conference Report, April 1965, 46)

———

Let us reach out to rescue those who need our help and lift them to the higher road and the better way. Let us focus our thinking on the needs of priesthood holders and their wives and children who have slipped from the path of activity. May we listen to the unspoken message from their hearts. You will find it to be familiar: "Lead me, guide me, walk beside me, / Help me find the way. / Teach me all that I must do / To live with him someday" (*Hymns,* no. 301).

The work of reactivation is no task for the idler or daydreamer. Children grow, parents age, and time waits for no man. Do not postpone a prompting; rather, act on it, and the Lord will open the way. ("The Sacred Call of Service," *Ensign,* May 2005, 55)

———

Many years ago, Bishop Marvin O. Ashton, who served as a counselor in the Presiding Bishopric, gave an illustration I'd like to share with you. Picture with me, if you will, a farmer driving a large open-bed truck filled with sugar beets en route to the sugar refinery. As the farmer drives along a bumpy dirt road, some of the sugar beets bounce from the truck and are strewn along the roadside. When he realizes he has lost some of the beets, he instructs his helpers, "There's just as much sugar in those which have slipped off. Let's go back and get them!"

In my application of this illustration, the sugar beets represent the members of the Church for whom we are responsible; and those that have fallen out of the truck represent the men and women, youth and children who, for whatever reason, have fallen from the path of activity. Paraphrasing the farmer's comments concerning the sugar beets, I say of these souls, precious to our Father and our Master: "There's just as much value in those who have slipped off. Let's go back and get them!"

Right now, today, some of them are caught in the current of popular opinion. Others are torn by the tide of turbulent times. Yet others are drawn down and drowned in the whirlpool of sin.

This need not be. We have the doctrines of truth. We have the programs. We have the people. We have the power. Our mission is more than meetings. Our service is to save souls. ("Sugar Beets and the Worth of a Soul," *Ensign,* July 2009, 5)

The ranks of . . . prospective elders have grown larger. This is because of those younger boys of the Aaronic Priesthood quorums who are lost along the Aaronic Priesthood pathway and also those grown men who are baptized but do not persevere in activity and faith so that they might be ordained elders.

I not only reflect on the hearts and souls of such individual men, but also sorrow for their sweet wives and growing children. These men await a helping hand, an encouraging word, and a personal testimony of truth expressed from a heart filled with love and a desire to lift and to build. ("Anxiously Engaged," *Ensign,* November 2004, 58)

RELIEF SOCIETY
(SEE ALSO WOMEN)

Women of Relief Society, you truly are angels of mercy. This is demonstrated on a grand scale through the humanitarian outreach to the cold, the hungry, and to suffering wherever it is found. Your labors are also very much in evidence in our wards and in our stakes and missions. Every bishop in the Church could testify of this truth. ("'Be Thou an Example,'" *Ensign,* November 2001, 99)

You, my beloved sisters, know who you are and what God expects you to become. Your challenge is to bring all for whom you are responsible to a knowledge of this truth. The Relief Society of this, the Lord's Church, can be the means to achieve such a goal. . . .

A love for the Savior, a reverence for His name, and genuine respect one for another will provide a fertile seedbed for a testimony to grow.

Learning the gospel, bearing a testimony, leading a family are rarely if ever simple processes. Life's journey is characterized by bumps in the road, swells in the sea—even the turbulence of our times. ("If Ye Are Prepared Ye Shall Not Fear," *Ensign,* November 2004, 115)

———

The women of Relief Society stand side by side as sisters. May you ever be there to care for each other, to recognize one another's needs. May you be sensitive to the circumstances of each, realizing that some women are facing particular challenges, but that every woman is a valued daughter of our Heavenly Father. ("If Ye Are Prepared Ye Shall Not Fear," *Ensign,* November 2004, 116)

———

Remember the past; learn from it. Contemplate the future; prepare for it. Live in the present; serve in it. Therein is the mighty strength of the Relief Society of this church. ("The Mighty Strength of the Relief Society," *Ensign,* November 1997, 94)

———

From the beginning, the Prophet Joseph Smith recognized the importance of organizing the women of the Church after the pattern of the priesthood. As he did so, the Prophet declared: "And I now turn the key in your behalf in the name of the Lord, and this Society shall rejoice, and knowledge and intelligence shall flow down from this time henceforth" (*History of the Church* [1932–1952], 4:607).

In planning the curriculum for women of the Church, we have been guided by the Prophet's statements, as well as the instruction provided by those who succeeded him in Church leadership. We have, with resolute care, followed these guidelines:

1. Every woman has been endowed by God with distinctive characteristics, gifts, and talents in order that she may fulfill a specific mission in the eternal plan.
2. The priesthood is the central power of the Church. "The priesthood is for the benefit of all members of the Church. Men have no greater claim than women upon the blessings that issue from the priesthood and accompany its possession" (John A. Widtsoe, *Priesthood and Church Government* [1939], 83).
3. The home is the basic organization to teach an individual to walk uprightly before the Lord.
4. Compassionate service and a sensitivity to the needs of others are the principal purposes for which a women's program was organized.

(General Relief Society Conference, September 30, 1970)

REPENTANCE

We have all made incorrect choices. If we have not already corrected such choices, I assure you that there is a way to do so. The process is called repentance. I plead with you to correct your mistakes. Our Savior died to provide you and me that blessed gift. Although the path is not easy, the promise is real: "Though your sins be as scarlet, they shall be as white as snow" (Isaiah 1:18). "And I, the Lord, remember them no more" (D&C 58:42). Don't put your eternal life at risk. If you have sinned, the sooner you begin to make your way back, the sooner you will find the sweet peace and joy that come with the miracle of forgiveness. ("The Three Rs of Choice," *Ensign,* November 2010, 69)

———

Should there be anything amiss in your life, there is open to you a way out. Cease any unrighteousness. Talk with your bishop. Whatever the problem, it can be worked out through proper repentance. You can become clean once again. ("Priesthood Power," *Ensign,* May 2011, 67)

———

Our Heavenly Father rejoices for those who keep His commandments. He is concerned also for the lost child, the tardy teenager, the wayward youth, the delinquent parent. Tenderly He speaks to these, and indeed to all: "Come back. Come up. Come in. Come home. Come unto me." I pray all mankind may accept His divine invitation to exaltation. ("An Invitation to Exaltation," Satellite Broadcast, March 4, 1984)

———

There are those who feel that their own neglect, their bad habits, their shunning of the righteous life have caused God to abandon them, that He will no longer hear their pleadings, nor see their plight, nor feel compassion towards them. Such feelings are not compatible with the word of the Lord. . . .

Should there be anyone who feels he is too weak to change the onward and downward moving course of his life, or should there be those who fail to resolve to do better because of that greatest of fears, the fear of failure, there is no more comforting assurance to be had than the words of the Lord: "My grace is sufficient for all men that humble themselves before me; for if they humble themselves before me, and have faith in me, then will I make weak things become strong unto them" (Ether 12:27). ("The Precious Gift of Sight," Conference Report, April 1965, 47–48)

———

The wayward son, the willful daughter, the pouting husband, the nagging wife—all can change. There can occur a parting of the clouds, a break in the storm. Maturity comes, friendships alter, circumstances vary. "Cast in concrete" need not describe human behavior.

From the perspective of eternity, our sojourn in this life is ever so brief. Detours are costly; they must be shunned. The spiritual nature within us should not be dominated by the physical. It behooves each of us to remember who he or she is and what God expects him or her to become. ("The Will Within," *Ensign,* May 1987, 67)

RESPONSIBILITY

———

Responsibility was taught rather effectively in this lesson from World War II. At a large Air Force base, men were taught to jump from high flying planes, depending for their lives on the parachute each wore. Some died when chutes failed to open. Those who packed them had not been careful. The result was tragedy. Then a solution was devised. Each packed parachute would bear the number of him who packed it; then periodically, and without prior notice, the base commander would assemble all who had packed the chutes. Each would be handed a parachute he had personally packed. These men would then board a plane and, upon a given signal, while high in the sky would themselves jump, depending for their lives on the very chute each had packed. The results were gratifying. Not a single death occurred—then or later. ("Be All That You Can Be," BYU–Hawaii Commencement, December 14, 2002)

———

In our chosen fields, the obstacles confronting us may be mountainous in their appearance—even impassable in their challenge to our abilities. Press onward we must, for we understand full well that attacking is not solving. Complaining is not thinking. Ridiculing is not reasoning. Accountability is not for the intention but for the deed. No man is proud simply of what he intends to do. ("Be All That You Can Be," BYU–Hawaii Commencement, December 14, 2002)

———

Can we not be men and women of integrity, of principle, of honor? Not fence straddlers, but men of courage and conviction. Seek not freedom from responsibility, but the freedom and the willingness to accept responsibility. ("Constant Truths in Changing Times," BYU Commencement, May 26, 1967)

RESURRECTION

———

We understand we have come to earth to learn, to live, to progress in our eternal journey toward perfection. Some remain on earth but for a moment, while others live long upon the land. The measure is not how long we live, but rather how well we live.

Then comes death . . . followed by that glorious day of resurrection, when spirit and body will be reunited, never again
to be separated. "I am the resurrection, and the life," said
the Christ to the grieving Martha. "He that believeth in me,
though he were dead, yet shall he live:

"And whosoever liveth and believeth in me shall never die"
(John 11:25–26). . . .

"In my Father's house are many mansions: if it were not so,
I would have told you. I go to prepare a place for you . . . that
where I am, there ye may be also" (John 14:2–3).

This transcendent promise became a reality when Mary
and the other Mary approached the garden tomb—that cem-
etery which had but one occupant. . . . Let Luke, the physician,
describe their experience:

"Now upon the first day of the week, very early in the morning, they came unto the sepulchre. . . .

"And they found the stone rolled away. . . .

" . . . they entered in, and found not the body of the Lord
Jesus.

" . . . as they were much perplexed thereabout, behold, two
men stood by them in shining garments:

"And . . . said unto them, Why seek ye the living among the
dead?" (Luke 24:1–5).

"He is not here: for he is risen" (Matthew 28:6). ("He Is
Risen," *Ensign*, November 1981, 18)

———

Against the philosophy rampant in today's world—a doubting of the authenticity of the Sermon on the Mount, an abandonment of Christ's teaching, a denial of God, and a rejection
of His laws . . . true believers everywhere treasure the testimonies of eyewitnesses to His resurrection. . . .

Saul, on the road to Damascus, had a vision of the risen,
exalted Christ. Peter and John also testified of the risen Christ.

And in our dispensation, the Prophet Joseph Smith bore eloquent testimony of the Son of God, for he saw Him and heard the Father introduce Him: *"This is my Beloved Son. Hear Him!"* (Joseph Smith—History 1:17). ("Meeting Life's Challenges," *Ensign,* November 1993, 70)

——

Preceding almost every declaration of eternal truth has been a universal question; for instance, what man has not asked himself as did Job of old, "If a man die, shall he live again?" (Job 14:14). And what man has not found comfort in the answer which the angel gave to Mary Magdalene and Mary, the mother of James, when they approached the tomb to care for the body of the Master. He said, "Why seek ye the living among the dead? He is not here, but is risen" (Luke 24:5–6). ("In Search of Truth," Conference Report, October 1964, 17)

——

Through tears and trials, through fears and sorrows, through the heartache and loneliness of losing loved ones, there is assurance that life is everlasting. Our Lord and Savior is the living witness that such is so.

With all my heart and the fervency of my soul, I lift up my voice in testimony as a special witness and declare that God does live. Jesus is His Son, the Only Begotten of the Father in the flesh. He is our Redeemer; He is our Mediator with the Father. He it was who died on the cross to atone for our sins. He became the firstfruits of the Resurrection. Because He died, all shall live again. "Oh, sweet the joy this sentence gives: 'I know that my Redeemer lives!'" (*Hymns,* no. 136). May the whole world know it and live by that knowledge. ("I Know That My Redeemer Lives!" *Ensign,* May 2007, 25)

REVELATION

———

Let us *look heavenward*. Doing so is much more inspiring. From the heavens came the gentle invitation, "Look to God and live" (Alma 37:47). We have not been left to wander in darkness and in silence uninstructed, uninspired, without revelation. . . .

From the scriptures, from the prophets, comes counsel for our time as we look heavenward. ("Be All That You Can Be," BYU–Hawaii Commencement, December 14, 2002)

———

The boy prophet, Joseph Smith, sought heavenly help by entering a grove which then became sacred. Do we need similar strength? Does each need to seek his own Sacred Grove? A place where communion between God and man can go forth unimpeded, uninterrupted, and undisturbed is such a grove. ("Be All That You Can Be," BYU–Hawaii Commencement, December 14, 2002)

———

How grateful we should be that revelation, the clear and uncluttered channel of truth, is still open. Our Heavenly Father continues to inspire His prophets. This inspiration can serve as a sure guide in making life's decisions. It will lead us to truth. ("In Search of Truth," Conference Report, October 1964, 18)

RIGHTEOUSNESS
(SEE ALSO DISCIPLESHIP)

———

As we pursue our quest for eternal life, we will come to many forks and turnings in the road. We cannot venture into the uncertainties of the future without reference to the certainties of the past. Your challenge is to join the forces of the old and the new—experience and experiment, history and destiny, the world of man and the world of science—but always in accordance with the never-changing word of God. In short, He becomes your pilot on this eternal journey. He knows the way. His counsel can keep us from the pitfalls threatening to engulf us and lead us rather to the way of life eternal.

As we face the temptations of our times, the confusion of choice, the embarrassment of error, the pursuit of perfection, our Heavenly Father is there to listen, to love, to inspire. Our Father to whom we earnestly pray is not an ethereal substance or a mysterious and incomprehensible being. Rather, He has eyes with which to view our actions, lips with which to speak to us, ears to hear our plea, and a heart to understand our love. ("The Race for Eternal Life," Ricks College Baccalaureate, May 10, 1967)

———

The unsatisfied yearnings of the soul will not be met by a never-ending quest for joy midst the thrills of sensation and vice. Vice never leads to virtue. Hate never points to love. Cowardice never reflects courage. Doubt never inspires faith.

It [should not be] difficult to withstand the mockings and unsavory remarks of foolish ones who would ridicule chastity, honesty, and obedience to God's commands. The world has ever belittled adherence to principle. Times change. Practices persist. When Noah was instructed to build an ark, the foolish populace looked at the cloudless sky, then scoffed and jeered—until the rain came.

In the Western Hemisphere, those long centuries ago, people doubted, disputed, and disobeyed until the fire consumed Zarahemla, the earth covered Moronihah, and water engulfed the land of Moroni. Jeering, mocking, ribaldry, and sin were no more. They had been replaced by sullen silence, dense darkness. The patience of God had expired, His timetable fulfilled.

Must we learn such costly lessons over and over again? When we fail to profit from the experiences of the past, we are doomed to repeat them with all their heartache, suffering, and anguish. Haven't we the wisdom to obey Him who designed the plan of salvation—rather than that serpent who despised its beauty?

In the words of the poet, "Wouldst thou be gathered to Christ's chosen flock, shun the broad way too easily explored, And let thy path be hewn out of the rock, The living rock of God's eternal word" (William Wordsworth, "Inscription on a Rock at Rydal Mount").

Can we not follow the Prince of Peace, that pioneer who literally showed the way for others to follow? His divine plan can save us from the Babylons of sin, complacency, and error. His example points the way. When faced with temptation, He shunned it. When offered the world, He declined it. When asked for His life, He gave it! ("Come, Follow Me," Conference Report, April 1967, 57–58)

———

We have come to the earth in troubled times. The moral compass of the masses has gradually shifted to an "almost anything goes" position.

I've lived long enough to have witnessed much of the

metamorphosis of society's morals. Where once the standards of the Church and the standards of society were mostly compatible, now there is a wide chasm between us, and it's growing ever wider.

Many movies and television shows portray behavior which is in direct opposition to the laws of God. Do not subject yourself to the innuendo and outright filth which are so often found there. The lyrics in much of today's music fall in the same category. The profanity so prevalent around us today would never have been tolerated in the not-too-distant past. Sadly, the Lord's name is taken in vain over and over again. Recall with me the commandment—one of the ten—which the Lord revealed to Moses on Mount Sinai: "Thou shalt not take the name of the Lord thy God in vain; for the Lord will not hold him guiltless that taketh his name in vain"(Exodus 20:7). I am sorry that any of us is subjected to profane language, and I plead with you not to use it. I implore you not to say or to do anything of which you cannot be proud.

Stay completely away from pornography. Do not allow yourself to view it, ever. It has proven to be an addiction which is more than difficult to overcome. Avoid alcohol and tobacco or any other drugs, also addictions which you would be hard pressed to conquer.

What will protect you from the sin and evil around you? I maintain that a strong testimony of our Savior and of His gospel will help see you through to safety. If you have not read the Book of Mormon, read it. If you do so prayerfully and with a sincere desire to know the truth, the Holy Ghost will manifest its truth to you. If it is true—and it *is*—then Joseph Smith was a prophet who saw God the Father and His Son, Jesus Christ. The Church is true. If you do not already have a testimony of these things, do that which is necessary to obtain one. It is essential for you to have your own testimony, for the testimonies of others will carry you only so far. Once obtained, a testimony needs to be kept vital and alive through obedience to the commandments of God and through regular prayer and scripture study. Attend church. You young [people], attend seminary or institute if such is available to you. ("Priesthood Power," *Ensign*, May 2011, 66–67)

———

The Savior of mankind described Himself as being in the world but not of the world (see John 17:14; D&C 49:5). We also can be in the world but not of the world as we reject false concepts and false teachings and remain true to that which God has commanded. ("Priesthood Power," *Ensign*, May 2011, 67)

———

Young men [and women] . . . there are many tools to help you learn the lessons which will be beneficial to you as well as helping you to live the life you will need to have lived to be worthy. One such tool is the booklet entitled *For the Strength of Youth*, published under the direction of the First Presidency and Quorum of the Twelve Apostles. It features standards from the writings and teachings of Church leaders and from scripture, adherence to which will bring the blessings of our Heavenly Father and the guidance of His Son to each of us. In addition, there are lesson manuals, carefully prepared after prayerful consideration. Families have family home evenings, where gospel principles are taught. Almost all of you have the opportunity to attend seminary classes taught by dedicated teachers who have much to share.

Begin to prepare for a temple marriage as well as for a mission. Proper dating is a part of that preparation. In cultures where dating is appropriate, do not date until you are sixteen years old. "Not all teenagers need to date or even want to. . . . When you begin dating, go in groups or on double dates. . . . Make sure your parents meet [and become acquainted with] those you date." Because dating is a preparation for marriage, "date only those who have high standards"(*For the Strength of Youth* [booklet, 2001], 24, 26).

Be careful to go to places where there is a good environment, where you won't be faced with temptation.

A wise father said to his son, "If you ever find yourself in a place where you shouldn't ought to be, get out!" Good advice for all of us.

Servants of the Lord have always counseled us to dress appropriately to show respect for our Heavenly Father and for ourselves. The way you dress sends messages about yourself to others and often influences the way you and others act. Dress in such a way as to bring out the best in yourself and those around you. Avoid extremes in clothing and appearance, including tatoos and piercings.

Everyone needs good friends. Your circle of friends will greatly influence your thinking and behavior, just as you will theirs. When you share common values with your friends, you can strengthen and encourage each other. Treat everyone with kindness and dignity. Many nonmembers have come into the Church through friends who have involved them in Church activities.

. . . A Latter-day Saint young man lives as he teaches and as he believes. He is honest with others. He is honest with himself. He is honest with God. He is honest by habit and as a matter of course. When a difficult decision must be made, he never asks himself, "What will others think?" but rather, "What will I think of myself?" . . .

How you speak and the words you use tell much about the image you choose to portray. Use language to build and uplift those around you. Profane, vulgar, or crude language and inappropriate or off-color jokes are offensive to the Lord. Never misuse the name of God or Jesus Christ. The Lord said, "Thou shalt not take the name of the Lord thy God in vain" (Exodus 20:7).

Our Heavenly Father has counseled us to seek after "anything virtuous, lovely, or of good report or praiseworthy" (Articles of Faith 1:13). Whatever you read, listen to, or watch makes an impression on you.

Pornography is especially dangerous and addictive. Curious exploration of pornography can become a controlling habit, leading to coarser material and to sexual transgression. Avoid pornography at all costs. . . .

The Apostle Paul declared: "Know ye not that ye are the temple of God, and that the Spirit of God dwelleth in you? . . . The temple of God is holy, which temple ye are" (1 Corinthians 3:16, 17). It is our responsibility to keep our temples clean and pure.

Hard drugs, wrongful use of prescription drugs, alcohol, coffee, tea, and tobacco products destroy your physical, mental, and spiritual well-being. Any form of alcohol is harmful to your spirit and your body. Tobacco can enslave you, weaken your lungs, and shorten your life. . . .

Because sexual intimacy is so sacred, the Lord requires self-control and purity before marriage as well as full fidelity after marriage. In dating, treat your date with respect and expect your date to show that same respect for you. Tears inevitably follow transgression.

President David O. McKay, ninth president of the Church, advised, "I implore you to think clean thoughts." He then made this significant declaration of truth: "Every action is preceded by a thought. If we want to control our actions, we must control our thinking." Brethren, fill your minds with good thoughts, and your actions will be proper. May each of you be able to echo in truth the line from Tennyson spoken by Sir Galahad: "My strength is as the strength of ten, because my heart is pure" (Alfred Lord Tennyson, in John Bartlett, *Familiar Quotations* [1952], 647). . . .

When you were confirmed a member of the Church, you received the right to the companionship of the Holy Ghost. He can help you make good choices. When challenged or tempted, you do not need to feel alone. ("Preparation Brings Blessings," *Ensign,* May 2010, 64–66)

———

Each of us is a miracle of engineering. Our creation, however, was not limited by human genius. Man can devise the most complex machines, but he cannot give them life or bestow upon them the powers of reason and judgment. Why? Because these are divine gifts, bestowed solely at God's discretion. Our Creator has provided us with a circulatory system to keep all channels constantly clean and serviceable, a digestive system to preserve strength and vigor, and a nervous system to keep all parts in constant communication and coordination. God gave man life, and with it, the power to think, to reason, to decide, and to love.

Like the vital rudder of a ship, we have been provided a way to determine the direction we travel. The lighthouse of the Lord beckons to all as we sail the seas of life. Our home port is the celestial kingdom of God. Our purpose is to steer an undeviating course in that direction. A man without a purpose is like a ship without a rudder—never likely to reach home port. To us comes the signal: Chart your course, set your sail, position your rudder, and proceed.

As with the ship, so it is with man. The thrust of the turbines, the power of the propellers are useless without that sense of direction, that harnessing of the energy, that directing of the power provided by the rudder, hidden from view, relatively small in size, but absolutely essential in function.

Our Father provided the sun, the moon, the stars—heavenly galaxies to guide mariners who sail the lanes of the sea. To all who walk the pathways of life, He cautions: Beware the detours, the pitfalls, the traps. Cunningly positioned are those clever pied pipers of sin beckoning here or there. Do not be deceived. Pause to pray. Listen to that still, small voice which speaks to the depths of our souls the Master's gentle invitation: "Come, follow me" (Luke 18:22). We turn from destruction, from death. We find happiness and life everlasting. ("Sailing Safely the Seas of Life," *Ensign,* May 1982, 60)

———

We are the product of all we read, all we view, all we hear and all we think. I join you in a united determination to so *think,* to so *read* and to so *hear*—and I might also add to so *feel*—that we may evidence that we are on the Lord's side. (All-Church Coordinating Council, November 15, 1988)

SACRIFICE

———

The call to serve has ever characterized the work of the Lord. It rarely comes at a convenient time. It brings humility, it provokes prayer, it inspires commitment. The call came—to Kirtland. Revelations followed. The call came—to Missouri. Persecution prevailed. The call came—to Nauvoo. Prophets died. The call came—to the basin of the Great Salt Lake. Hardship beckoned.

That long journey, made under such difficult circumstances, was a trial of faith. But faith forged in the furnace of trials and tears is marked by trust and testimony. Only God can count the sacrifice; only God can measure the sorrow; only God can know the hearts of those who serve Him—then and now. ("Tears, Trials, Trust, Testimony," *Ensign,* May 1987, 43–44)

SAFETY

You have access to the lighthouse of the Lord. There is no fog so dense, no night so dark, no mariner so lost, no gale so strong as to render useless the lighthouse of the Lord. It beckons through the storms of life. It seems to call to you and me: "This way to safety; this way to home." ("Life's Greatest Decisions," Church Educational System Fireside Satellite Broadcast, September 7, 2003)

Today in our hurried and hectic lives, we could well go back to an earlier time for the lesson taught us regarding crossing dangerous streets. "Stop, look, and listen" were the watchwords. Could we not apply them now? Stop from a reckless road to ruin. Look upward for heavenly help. Listen for His invitation: "Come unto me, all ye that labour and are heavy laden, and I will give you rest" (Matthew 11:28). ("Patience—A Heavenly Virtue," *Ensign*, November 1995, 60)

We live at a time when many in the world have slipped from the moorings of safety found in compliance with the commandments. It is a time of permissiveness, with society in general routinely disregarding and breaking the laws of God. We often find ourselves swimming against the current, and sometimes it seems as though the current could carry us away.

I am reminded of the words of the Lord found in the book of Ether in the Book of Mormon. Said the Lord, "Ye cannot cross this great deep save I prepare you against the waves of the sea, and the winds which have gone forth, and the floods which shall come" (Ether 2:25). My brothers and sisters, He has prepared us. If we heed His words and live the commandments, we will survive this time of permissiveness and wickedness—a time which can be compared with the waves and the winds and the floods that can destroy. He is ever mindful of us. He loves us and will bless us as we do what is right. ("Closing Remarks," *Ensign,* November 2009, 109)

SCOUTING

Where there is one man who is willing and able to build a boy, there are many more who, through greed, selfishness, and lust for power, lurk in the shadows of gloom, away from the light of truth, to tear a boy down. I speak of those who peddle pornography, who belittle morality, who violate law, and for filthy lucre sell a boy those products that destroy. Those who put sin on a pedestal, who conceal truth, who glamorize error, who look upon a fair-haired boy as a commodity for exploitation.

The "get-rich-quick" theories, the philosophy of something for nothing, confusion of proper goals and objectives, have all combined to make our building task more difficult. The foundations of love and life-established principles are crumbling before our very eyes. They are being eroded by the forces of Lucifer. Unfortunately, some of our precious youth are even now sliding to their destruction down the slippery slopes of sin. . . . Fellow Scouters, this is our duty, our responsibility, our opportunity—to guide, to build, to inspire our boys. . . .

The Master Teacher, the best Builder of all, gave us the formula: "He that findeth his life shall lose it: and he that loseth his life for my sake shall find it" (Matthew 10:39). ("Builders of

Boys," Forty-Seventh Annual Scouters Convention, February 14, 1966)

———

Scouting's motto, "Be Prepared," has universal application. Being prepared does not mean learning a set of hard and fast rules. Scouting must help boys to live in a world of change, to live with uncertainty and yet to act with confidence. It must help them to be prepared to modify yesterday's understandings in the light of today's knowledge so that they can move confidently into tomorrow's world. ("Scouting—Builder of Boys, Molder of Men," Satellite Broadcast, Scouting's Seventy-Fifth Anniversary, February 10, 1985)

———

In the lives of boys, many now men, we observe monuments to patience, to understanding, to effort, to kindness, to service, and to love. In reality, the greatest gift a boy can receive is the knowledge that a man cares enough to share a part of his life with him. This is the spirit of Scouting. ("Scouting—Builder of Boys, Molder of Men," Satellite Broadcast, Scouting's Seventy-Fifth Anniversary, February 10, 1985)

———

It is the mission of the Boy Scouts of America to serve others by helping to instill values in young people and, in other ways, to prepare them to make ethical choices over their lifetime in achieving their full potential.

The values we strive to instill are based on those found in the Scout Oath and Law:

> On my honor I will do my best
> To do my duty to God and my country

And to obey the Scout Law,
To help other people at all times;
To keep myself physically strong, mentally awake
And morally strait.

A Scout is: trustworthy, loyal, helpful, friendly, courteous, kind, obedient, cheerful, thrifty, brave, clean, and reverent.

When that blueprint overlays and undergirds the members of the American family, hope will conquer despair, and faith will triumph over doubt. Such values, when learned and lived in our families, will be as welcome rain to parched soil. Love will be engendered; loyalty to one's best self enhanced; and those virtues of character, integrity and goodness fostered. ("Duty—Honor—Country," National Boy Scouts of America Duty to God Breakfast, May 29, 2003)

——

The paintings of Norman Rockwell on the cover of *The Saturday Evening Post* magazine or in *Boy's Life* always brought tender feelings to me. Of the two paintings I most admire, one is of a Scoutmaster sitting by the dying embers of the bonfire and observing his boys—fast asleep in their small tents. The sky is filled with stars, the tousled heads of the boys illumined by the fire's glow. The Scoutmaster's countenance reflects his love, his faith, and his devotion. . . .

The other painting is of a small lad, clad in the oversized Scout uniform of his older brother. He is looking at himself in a mirror which adorns the wall, his tiny arm raised in the Scout salute. It could well be entitled "Following in the Footsteps of Scouting."

In this world where some misguided men and women strive to tear down and destroy great movements such as Scouting, I am pleased to stand firm for an organization that teaches duty to God and country, that embraces the Scout Law. Yes, an organization whose motto is "Be prepared" and whose slogan is "Do a good turn daily." ("The Upward Reach," *Ensign,* November 1993, 47–48)

———

May I suggest for each of us builders of boys a Scouter's Standard, even a performance pledge:

I WILL LEARN
I WILL LOVE
I WILL SERVE

Let each of us learn the Scout oath and honor it. Let each of us learn the Scout law and live it. One of the tools of our trade will be the merit badge system of Scouting. Each Scout is encouraged to study for merit badges representing knowledge of trades, skills, and arts. In qualifying for these awards, the Scout meets many people of varying talents and occupations. He learns about many lines of activity. He broadens his horizon. He attains understanding. He achieves that most important quality: versatility. ("Builders of Boys," Satellite Fireside, February 14, 1988)

———

If ever there were a time when the principles of Scouting were vitally needed—that time is now. If ever there were a generation who would benefit by keeping physically strong, mentally awake, and morally straight—that generation is the present generation. ("Called to Serve," *Ensign,* November 1991, 47)

———

The well-trained Scout is a mirror image to his family of all that is good and decent. He is a source of justifiable pride to his parents. To his brothers and sisters he is a model to follow. ("Scouting: The Family's Treasured Friend," BSA National Meeting, May 15, 1992)

———

Boys of Scout age have seen greater strides into the mysteries of science than others have known in all history. This is not the age of small goals, mediocre accomplishment, or shallow thought. We must think big.

Don't restrict your thinking to today's problems. Plan for tomorrow's opportunities. Get clearly in mind your purpose in life. You are only limited by your thoughts and personal determination to convert these thoughts to realities. Scouting will help. (Boy Scout Gathering, Las Vegas, Nevada, October 14, 2006)

———

Each of you is precious in the sight of our Heavenly Father. He desires that you pray to Him; let prayer be a governing principle in your life. Each boy is uniquely different. Some are stronger physically than others. Some overcome handicaps through sheer effort and determination. Scouting brings out the best in each of us. (Boy Scout Gathering, Las Vegas, Nevada, October 14, 2006)

———

Boys of promise need men of purpose to guide them. Ours is that responsibility. Let us rededicate ourselves to the principle of loving service. Let us remember that there has never been a time when boys have needed, to a greater extent, the example of true leadership. We have the privilege to provide that example; and the lessons which we teach are lessons which shall endure and may well provide the means to guide a boy along that pathway which enables him to fulfill his divine destiny. . . .

May all of us engaged in the great cause of Scouting remember our responsibility to build better boys today for a brighter future tomorrow. ("Builders of Boys," Silver Beaver Award Night, February 8, 1977)

SCRIPTURES

———

The words of truth and inspiration found in our four standard works are prized possessions to me. I never tire of reading them. I am lifted spiritually whenever I search the scriptures. These holy words of truth and love give guidance to my life and point out to each of us the way to eternal perfection. ("Come Learn of Me," Satellite Broadcast, March 10, 1985)

———

The holy scriptures are for children, to fill their eager minds with sacred truth. They are for youth, to prepare them for the challenges of our fast-moving world. They are for the sisters, remembering President Spencer W. Kimball's advice: "We want our sisters to be scholars of the scriptures as well as our men" (in *Ensign,* November 1978, 102). They are for the brethren of the priesthood, that each may qualify for the description given in the Book of Mormon to the sons of Mosiah: "They were men of a sound understanding and they had searched the scriptures diligently, that they might know the word of God" (Alma 17:2). ("Come Learn of Me," Satellite Broadcast, March 10, 1985)

———

Become acquainted with the lessons the scriptures teach. Learn the background and setting of the Master's parables and the prophets' admonitions. Study them as though each were speaking to you, for such is the truth. ("A Time to Choose," *Ensign,* May 1995, 97)

———

Let the scriptures be your guide, and you will never find yourself traveling the road to nowhere. ("Patience—A Heavenly Virtue," *Ensign,* November 1995, 60)

———

We must be careful not to underestimate the capacity of children to read and to understand the word of God.

A few months ago we took our grandchildren on an escorted tour of the Church printing facilities. There, all of us saw the missionary edition of the Book of Mormon coming off the delivery line—printed, bound, and trimmed, ready for reading. I said to a young grandson, "The operator says that you can remove one copy of the Book of Mormon to be your very own. You select the copy, and it will then be yours."

Removing one finished copy of the book, he clutched it to his breast and said with sincerity, "I love the Book of Mormon. This is *my* book."

I really don't remember other events of that day, but none of us who were there will ever forget the honest expression from the heart of a child. ("Hallmarks of a Happy Home," *Ensign,* November 1988, 70)

———

The way to teach scripture to the membership of the Church is to help them internalize the lessons of the scriptures. We must realize that the lesson of Joseph and Potiphar's wife applies to us today, that the lesson of the ninth section of the Doctrine and Covenants applies to any decision we need to make on earth today, that the lesson of Nephi applies to the attitude we should have toward the work to which we have been called. (All-Church Coordinating Council, November 15, 1988)

———

A pattern for our decision making, whether we are young or old, is set forth in the scriptures. When our youth read the scriptures, when they understand the scriptures, and when they live the scriptures, they will stand firm for truth. ("Duty Calls," Regional Representatives Seminar, March 30, 1990)

———

The Holy Bible is an inspiration to me. This sacred book has inspired the minds of men and has motivated readers to live the commandments of God and to love one another. It is printed in greater quantities, is translated into more languages, and has touched more human hearts than any other volume. ("My Brother's Keeper," *Ensign,* May 1990, 46)

———

Let us study the scriptures and "meditate therein day and night," as counseled by the Lord in the book of Joshua (Joshua 1:8). . . .

Spending time each day in scripture study will, without doubt, strengthen our foundations of faith and our testimonies of truth.

Recall with me the joy Alma experienced as he was journeying from the land of Gideon southward to the land of Manti and met the sons of Mosiah. Alma had not seen them for some time, and he was overjoyed to discover that they were "still his brethren in the Lord; yea, and they had waxed strong in the knowledge of the truth; for they were men of a sound understanding and they had searched the scriptures diligently, that they might know the word of God" (Alma 17:1–2).

May we also know the word of God and conduct our lives accordingly. ("How Firm a Foundation," *Ensign,* November 2006, 67, 68)

Each one of us has the responsibility to find out for himself whether or not this gospel of Jesus Christ is true. If we read the Book of Mormon, read the standard works, and put the teachings to the test, then we shall know of the doctrine, whether it be of man or whether it be of God, for this is our promise. ("Life's Greatest Questions," BYU Fireside, February 6, 1977)

Study diligently. Every holder of the priesthood should participate in daily scripture study. Crash courses are not nearly so effective as the day-to-day reading and application of the scriptures in our lives. . . .

I promise you, whether you hold the Aaronic or the Melchizedek Priesthood, that if you will study the scriptures diligently, your power to avoid temptation and to receive direction of the Holy Ghost in all you do will be increased. ("Be Your Best Self," *Ensign,* May 2009, 68)

There is safety in the scriptures. Do not postpone reading them. If you have small children at home, do not put off teaching them from the scriptures. They understand more than we might imagine. (Bolivia Stake Conference Broadcast, March 16, 2008)

SELF-DISCIPLINE

One of the imperative requirements of life is to be able to make choices. In order to do so one must know how to look at things and oneself. One must also learn that to live means being able to cope with difficulties; problems are a normal part of life and the great thing is to avoid being flattened by them.

The battle for self-mastery may leave you a bit bruised and battered, but always a better man or woman. ("In Quest of the Abundant Life," Utah State University Baccalaureate, June 2, 1967)

———

In our science-oriented age we conquer space, but cannot control self; hence, we forfeit peace. ("In Quest of the Abundant Life," Utah State University Baccalaureate, June 2, 1967)

———

Self-discipline is a rigorous process at best; too many of us want it to be effortless and painless. Should temporary setbacks afflict us, a very significant part of our struggle for self-discipline is the determination and the courage to try again. ("Pathways to Perfection," *Ensign,* May 2002, 100)

———

Have discipline in your preparations. Have checkpoints where you can determine if you're on course.

I hope that you are not afraid of tough classes. I never did have a "cinch" class. I hope that you are not afraid of lengthy periods of preparation. Burn the midnight oil. ("Life's Greatest Decisions," Church Educational System Fireside Satellite Broadcast, September 7, 2003)

Basic courtesy is required of you and me. There isn't room for anger, there isn't room for disappointment. . . . I think it is far better to be courteous to all around us and make that second effort than to fly off the handle and show our displeasure through a lack of tact and a lack of good self-discipline. Let us be courteous to all of our associates, to subordinates, to superiors, and we shall indeed find it is one of the watchwords to success. (BYU College of Business, March 14, 1973)

SELFISHNESS

The Apostle Paul observed in his charge to the elders, "Remember the words of the Lord Jesus, how he said, It is more blessed to give than to receive" (Acts 20:35).

This is a truth more profound than most of us realize. Furthermore, it is a very practical truth. Many of the problems of our times arise out of an excess of receiving. ("In Quest of the Abundant Life," Utah State University Baccalaureate, June 2, 1967)

In the helter-skelter competitiveness of life, there is a tendency to think only of ourselves. To succumb to this philosophy narrows one's vision and distorts a proper view of life. When concern for others replaces concern for self, our own progress is enhanced. ("Go for It!" *Ensign*, May 1989, 44)

SELF-RELIANCE

Are we prepared for the emergencies of our lives? Are our skills perfected? Do we live providently? Do we have on hand our reserve supply? Are we obedient to the commandments of God? Are we responsive to the teachings of prophets? Are we prepared to give of our substance to the poor, the needy? Are we square with the Lord? ("A Provident Plan—A Precious Promise," *Ensign*, May 1986, 64)

We live in turbulent times. Often the future is unknown; therefore, it behooves us to prepare for uncertainties. Statistics reveal that at some time, because of the illness or death of your husband or because of economic necessity, you [wives] may find yourself in the role of financial provider. I urge you to pursue your education and learn marketable skills so that, should an emergency arise, you are prepared to provide.

Your talents will expand as you study and learn. You will be able to better assist your children in their learning, and you will have peace of mind in knowing that you have prepared yourself for the eventualities that you may encounter in life. ("Be Thou an Example," *Ensign*, November 2001, 99)

SERVICE

While driving to the office one morning, I passed a dry-cleaning establishment which had a sign by the side of the front door. It read, "It's the Service That Counts." I suppose in a highly competitive field such as the dry-cleaning business and many others, the differentiating factor which distinguishes one store from another is, in actual fact, service.

The message from the small sign simply would not leave my mind. Suddenly I realized why. In actual fact it is the service that counts—the Lord's service. ("The Joy of Service," *New Era,* October 2009, 2)

———

As we look heavenward, we inevitably learn of our responsibility to reach outward. To find real happiness, we must seek for it in a focus outside ourselves. No one has learned the meaning of living until he has surrendered his ego to the service of his fellow man. Service to others is akin to duty, the fulfillment of which brings true joy. We do not live alone—in our city, our nation, or our world. There is no dividing line between our prosperity and our neighbor's wretchedness. "Love thy neighbor" is more than a divine truth. It is a pattern for perfection. This truth inspires the familiar charge, "Go forth to serve." Try as some of us may, we cannot escape the influence our lives have upon the lives of others. Ours is the opportunity to build, to lift, to inspire, and indeed to lead. . . .

The Prophet Joseph Smith taught that a true Latter-day Saint is "to feed the hungry, to clothe the naked, to provide for the widow, to dry up the tear of the orphan, to comfort the afflicted, whether in this church or in any other, or in no church at all, wherever he finds them" (*Times and Seasons,* March 15, 1842, 732). ("The Joy of Service," *New Era,* October 2009, 4)

———

We look to the Savior as our example of service. Although He came to earth as the Son of God, He humbly served those around Him. He came forth from heaven to live on earth as mortal man and to establish the kingdom of God. His glorious gospel reshaped the thinking of the world. He blessed the sick; He caused the lame to walk, the blind to see, the deaf to hear. He even raised the dead to life. ("The Joy of Service," *New Era*, October 2009, 6)

———

It is an immutable law that the more you give away, the more you receive. You make a living by what you get, but you make a life by what you give. ("In Quest of the Abundant Life," Utah State University Baccalaureate, June 2, 1967)

———

Man does not run the race of life by himself. When you help another in his race of life you really serve your God. King Benjamin stated the principle so beautifully, "When ye are in the service of your fellow beings ye are only in the service of your God" (Mosiah 2:17). . . .

Balanced service is a virtue to be cherished. There is to be time in your life to serve God, to serve your family, to serve your country and community, to serve your employer. . . . "Service with a smile" is far more than a department store slogan. It is a way of life and a path to happiness. ("The Race for Eternal Life," Ricks College Baccalaureate, May 10, 1967)

———

Serve faithfully. Never let it be said of us that we didn't have sufficient time. Time is precious, but life is priceless. ("Builders of Faith in Children of God," Interfaith Service, Lethbridge, Alberta, Canada, June 10, 1967)

In this marvelous dispensation of the fulness of times, our opportunities to give of ourselves are indeed limitless, but they are also perishable. There are hearts to gladden. There are kind words to say. There are gifts to be given. There are deeds to be done. There are souls to be saved. "Go gladden the lonely, the dreary; go comfort the weeping, the weary; go scatter kind deeds on your way. Oh, make the world brighter today." . . .

We need not think such opportunities are found only in far away places with strange sounding names. Most will be discovered close at hand.

Perhaps we could well begin with our own families. Are we as parents setting before our precious children an example worthy of emulation? Do our actions conform to the teachings of the Master?

We can make our houses homes and our homes heavens when the Savior becomes the center of our lives and His example of love and service finds meaningful expression in our own lives. ("The Search for Jesus," Centennial Service, Lethbridge, Alberta, Canada, June 11, 1967)

During your life you may achieve wealth or fame or social standing. Real success, however, comes from helping others. Said Ralph Waldo Emerson, noted thinker, lecturer, essayist, and poet, "To know even one life breathed easier because you have lived. This is to have succeeded."

There are opportunities to serve which are open to everyone. The blind and the handicapped need friendship; the aged are hungry for companionship; the young need understanding guidance; the gifted are starved for encouragement. These benefits can't be conferred by reaching for your checkbook. Personal service is direct and human.

Said a wise man many years ago, "We can't do everything

for everyone everywhere, but we can do something for someone somewhere" (Richard L. Evans).

Our service to others may not be dramatic, but we can bolster human spirits, clothe cold bodies, feed hungry people, comfort grieving hearts, and lift to new heights precious souls.

Albert Schweitzer, the noted theologian and missionary physician, declared, "I don't know what your destiny will be, but one thing I know: the only ones among you who will be really happy are those who have sought and found how to serve." ("Three Bridges to Cross," Dixie State College Commencement, May 6, 2011)

———

Though we may not necessarily forfeit our lives in service to our God, we can certainly demonstrate our love for Him by how well we serve Him. He who hears our silent prayers, He who observes our unheralded acts, will reward us openly when the need comes. (BYU Fourteen-Stake Fireside, October 11, 1981)

———

One hundred years from now it will not matter what kind of a car you drove, what kind of a house you lived in, how much you had in the bank account, nor what your clothes looked like. But the world may be a little better because you were important in the life of a boy or a girl. ("In Quest of the Abundant Life," Utah State University Baccalaureate, June 2, 1967)

———

Let us ask ourselves the questions: "Have I done any good in the world today? Have I helped anyone in need?" (*Hymns,* no. 223). What a formula for happiness! What a prescription for contentment, for inner peace—to have inspired gratitude in another human being. ("Now Is the Time," *Ensign*, November 2001, 60)

———

May we go the extra mile to include in our lives any who are lonely or downhearted or who are suffering in any way. May we "[cheer] up the sad and [make] someone feel glad" (*Hymns*, no. 223). May we live so that when that final summons is heard, we may have no serious regrets, no unfinished business, but will be able to say with the Apostle Paul, "I have fought a good fight, I have finished my course, I have kept the faith" (2 Timothy 4:7). ("Now Is the Time," *Ensign*, November 2001, 61)

———

Though exaltation is a personal matter, and while individuals are saved not as a group but indeed as individuals, yet one cannot live in a vacuum. Membership in the Church calls forth a determination to serve. A position of responsibility may not be of recognized importance, nor may the reward be broadly known. Service must come from willing minds, ready hands, and pledged hearts.

Occasionally discouragement may darken our pathway; frustration may be a constant companion. In our ears there may sound the sophistry of Satan as he whispers, "You cannot save the world; your small efforts are meaningless. You haven't time to be concerned for others." Trusting in the Lord, let us turn our heads from such falsehoods and make certain our feet are firmly planted in the path of service and our hearts and souls dedicated to follow the example of the Lord. In moments when the light of resolution dims and when the heart grows faint, we can take comfort from His promise: "Be not weary in well-doing. . . . Out of small things proceedeth that which is great.

"Behold, the Lord requireth the heart and a willing mind" (D&C 64:33–34). ("The Path to Peace," *Ensign,* May 1994, 62)

———

Your service to God and to your fellow men will not be restricted to the pulpit, the classroom, or your home teaching visits. Your own personal influence and demonstration of service to God can be the light which brings happiness into the lives of others. ("A Chosen Generation," Germanic Youth Conference, July 28, 1968)

———

Jesus was the epitome of service. It was said of Him that He "went about doing good" (Acts 10:38). Do we, my brethren, do likewise? Our opportunities are many, but some are perishable and fleeting. Brethren, what supernal joy you feel when someone recalls counsel you gave, an example you lived, a truth you taught, the influence you had in prompting another to do good. ("In Harm's Way," *Ensign,* May 1998, 48)

———

Share your talents. Each of you, single or married, regardless of age, has the opportunity to learn and grow. Expand your knowledge, both intellectual and spiritual, to the full stature of your divine potential. There is no limit to your influence for good. Share your talents, for that which we willingly share, we keep. But that which we selfishly keep, we lose. ("The Spirit of Relief Society," Relief Society Sesquicentennial Conference, March 14, 1992)

When we catch the vision regarding the worth of human souls, when we realize the truth of the adage, "God's sweetest blessings always flow through hands that serve Him here below," then we have quickened within our souls the desire to do good, the willingness to serve, and the yearning to lift to a higher plane the children of God. . . . The bottom line of living is giving. ("Windows," *Ensign,* November 1989, 69)

May all of us . . . make a renewed effort to qualify for the Lord's guidance in our lives. There are so many out there who plead and pray for help. There are those who are discouraged, those who long to return but who don't know how to begin.

. . . Let us have ready hands, clean hands, and willing hands, that we may participate in providing what our Heavenly Father would have others receive from Him. ("True to Our Priesthood Trust," *Ensign,* November 2006, 58)

God bless all who endeavor to be their brother's keeper, who give to ameliorate suffering, who strive with all that is good within them to make a better world. Have you noticed that such individuals have a brighter smile? Their footsteps are more certain. They have an aura about them of contentment and satisfaction, even dedication, for one cannot participate in helping others without experiencing a rich blessing himself. ("My Brother's Keeper," Los Angeles Rotary International, January 19, 2007)

I have observed in studying the life of the Master that His lasting lessons and His marvelous miracles usually occurred when He was doing His Father's work. On the way to Emmaus He appeared with a body of flesh and bones. He partook of food and testified of His divinity. All of this took place after He had exited the tomb.

At an earlier time, it was while He was on the road to Jericho that He restored sight to one who was blind.

The Savior was ever up and about—teaching, testifying, and saving others. Such is our individual duty. ("Anxiously Engaged," *Ensign*, November 2004, 56)

———

Most service given . . . is accomplished quietly, without fanfare. A friendly smile, a warm handclasp, a sincere testimony of truth can literally lift lives, change human nature, and save precious souls. ("To Learn, to Do, to Be," *Ensign*, November 2008, 62)

———

The Savior taught His disciples, "For whosoever will save his life shall lose it: but whosoever will lose his life for my sake, the same shall save it" (Luke 9:24).

I believe the Savior is telling us that unless we lose ourselves in service to others, there is little purpose to our own lives. Those who live only for themselves eventually shrivel up and figuratively lose their lives, while those who lose themselves in service to others grow and flourish—and in effect save their lives. ("What Have I Done for Someone Today?" *Ensign*, November 2009, 85)

———

I am confident it is the *intention* of each member of the Church to serve and to help those in need. At baptism we covenanted to "bear one another's burdens, that they may be light" (Mosiah 18:8). How many times has your heart been touched as you have witnessed the need of another? How often have you *intended* to be the one to help? And yet how often has day-to-day living interfered and you've left it for others to help, feeling that "oh, surely someone will take care of that need."

We become so caught up in the busyness of our lives. Were we to step back, however, and take a good look at what we're doing, we may find that we have immersed ourselves in the "thick of thin things." In other words, too often we spend most of our time taking care of the things which do not really matter much at all in the grand scheme of things, neglecting those more important causes. . . .

My brothers and sisters, we are surrounded by those in need of our attention, our encouragement, our support, our comfort, our kindness—be they family members, friends, acquaintances, or strangers. We are the Lord's hands here upon the earth, with the mandate to serve and to lift His children. He is dependent upon each of us. ("What Have I Done for Someone Today?" *Ensign,* November 2009, 85, 86)

———

My thoughts [turn] backward in time—back to the Holy Land; . . . back to Him who on that special mountain taught His disciples the true spirit of giving when He counseled, "Take heed that ye do not your alms before men, to be seen of them. . . .

"But when thou doest alms, let not thy left hand know what thy right hand doeth" (Matthew 6:1, 3).

The classics of literature, as well as the words from holy writ, teach us the endurability of anonymity. A favorite of mine [from literature] is Charles Dickens' *A Christmas Carol.* . . . After a fretful night—wherein Scrooge was shown by the Ghost of Christmas Past, the Ghost of Christmas Present, and the Ghost of Christmas Yet to Come the true meaning of living, loving, and giving—he awakened to discover anew the freshness of life, the power of love, and the spirit of a true gift. He remembered the plight of the Bob Cratchit family, arranged with a lad to purchase the giant turkey . . . and sent the gift to the Cratchits. Then, with supreme joy, the reborn Ebenezer Scrooge exclaims to himself, "He shan't know who sends it." Again, the word *anonymous* [applies]. . . .

May we look upward as we press forward in the service of our God and our fellowmen. And may we incline an ear toward Galilee, that we might hear perhaps an echo of the Savior's teachings [as he spoke of good deeds]: . . . "See thou tell no man" (Matthew 8:4). Our hearts will be lighter, our lives brighter, and our souls richer.

Loving service anonymously given may be unknown to man—but the gift and the giver are known to God. ("'Anonymous,'" *Ensign*, May 1983, 55–57)

Sin

Some foolish persons turn their backs on the wisdom of God and follow the allurement of fickle fashion, the attraction of false popularity and the thrill of the moment. Their course of conduct so resembles the disastrous experience of Esau, who exchanged his birthright for a mess of pottage.

And what are the results of such action? I testify to you tonight that turning away from God brings broken covenants, shattered dreams, vanished ambitions, evaporated plans, unfulfilled expectations, crushed hopes, misused drives, warped character, and wrecked lives.

Such a quagmire of quicksand I plead with you to avoid. You are of a noble birthright. ("Decisions Determine Destiny," LDS Student Association Young Women's Meeting, Logan, Utah, May 16, 1968)

———

Like the leprosy of yesteryear are the plagues of today. They linger; they debilitate; they destroy. They are to be found everywhere. Their pervasiveness knows no boundaries. We know them as selfishness, greed, indulgence, cruelty, and crime, to identify but a few. Surfeited with their poison, we tend to criticize, to complain, to blame, and, slowly but surely, to abandon the positives and adopt the negatives of life. ("An Attitude of Gratitude," *Ensign*, May 1992, 54)

SINGLES

———

I suggest three points to ponder with regard to the single members in the Church:

1. They need activity. We have the responsibility to supply it. If you could be with me in some of the Scandinavian youth conferences, called "Festinord," you would see the joy that comes to the young people when they realize that there are more people in their circumstances than they ever realized.
2. They seek improved gospel scholarship. Those over 30 frequently seek gospel scholarship more than activity. Firesides and study groups can be most helpful. Gospel Doctrine classes in Sunday School will be essential.
3. They need service. Give them an opportunity to serve.

(General Conference, Friday Evening Leadership Session, April 4, 1986)

———

The Church has need of every member! Church leaders and members alike need to give acceptance and full fellowship to singles—all of them: the never married, the widowed, and the divorced. They need to be lifted up in their own self-image and in the eyes of others. The Church setting for them needs to be one of caring, nurturing, and involvement. Let us remember that everyone is a member of a family, even though everyone does not happen to be married. ("The Perfection of the Saints," Regional Representatives Seminar, April 1, 1988)

———

Many members of Relief Society do not have husbands. Death, divorce, and indeed lack of opportunity to marry have, in many instances, made it necessary for a woman to stand alone. In reality, she need not stand alone, for a loving Heavenly Father will be by her side to give direction to her life and provide peace and assurance in those quiet moments where loneliness is found and where compassion is needed. ("The Spirit of Relief Society," Relief Society Sesquicentennial Conference, March 14, 1992)

SPIRITUALITY

———

Spirituality is not like a water faucet that can be turned off or turned on at will. Some . . . make the fatal error of assuming that religion is for [others] and "perhaps someday for me." Such thinking is not based on fact or experience, for we are daily becoming what we shall be ultimately. ("Leadership—Our Challenge Today," Explorer-Ensign Leadership Conference, August 18, 1967)

Spirituality is not bestowed simply by wishing; rather, it comes quietly and imperceptibly by serving. The Lord counseled, "Therefore, if ye have desires to serve God ye are called to the work" (D&C 4:3). . . .

Somehow I feel that if we will always remember who it is we serve, and on whose errand we are, we will draw closer to the source of the inspiration we seek—even our Master and Savior. ("The Priesthood—A Sacred Trust," *Ensign,* May 1994, 50, 51)

In all of our training, in our teaching, and in our daily lives, let us not neglect the importance of spirituality. Are our lives in order? Can we call down the power of heaven? Are we entitled to the companionship of the Spirit of the Lord? ("Only a Teacher," Regional Representatives Seminar, March 31, 1989)

STANDARDS

Styles in clothing change; and fads come and go; but if the dress styles are immodest, it is important that our young women avoid them. When you dress modestly, you show respect for your Heavenly Father and for yourself. At this time, when dress fashions are styled after the skimpy clothing some of the current movie and music idols are wearing, it may be difficult to find modest apparel in clothing stores. However, it is possible, and it is important. . . . You know the truth; live it. ("Be Thou an Example," *Ensign,* May 2005, 114–15)

———

In the . . . decades since the end of World War II standards of morality have lowered and lowered. Today we have more people in jail, in reformatories, on probation, and in trouble than ever before. From the padded expense account to grand larceny, petty crimes to crimes of passion, the figures are higher than ever and going higher. Crime spirals upward! Decency careens downward! Many are on a giant roller coaster of disaster, seeking the thrills of the moment while sacrificing the joys of eternity. ("Come, Follow Me," Conference Report, April 1967, 57)

———

Maintain an eternal perspective. Let there be a temple marriage in your future. There is no scene so sweet, no time so sacred as that very special day of your marriage. Then and there you glimpse celestial joy. Be alert; do not permit temptation to rob you of this blessing.

In the delightful musical *Camelot,* as the plot thickens and Queen Guinevere becomes infatuated with Lancelot, her husband King Arthur pleads with her—and in reality with each of us—"We must not let our passions destroy our dreams." ("The Lighthouse of the Lord," General Young Women Meeting, March 22, 1980)

SUCCESS

———

Success is the ratio of your accomplishments to your capacities. ("Timeless Truths for a Changing World," BYU Women's Conference, May 4, 2001)

In our journey on earth, we discover that life is made up of challenges—they just differ from one person to another. We are success oriented, striving to become "wonder women" and "super men." Any intimation of failure can cause panic, even despair. Who among us cannot remember moments of failure? . . .

Our responsibility is to rise from mediocrity to competence, from failure to achievement. Our task is to become our best selves. One of God's greatest gifts to us is the joy of trying again, for no failure ever need be final. ("The Will Within," *Ensign,* May 1987, 68)

Life was never intended to . . . be an easy course, or filled only with success. There are those games which we lose, those races in which we finish last, and those promotions which never come. Such experiences provide an opportunity for us to show our determination and to rise above disappointment. ("Go for It!" *Ensign,* May 1989, 44)

TEACHERS AND TEACHING

Jesus made *parables* a part of nearly every teaching situation. So often did He use this teaching device that evangelists recorded at one point that "without a parable spake he not unto them" (Mark 4:34). Jesus said He used parables in teaching because they conveyed to the hearer religious truth exactly in proportion to his faith and intelligence. To the unlearned the parable had story interest and some teaching value. To the spiritual, it conveyed much more, including the mysteries or secrets of the kingdom of heaven. Thus the parable is suited alike to simple and learned. It teaches all people to find divine truth in common things.

For the purpose of teaching in our day, the Savior's parables have the added advantage of taking on more and more meaning as we understand more about the objects and symbols He used in his parables. These stories also can be suited to a variety of applications. ("How to Communicate Effectively," General Authority Training Meeting, December 1967)

———

Guidelines for making a concise presentation:

1. Study and research until you know you have information that is worthy of presentation.
2. Write your thoughts on paper as they come, without concern for style or polish.
3. Arrange ideas in logical order. Some prefer a formula for organizing material into logical sequence such as PREP—Point, Reason, Example, Point. The name of a well-known opera has been used as a letter key to a motivation formula. AIDA in this instance stands for: Gain *Attention;* Sustain *Interest;* Incite *Desire;* Get *Action.*
4. Eliminate irrelevant ideas, illustrations and humor which reaches too far for an application. Because of the difficulty of getting full attention, there is a temptation with some to include interesting material even though it is not entirely relevant.
5. When the organizing stage has been completed, reduce every sentence to the fewest necessary words.
6. Last, learn the material well enough to present it as it has been prepared.

("How to Communicate Effectively," General Authority Training Meeting, December 1967)

———

The mark of a master teacher is indelible. It makes no difference whether or not he is teaching literature or mathematics or science or any other subject of the curriculum. He must win from his students the faith that moves mountains.

When he succeeds, near-miracles happen. Suddenly a pupil is awakened to an enthusiastic interest in some aspect of learning and begins to read widely without being urged.

Another discovers in himself powers that he did not know he had.

Another decides to seek better companions.

In a flash of inspiration, still another makes a decision that leads to a lifetime career. ("Yesterday, Today, and Tomorrow," Weber State College Baccalaureate, May 31, 1968)

———

Some time ago I overheard what I am confident is an oft-repeated conversation. Three very young boys were discussing the relative virtues of their fathers. One spoke out: "My dad is bigger than your dad," to which another replied, "Well, my dad is smarter than your dad." The third boy countered: "My dad is a doctor"; then, turning to one boy, he taunted in derision, "and your dad is only a teacher."

The call of a mother terminated the conversation, but the words continued to echo in my ears. Only a teacher. Only a teacher. Only a teacher. One day, each of those small boys will come to appreciate the true worth of inspired teachers and will acknowledge with sincere gratitude the indelible imprint which such teachers will leave on their personal lives. ("Only a Teacher," Conference Report, April 1970, 97)

———

The teacher not only shapes the expectations and ambitions of her pupils, but she also influences their attitudes toward their future and themselves. If she is unskilled, she leaves scars on the lives of youth, cuts deeply into their self-esteem, and distorts their image of themselves as human beings. But if she loves her students and has high expectations of them, their self-confidence will grow, their capabilities will develop, and their future will be assured. ("Only a Teacher," Conference Report, April 1970, 98)

———

In the home, the school, or the house of God, there is one teacher whose life overshadows all others. He taught of life and death, of duty and destiny. He lived not to be served, but to serve; not to receive, but to give; not to save His life, but to sacrifice it for others. He described a love more beautiful than lust, a poverty richer than treasure. It was said of this teacher that He taught with authority and not as do the scribes. In today's world, when many men are greedy for gold and for glory, and dominated by a teaching philosophy of "publish or perish," let us remember that this teacher never wrote—once only He wrote on the sand, and wind destroyed forever His handwriting. His laws were not inscribed upon stone, but upon human hearts. I speak of the master teacher, even Jesus Christ, the Son of God, the Savior and Redeemer of all mankind.

When dedicated teachers respond to His gentle invitation, "Come learn of me," they learn, but they also become partakers of His divine power. ("Only a Teacher," Conference Report, April 1970, 99)

———

The goal of gospel teaching today . . . is not to "pour information" into the minds of class members. It is not to show how much the teacher knows, nor is it merely to increase knowledge about the Church. *The basic goal of teaching in the Church is to help bring about worthwhile changes in the lives of boys and girls, men and women. The aim is to inspire the individual to think about, feel about, and then do something about living gospel principles.* ("Thou Art a Teacher Come from God," Conference Report, October 1970, 107)

———

To you who are administrators and teachers, you will stand before those who have struggled and saved and planned so that they might be your students. Treat them with dignity and provide them your very best. You not only teach a subject; you also mold human nature. You light the lamp of learning, that your students will better understand their earthly mission. You, through your spirit, your faith, and your love, will bless generations yet to be born. Your opportunities are not dissimilar to the Master Teacher—even Jesus Christ, the Son of God. (Dedication of the Jacob Spori Building, BYU–Idaho, August 22, 2003)

———

Who is the teacher you best remember from your youth? I would guess that in all probability it was the one who knew your name, who welcomed you to class, who was interested in you as a person, and who truly cared. When a leader walks the pathway of mortality with a precious youth alongside, there develops a bond of commitment between the two that shields the youth from the temptations of sin and keeps him or her walking steadfastly on the path that leads onward, upward, and unswervingly to eternal life. Build a bridge to each youth. ("They Will Come," *Ensign,* May 1997, 46)

———

The Church has always had a vital interest in public education and encourages its members to participate in parent-teacher activities and other events designed to improve the education of our youth.

There is no more important aspect of public education than the teacher who has the opportunity to love, to teach, and to inspire eager boys and girls and young men and young women. . . . I trust we shall recognize their importance and their vital mission by providing adequate facilities, the finest of books, and salaries which show our gratitude and our trust. ("Precious Children—A Gift from God," *Ensign,* November 1991, 67)

———

Each of us remembers with affection the teachers of our youth. I think it amusing that my elementary school music teacher was a Miss Sharp. She had the capacity to infuse within her pupils a love for music and taught us to identify musical instruments and their sounds. I well recall the influence of a Miss Ruth Crow who taught the subject of health. Though these were depression times, she insured that each sixth-grade student had a dental health chart. She personally checked each pupil for dental health and made certain that through public or private resources, no child went without proper dental care. As Miss Burkhaus, who taught geography, rolled down the maps of the world and, with her pointer, marked the capital cities of nations and the distinctive features of each country, language, and culture, little did I anticipate or dream that one day I would visit these lands and peoples.

Oh, the importance in the lives of our children of teachers who lift their spirits, sharpen their intellects, and motivate their very lives! ("Precious Children—A Gift from God," *Ensign,* November 1991, 67–68)

The classroom at church adds a vital dimension to the education of every child and youth. In this setting each teacher can provide an upward reach to those who listen to her lessons and feel the influence of her testimony. In Primary, Sunday School, Young Women meetings and those of the Aaronic Priesthood, well-prepared teachers, called under the inspiration of the Lord, can touch each child, each youth. . . . A word of encouragement here and a spiritual thought there can affect a precious life and leave an indelible imprint upon an immortal soul. . . .

The humble and inspired teacher in the church classroom can instill in her pupils a love for the scriptures. Why, the teacher can bring the Apostles of old and the Savior of the world not only into the classroom but also into the hearts, the minds, the souls of our children. ("Precious Children—A Gift from God," *Ensign*, November 1991, 68)

We are all teachers. We should ever remember that we not only teach with words; we teach also by who we are and how we live our lives. As we teach others, may we follow the example of the perfect teacher, our Lord and Savior Jesus Christ. He left His footprints in the sands of the seashore, but left His teaching principles in the hearts and in the lives of all whom He taught. He instructed His disciples of that day, and to us He speaks the same words, "Follow thou me." May we go forward in the spirit of obedient response, that it may be said of each of us as it was spoken of the Redeemer, "Thou art a teacher come from God." (Worldwide Priesthood Leadership Satellite Broadcast, February 10, 2007)

TECHNOLOGY

We live in a changing world. Technology has altered nearly every aspect of our lives. We must cope with these advances—even these cataclysmic changes—in a world of which our forebears never dreamed.

Remember the promise of the Lord: "If ye are prepared ye shall not fear" (D&C 38:30). Fear is a deadly enemy of progress. ("In Search of Treasure," *Ensign,* May 2003, 20)

You have come to this earth at a glorious time. The opportunities before you are nearly limitless. Almost all of you live in comfortable homes, with loving families, adequate food, and sufficient clothing. In addition, most of you have access to amazing technological advances. You communicate through cell phones, text messaging, instant messaging, e-mailing, blogging, Facebook, and other such means. You listen to music on your iPods and MP3 players. This list, of course, represents but a few of the technologies which are available to you. . . .

Although this is a remarkable period when opportunities abound, you also face challenges which are unique to this time. For instance, the very technological tools I have mentioned provide opportunities for the adversary to tempt you and to ensnare you in his web of deceit, thereby hoping to take possession of your destiny. ("May You Have Courage," *Ensign,* May 2009, 123–24)

TEMPLES AND TEMPLE WORK

The first temple to be built in this dispensation was the temple at Kirtland, Ohio. The Saints at the time were impoverished, and yet the Lord had commanded that a temple be built, so build it they did. Wrote Elder Heber C. Kimball of the experience, "The Lord only knows the scenes of poverty, tribulation and distress which we passed through to accomplish it" (in Orson F. Whitney, *Life of Heber C. Kimball* [1945], 67). And then, after all that had been painstakingly completed, the Saints were forced to leave Ohio and their beloved temple. They eventually found refuge—although it would be temporary—on the banks of the Mississippi River in the state of Illinois. They named their settlement Nauvoo, and willing to give their all once again and with their faith intact, they erected another temple to their God. Persecutions raged, however, and with the Nauvoo Temple barely completed, they were driven from their homes once again, seeking refuge in a desert place.

The struggle and the sacrifice began once again as they labored for forty years to erect the Salt Lake Temple. . . .

Some degree of sacrifice has ever been associated with temple building and with temple attendance. Countless are those who have labored and struggled in order to obtain for themselves and for their families the blessings which are found in the temples of God. ("The Holy Temple—A Beacon to the World," *Ensign,* May 2011, 92)

———

The Lord has never, to my knowledge, indicated that His work was simply the work that was going on here in mortality. His work embraces eternity, and if He indicated, as He did in the 88th section [of the Doctrine and Covenants], that He would hasten His work in His time, . . . I am simple enough to believe in my faith that our Heavenly Father is hastening His work in the spirit world and that He is bringing many souls into a period of preparation and readiness, that we might go into the temple of God and perform the sacred ordinances which will bring to those spirit children who have gone beyond, having lived in mortality, the same opportunities that you and I have. I firmly believe that He is hastening His work in the spirit world. (Los Angeles Temple Genealogical Library Dedication, June 20, 1964)

———

Why are so many willing to give so much in order to receive the blessings of the temple? Those who understand the eternal blessings which come from the temple know that no sacrifice is too great, no price too heavy, no struggle too difficult in order to receive those blessings. There are never too many miles to travel, too many obstacles to overcome, or too much discomfort to endure. They understand that the saving ordinances received in the temple that permit us to someday return to our Heavenly Father in an eternal family relationship and to be endowed with blessings and power from on high are worth every sacrifice and every effort. ("The Holy Temple—A Beacon to the World," *Ensign,* May 2011, 92)

———

The world can be a challenging and difficult place in which to live. We are often surrounded by that which would drag us down. As you and I go to the holy houses of God, as we remember the covenants we make within, we will be more able to bear every trial and to overcome each temptation. In this sacred sanctuary we will find peace; we will be renewed and fortified. ("The Holy Temple—A Beacon to the World," *Ensign,* May 2011, 93)

———

Each [of our temples] stands as a beacon to the world, an expression of our testimony that God, our Eternal Father, lives, that He desires to bless us and, indeed, to bless His sons and daughters of all generations. Each of our temples is an expression of our testimony that life beyond the grave is as real and as certain as is our life here on earth. I so testify. ("The Holy Temple—A Beacon to the World," *Ensign,* May 2011, 94)

———

Temples . . . are built with stone, glass, wood, and metal. But they are also a product of faith and an example of sacrifice. The funds to build temples come from all tithe payers and consist of the widow's mite, children's pennies, and workmen's dollars—all sanctified by faith. ("Days Never to Be Forgotten," *Ensign,* November 1990, 69)

There is much to be done in our temples in behalf of those who wait beyond the veil. As we do the work for them, we will know that we have accomplished what they cannot do for themselves. . . .

If you have not yet been to the temple or if you *have* been but currently do not qualify for a recommend, there is no more important goal for you to work toward than being worthy to go to the temple. Your sacrifice may be bringing your life into compliance with what is required to receive a recommend, perhaps by forsaking long-held habits which disqualify you. It may be having the faith and the discipline to pay your tithing.

Whatever it is, qualify to enter the temple of God. Secure a temple recommend and regard it as a precious possession, for such it is.

Until you have entered the house of the Lord and have received all the blessings which await you there, you have not obtained everything the Church has to offer. The all-important and crowning blessings of membership in the Church are those blessings which we receive in the temples of God. ("The Holy Temple—A Beacon to the World," *Ensign,* May 2011, 92–93)

———

For those who have died without a knowledge of the truth, a way has been provided. Sacred ordinances can be performed by the faithful living for the waiting dead. Houses of the Lord known as temples dot the land. As Elijah the prophet testified, the hearts of the fathers have been turned to the children, and the children to the fathers (see D&C 110:14–15). None shall be denied. All shall have opportunity for eternal blessings. ("An Invitation to Exaltation," Satellite Broadcast, March 4, 1984)

———

My young friends who are in your teenage years, always have the temple in your sights. Do nothing which will keep you from entering its doors and partaking of the sacred and eternal blessings there. I commend those of you who already go to the temple regularly to perform baptisms for the dead, arising in the very early hours of the morning so you can participate in such baptisms before school begins. I can think of no better way to start a day. ("The Holy Temple—A Beacon to the World," *Ensign,* May 2011, 93)

———

To you who are worthy and able to attend the temple, I would admonish you to go often. The temple is a place where we can find peace. There we receive a renewed dedication to the gospel and a strengthened resolve to keep the commandments.

What a privilege it is to be able to go to the temple, where we may experience the sanctifying influence of the Spirit of the Lord. Great service is given when we perform vicarious ordinances for those who have gone beyond the veil. In many cases we do not know those for whom we perform the work. We expect no thanks, nor do we have the assurance that they will accept that which we offer. However, we serve, and in that process we attain that which comes of no other effort: we literally become saviors on Mount Zion. As our Savior gave His life as a vicarious sacrifice for us, so we, in some small measure, do the same when we perform proxy work in the temple for those who have no means of moving forward unless something is done for them by those of us here on the earth. ("Until We Meet Again," *Ensign*, May 2009, 113–14)

———

Temple building increases family history work, and no person can go to the temple for himself or for another without learning something. As we learn, we come to know, and when we come to know, we come to do, and that is our purpose— to serve our Heavenly Father and help others along the way. I'm grateful for the temples of our Heavenly Father. (General Authority Training Meeting, September 30, 2009)

TEMPTATION

———

[The Apostle] Paul indicated that no temptation comes to man but that a way is prepared for him to escape the temptation (see 1 Corinthians 10:13). We do not quote that scripture very frequently these days. Rather, we prefer to echo the words used on television by a comedian: "The devil made me do it!" I think a lot of people like to say, "The devil made me do it," rather than admitting that for every temptation that comes to man, there is a way to escape the temptation. (All-Church Coordinating Council, November 15, 1988)

———

On a . . . visit to Tonga, . . . entering a typical classroom, I noticed the rapt attention that the children gave their native instructor. His textbook and theirs lay closed upon the desks. In his hand he held a strange-appearing lure fashioned from a round stone and large seashells. This I learned was a *maka-feke* or octopus trap.

Tongan fishermen glide over the reef, paddling their outrigger canoes with one hand and dangling the *maka-feke* over the side. Octopuses dash out from their rocky lairs and seize the lure, mistaking it for an ocean crab. So tenacious is their grasp and so firm is their instinct not to relinquish the precious prize that fishermen can flip them right into the canoe.

It was an easy transition for the teacher to point out to eager and wide-eyed youth that the Evil One, even Satan, often fashions a *maka-feke* to ensnare unsuspecting persons and to take possession of their destiny.

Before some he dangles the *maka-feke* of tobacco with the cunning call, "This is the way to social ease." He who grasps, like the octopus, finds it difficult to relinquish the bait.

Before others he presents the *maka-feke* of alcohol with
the chant: "Here is the way to unwind and forget your cares."
The unsuspecting victim finds himself not carefree, but held
captive.

The new morality is a cleverly designed *maka-feke.* In a head-
long dash for what they envision will be social acceptance, the
weak-willed, deceived by a counterfeit bait, discover not social
acceptance, but experience social rejection. ("The Miracle
of the Friendly Islands," Conference Report, October 1968,
79–80)

———

We must not detour from our determined course. In our
journey we will encounter forks and turnings in the road.
There will be the inevitable trials of our faith and the temptations of our times. We simply cannot afford the luxury of a
detour, for certain detours lead to destruction and spiritual
death. Let us avoid the moral quicksands that threaten on every side, the whirlpools of sin, and the crosscurrents of uninspired philosophies. ("An Invitation to Exaltation," Satellite
Broadcast, March 4, 1984)

———

You will meet temptation; withstand it.

The Prophet Joseph Smith faced temptation. Can you
imagine the ridicule, the scorn, the mocking that must have
been heaped upon him as he declared that he had seen a vision? I suppose it became almost unbearable for the boy. He
no doubt knew that it would be easier to retract his statements
concerning the vision and just get on with a normal life. He did
not, however, give in. These are his words: "I had actually seen
a light, and in the midst of that light I saw two Personages, and
they did in reality speak to me; and though I was hated and

persecuted for saying I had seen a vision, yet it was true. . . . I had seen a vision; I knew it, and I knew that God knew it, and I could not deny it" (Joseph Smith—History 1:25). Joseph Smith taught courage by example. He faced temptation and withstood it. ("Be Thou an Example," *Ensign,* May 2005, 112–13)

———

The world can at times be a frightening place in which to live. The moral fabric of society seems to be unraveling at an alarming speed. None—whether young or old or in-between—is exempt from exposure to those things which have the potential to drag us down and destroy us. Our youth, our precious youth, in particular, face temptations we can scarcely comprehend. The adversary and his hosts seem to be working nonstop to cause our downfall.

We are waging a war with sin, my brothers and sisters, but we need not despair. It is a war we can and will win. Our Father in Heaven has given us the tools we need in order to do so. He is at the helm. We have nothing to fear. He is the God of light. He is the God of hope. I testify that He loves us—each one. ("Looking Back and Moving Forward," *Ensign,* May 2008, 90)

TESTIMONY

———

A study of the scriptures will help our testimonies and the testimonies of our family members. Our children today are growing up surrounded by voices urging them to abandon that which is right and to pursue, instead, the pleasures of the world. Unless they have a firm foundation in the gospel of Jesus Christ, a testimony of the truth, and a determination to live righteously, they are susceptible to such influences. It is our responsibility to fortify and protect them. ("Three Goals to Guide You," *Ensign,* November 2007, 118)

———

When our testimonies are reflected by our service, they shine with unequaled brilliance. ("Pathway to Life Eternal," BYU Devotional, February 27, 1968)

———

We really don't know how much good we can do until we put forth the effort to achieve our objectives. Our testimonies can penetrate the hearts of others and can bring to them the blessings which will prevail in this troubled world and which will guide them to exaltation. (BYU Sixteen-Stake Fireside, November 16, 1986)

———

Each one of us has the responsibility to find out for himself or herself that this gospel of Jesus Christ is true. If we study the scriptures and put the teachings to the test, then we shall know the truthfulness of the doctrine, for this is our promise.

Once we have such knowledge, it is up to us to decide what we will do with it. ("Life's Greatest Decisions," Church Educational System Fireside Satellite Broadcast, September 7, 2003)

———

You possess a testimony; share it. Never underestimate the far-reaching influence of your testimony. You can strengthen one another; you have the capacity to notice the unnoticed.

When you have eyes to see, ears to hear, and hearts to feel, you can reach out and rescue others. . . .

You can share your testimony in many ways—by the words you speak, by the example you set, by the manner in which you live your life. ("Be Thou an Example," *Ensign,* May 2005, 115)

———

Because the trend in society today is away from the values and principles the Lord has given us, you will almost certainly be called upon to defend that which you believe. Unless the roots of your testimony are firmly planted, it will be difficult for you to withstand the ridicule of those who challenge your faith. When firmly planted, your testimony of the gospel, of the Savior, and of our Heavenly Father will influence all that you do throughout your life. The adversary would like nothing better than for you to allow derisive comments and criticism of the Church to cause you to question and doubt. Your testimony, when constantly nourished, will keep you safe. ("May You Have Courage," *Ensign,* May 2009, 126)

TIME

———

Time is the raw material of life. Every day unwraps itself like a gift, bringing us the opportunity to spin a fabric of health, pleasure, and content, and to evolve into something better than we are at its beginning.

Every passing instant is a juncture of many roads open to our choice. Shall we do this or that? Go this way or that? We cannot stand still. Choosing between alternatives in the use of time is evidence of one of the noblest of God's gifts—freedom of choice. ("Yesterday, Today, and Tomorrow," Weber State College Baccalaureate, May 31, 1968)

———

Success is contingent upon our effective use of the time given us. When we cease peering backwards into the mists of our past, and craning forward into the fog that shrouds the future, and concentrate upon doing what lies clearly at hand, then we are making the best and happiest use of our time. ("Timeless Truths for a Changing World," BYU Women's Conference, May 4, 2001)

———

Make time serve you. Don't just spend time—utilize it. ("Eternal Flight," Church Educational System Fireside Satellite Broadcast, February 4, 1996)

TITHING

———

Always be active in the Church. I will give you a formula which will guarantee to a large extent your success in fulfilling that commitment. It is simple. It consists of just three words: Pay your tithing. Every bishop could tell you from his personal experience that when the members of the Church pay tithing, honestly, faithfully, they have little difficulty keeping the other commandments of God. I call it a benchmark commandment. ("Life's Greatest Decisions," Church Educational System Fireside Satellite Broadcast, September 7, 2003)

———

The honest payment of tithing provides a person the inner strength and commitment to comply with the other commandments. . . .

All of us can afford to pay tithing. In reality, none of us can afford not to pay tithing. The Lord will strengthen our resolve. He will open a way to comply. ("Be Thou an Example," *Ensign*, November 1996, 44)

TRUTH

———

When compared to eternal verities, the questions of daily living are really rather trivial. What shall we have for dinner? Is there a good movie playing tonight? Have you seen the television log? Where shall we go on Saturday? These questions pale in their significance when times of crisis arise, when loved ones are wounded, when pain enters the house of good health, or when life's candle dims and darkness threatens. Then, truth and trivia are soon separated. The soul of man reaches heavenward, seeking a divine response to life's greatest questions: *Where did we come from? Why are we here? Where do we go after we leave this life?* Answers to these questions are not discovered within the covers of academia's textbooks, by dialing information, in tossing a coin, or through random selection of multiple-choice responses. These questions transcend mortality. They embrace eternity. ("An Invitation to Exaltation," Satellite Broadcast, March 4, 1984)

———

You do not find truth groveling through error. Truth is found by searching, studying, and living the revealed word of God. We learn truth when we associate with truth. We adopt error when we mingle with error.

The Lord instructed us concerning how we might distinguish between truth and error when He said: "That which doth not edify is not of God, and is darkness.

"That which is of God is light" (D&C 50:23–24). ("In Search of Truth," Conference Report, October 1964, 18)

———

Is the search for truth really this important? Is it so vital? Must it span the ages of time, encompass every field of endeavor, and penetrate every human heart? . . .

Even the law of the land jealously safeguards the principle of truth. In our courts of law, before a witness takes the stand to testify, he is placed under solemn oath: " . . . the testimony you are about to give . . . is the truth, the whole truth, and nothing but the truth. . . ." ("In Search of Truth," Conference Report, October 1964, 17)

———

To those who humbly seek, there is no need to stumble or falter along the pathway leading to truth. It is well marked by our Heavenly Father. We must first have a desire to know for ourselves. We must study. We must pray. We must do the will of the Father. And then we will know the truth, and the truth shall make us free. Divine favor will attend those who humbly seek it. ("In Search of Truth," Conference Report, October 1964, 19)

VALUES

———

There seems to be the beginning in our society of a return to basic virtues, an appreciation of the value of the traditional family, whether large or small, whether young or old. To me it [was] most encouraging to find week after week on listings of best-selling books the classic, *The Book of Virtues,* by William J. Bennett. It just may be that the world is sick of sin, discouraged by degradation, and fed up with falsehoods. When true values and basic virtues overlay and undergird the families of society, hope will conquer despair, and faith will triumph over doubt. ("The Family Must Endure," International Year of the Family Conference, March 19, 1995)

VISION

———

I don't believe that we can be wise without vision. Remember the ancient prophet who said, "Where there is no vision, the people perish" (Proverbs 29:18). You and I have a responsibility to have that kind of vision which will not be content with one step ahead or two steps ahead; but really to see the end from the beginning, to have a panoramic vision of our opportunities, would be the desire of the heart when one is in tune with the spirit of Christ.

We should realize, when we go abroad in the land to seek our opportunities, that really and truly we are not simply filling a job. We can indeed seek to excel. We can bring credit to the Church. We can be a pillar in the community. We can be the pivotal point around which other Latter-day Saints will have opportunities. In short, we can achieve for our families blessings and benefits if we have the vision to see the end from the beginning. . . . Our Heavenly Father has put within us a thirst for knowledge. We have the responsibility to seek out that knowledge that will give us true vision. (BYU College of Business, March 14, 1973)

WAR

Who among us will ever forget the touching and vivid pictures of husbands and fathers bidding goodbye to weeping wives and wondering children as fond farewells dominated every newscast and printed story. The children cried but did not know why. Wives wept because they did know the danger, the loneliness, the fear that awaited.

With the wave of a hand and a somewhat forced smile, the men and the women of the military went off to war. Their farewell expressions even now ring the conviction of their hearts: "I love my country"; "I'm proud to serve"; "I'll be home soon"; "Try not to worry."

But worry they did. Constant bombardment not only by bombs and missiles but by the press and over the television provoked the haunting questions, "Was the downed pilot my husband?" "Was the navigator taken captive my son?" . . .

At last the guns fell silent. Aircraft remained grounded. Mobile patrols halted. A quiet calm settled over the battlefield. The din of war succumbed to the silence of peace.

A scene on the cruel desert sands—and a sentence uttered from the heart—spoke volumes. An American soldier looked down at his vanquished enemy prisoner, touched the man's shoulder, and reassured him with the words, "It's all right; it's all right."

Every man and woman embroiled in that conflict thought of home, of family, and of friends. The embers of longing for loved ones glowed brightly and were found on every face. Love replaced hate, warmth filled every heart, and compassion overflowed every soul. ("Never Alone," *Ensign,* May 1991, 59)

———

Sister Monson and I were young teenagers in love at the time of World War II. During one summer she worked in Clearfield in the great warehouse where the personal effects of sailors who had lost their lives were handled—those whose mothers and fathers and family members would never again see them in mortality; and there were far too many, as she could recount. When I entered the Navy right at the end of the war, I witnessed the tragic sight of men coming back from the aircraft battles of the Pacific, many who had been terribly burned by high octane gasoline. War is terrible, from any perspective. (BYU Eighteen-Stake Fireside, March 3, 1991)

WELFARE AND HUMANITARIAN AID

———

Let us live within our means. Where necessary, let us reduce the level of our living. It was never intended that the offerings of a man with no car would be expended to sustain another with two cars. It simply is not realistic to assume that a standard of living bordering on opulence can or should be maintained in a time of emergency or serious need. It is not the purpose of [the welfare] program to provide a car for every garage or a garage for every car. In a time of personal or family crisis, business as usual cannot prevail. ("Back to Basics," Regional Representatives Seminar, April 3, 1981)

———

The Lord's storehouse includes the time, talents, skills, compassion, consecrated material, and financial means of faithful Church members. These resources are available to the bishop in assisting those in need. Our bishops have the responsibility to learn how to use properly these resources. May I suggest five basic guidelines:

1. A bishop is to seek out the poor as the Lord has commanded and administer to their needs. Do not suppose that someone else will do it. It is a bishop's priesthood duty. He may call on others to assist, but he is responsible.

2. A bishop should thoroughly analyze the circumstances surrounding each need for welfare assistance. He wisely calls on his Relief Society president to assist in the evaluation. He exercises discernment, sound judgment, balance, and compassion. Church resources represent a sacred trust, which becomes even more sacred as the bishop properly applies these resources in blessing the lives of others.

3. Those receiving welfare assistance work to the extent of their abilities for that which is received. There are many creative ways to provide work opportunities. Bishops, with help from their Welfare Services Committees, will want to provide such work, which will enhance the recipients' efforts to become self-reliant.

4. The assistance given by the bishop is temporary and partial. Remember, Church assistance is designed to help people help themselves. The rehabilitation of our members is the responsibility of the individual and the family, aided by the priesthood quorum and Relief Society.

> We are attempting to develop independence, not dependence. The bishop seeks to build integrity, self-respect, dignity, and soundness of character in each person assisted, leading to complete self-sufficiency.
>
> 5. We assist with basic life-sustaining goods and services, not the maintenance of current living standards. Individuals and families may need to alter their standards in doing all they can to meet their own needs. A Church dole would be worse than a government dole because it fails in the face of greater light and betrays a more honorable aim, more glorious potential.

(Regional Representatives Seminar, April 4, 1986)

———

Today, some are out of work, out of money, out of self-confidence. Hunger haunts their lives, and discouragement dogs their paths. But help is here—even food for the hungry, clothing for the naked, and shelter for the homeless.

Thousands of tons move outward from our Church storehouses weekly—even food, clothing, medical equipment, and supplies to the far corners of the earth and to empty cupboards and needy people closer to home. ("Patience—A Heavenly Virtue," *Ensign*, November 1995, 60–61)

———

In the fertile lowlands of eastern Guatemala, near the city of San Esteban, the Church and the Ezra Taft Benson Agriculture and Food Institute are helping poor rural farm families to increase agricultural production. By teaching techniques for improved soil preparation, fertilization, and irrigation, small farms achieve balanced cropping that provides better nutrition for families and additional feed for livestock.

At the outset, 160 families benefited from this instruction

and assistance. Within a short time, the number of families will reach 400. As knowledge and skills are imparted among neighbors, many thousands more stand to benefit.

Released from the confinement of poverty and want, they will then be better able to receive the spiritual gifts He holds in store for them. We, by our efforts to assist them, will better understand His words, "I was in prison, and ye came unto me" (Matthew 25:36).

The children in African nations are receiving immunizations in an effort to eradicate common communicable diseases by the end of the century. A specific project involves a cooperative effort with Rotary International's Polio Plus endeavor. The Church has purchased sufficient polio serum to immunize 300,000 children. Gas and electric refrigerators have been placed in rural health outposts to keep vaccines viable until they are administered to the children. You . . . and your families helped to bring this dream to reality.

Closer to [home], caring dentists joined together to provide free dental care to residents of an urban homeless shelter. These dentists, hygienists, and other professionals volunteer their time and skills. The Church has helped to provide the needed dental supplies.

These efforts not only relieve discomfort and pain, they also brighten the smiles, lift the spirits, and gladden the hearts of homeless patients. The words of the Master bring peace to the souls of all who participate in such endeavors: "I was a stranger, and ye took me in" (Matthew 25:35).

In the Philippines, the Church provides assistance to the Mabuhay Deseret Foundation, which aids hundreds of children to receive operations to repair deformed palates and lips and to correct untreated fractures or burns. Children once shunned now live normal lives. The spring of their step and the sound of their joy seem to echo, "I was sick, and ye visited me" (Matthew 25:36).

Generous contributions of wearing apparel to Deseret

Industries are being used to clothe men, women, and children around the world. Clothing is sorted, sized, and shipped to locations as far distant as Romania, Peru, Zimbabwe, and Sierra Leone, as well as to cities in North America. This clothing has warmed and comforted those exiled in refugee centers and orphanages. The bright patterns and sound fabrics considered surplus by the donors are now new and wonderful attire to the aged and impoverished. Meaning is given to the words, "I was . . . naked and ye clothed me" (Matthew 25:35–36).

The Church's humanitarian efforts are reaching the hungry and homeless of many American cities. Throughout the state of Utah, among the border towns of Texas, Arizona, and California, and into the communities of Appalachia, food and clothing are donated through private voluntary organizations or directly to children's homes, food banks, and soup kitchens. Much of this food starts its long journey on production projects managed by local agent stakes. Food is processed and packaged in Church canneries and distributed through storehouses, where Church welfare recipients and volunteers labor to assist their poor and needy neighbors within and outside the Church. Many could say with feeling, "I was an hungred, and ye gave me meat" (Matthew 25:35).

Far away in the foothills on the western slopes of Mt. Kenya, along the fringe of the colossal Rift Valley, pure water is coming to the thirsty people. A potable water project has changed the lives of 1,100 families. In cooperation with TechnoServe, a private voluntary organization, the Church is assisting in a project that will pipe drinkable water through twenty-five miles of pipes to waiting homes in a fifteen-village area. The simple blessing of safe drinking water recalls the words of the Savior, "I was thirsty, and ye gave me drink" (Matthew 25:35).

In behalf of the hundreds of thousands who have benefited by your generous fast offering contributions—children who now walk, who smile, who are fed and clothed; and parents who now may live normal lives with their children—I extend to you . . . the heartfelt expression of so many: "Thank you, and may God bless you." ("A Royal Priesthood," *Ensign*, May 1991, 48–49)

———

We have a responsibility to extend help as well as hope to the hungry, to the homeless, and to the downtrodden both at home and abroad. Such assistance is being provided for the blessing of all. In a host of cities, where need has outdistanced help, lives have been lifted, hearts have been touched, and the frown of despair has been transformed to the smile of confidence, thanks to the generosity of the Church membership in the payment of their fast offerings as the Lord has commanded. ("Conference Is Here," *Ensign*, May 1990, 4)

———

In the Republic of Belarus, beneath the city of Minsk, a series of tunnels honeycomb in what is called a "cellar." This bomb shelter was built in the 1960s and '70s for use in case of a nuclear attack. The tunnels were intended for tens of thousands of citizens to huddle together and wait for the devastation of nuclear war to settle itself upon the surface, giving them a chance to survive.

But today the bomb shelter is used for an entirely different purpose than the one for which it was built. Says Alexander Mikhalchenko, chairman of the State Committee on Archival Record Keeping of the Republic of Belarus, "We are using these shelters to store humanitarian shipments from The Church of Jesus Christ of Latter-day Saints—blankets, quilts, medical supplies, food, hygiene kits, wheelchairs, textbooks.

"All the assistance that comes to us is passed along into the hands of the people who need it the most. It goes to children in orphanages, patients in hospitals, old people in homes.

Charitable dinners are arranged. Everything goes—one hundred percent—to those purposes for which it is intended. Not one drop of the assistance goes anywhere else."

Over the last few years, a bond of friendship and trust has developed between the LDS Church and many of the people in Belarus. Halfway around the world from Belarus, the LDS Humanitarian Center prepares shipments for countries throughout the world. In a wonderful twist of irony, the building that houses the humanitarian center in Salt Lake City was originally built as a factory that made munitions for World War II. What a remarkable and miraculous age in which to live—where an old munitions factory in the United States and an austere bomb shelter in the former Soviet Union can be linked together by a single thread—the thread of compassion. But perhaps, after all, that is the wonder of unselfish love. More than any other element in the world, it has the ability to soften animosity, transform enemies into friends, and make us realize that in the end, we are brothers and sisters and not so very different after all. ("My Brother's Keeper," Los Angeles Rotary International, January 19, 2007)

———

No member of The Church of Jesus Christ of Latter-day Saints who has canned peas, topped beets, hauled hay, shoveled coal, or helped in any way to serve others ever forgets or regrets the experience of helping provide for those in need. Devoted men and women help to operate this vast and inspired welfare program. In reality, the plan would never succeed on effort alone, for this program operates through faith after the way of the Lord. ("The Way of the Lord," *Basic Principles of Welfare and Self-Reliance,* 11)

In response to the . . . question, "How is your welfare plan financed?" one needs but to describe the fast offering principle. The prophet Isaiah described the true fast by asking, "Is it not to deal thy bread to the hungry, and that thou bring the poor that are cast out to thy house? when thou seest the naked, that thou cover him; and that thou hide not thyself from thine own flesh?

"Then shall thy light break forth as the morning, and thine health shall spring forth speedily: and thy righteousness shall go before thee; the glory of the Lord shall be thy [reward].

"Then shalt thou call, and the Lord shall answer; thou shalt cry, and he shall say, Here I am. . . .

"And the Lord shall guide thee continually, and satisfy thy soul in drought: . . . and thou shalt be like a watered garden, and like a spring of water, whose waters fail not" (Isaiah 58:7–9, 11).

Guided by this principle, in a plan outlined and taught by inspired prophets of God, Latter-day Saints fast one day each month and contribute generously to a fast offering fund at least the equivalent of the meals forfeited and usually many times more. Such sacred offerings finance the operation of storehouses, supply cash needs of the poor, and provide medical care for the sick who are without funds. ("The Way of the Lord," *Ensign*, November 1977, 8)

One might ask, concerning those who assist in the welfare program, What prompts such devotion on the part of every worker? The answer can be stated simply: An individual testimony of the gospel of the Lord Jesus Christ, even a heartfelt desire to love the Lord with all one's heart, mind, and soul, and one's neighbor as oneself. ("The Way of the Lord," *Basic Principles of Welfare and Self-Reliance*, 13)

———

There are those throughout the world who are hungry; there are those who are destitute. Working together, we can alleviate suffering and provide for those in need. In addition to the service you give as you care for one another, your contributions to the funds of the Church enable us to respond almost immediately when disasters occur anywhere in the world. We are nearly always among the first on the scene to provide whatever assistance we can. We thank you for your generosity. ("Until We Meet Again," *Ensign,* November 2008, 106–7)

———

How often do we hear that it is our responsibility to work for that which we receive? I love to go to Welfare Square. It is a place to labor and learn, and those who receive help from the Church should, if possible, serve there or in a similar facility. Such service could also be given in chapels that could use a little attention or in the homes of deserving and needy members. (General Authority Training Meeting, September 30, 2009)

WIDOWS

———

The Epistle of James has long been a favorite book of the Holy Bible. I find his brief message heart-warming and filled with life. Each of us can quote that well-known passage, "If any of you lack wisdom, let him ask of God, that giveth to all men liberally, and upbraideth not; and it shall be given him" (James 1:5). How many of us, however, remember his definition of religion? "Pure religion and undefiled before God and the Father is this, To visit the fatherless and widows in their affliction, and to keep himself unspotted from the world" (James 1:27).

The word *widow* appears to have had a most significant meaning to our Lord. He cautioned His disciples to beware the example of the scribes, who feigned righteousness by their long apparel and their lengthy prayers, but who devoured the houses of widows (see Mark 12:38, 40).

To the Nephites came the direct warning, "I will come near to you in judgment; and I will be a swift witness against . . . those that oppress the . . . widow" (3 Nephi 24:5).

To the Prophet Joseph Smith He directed, "The storehouse shall be kept by the consecrations of the church; and widows and orphans shall be provided for, as also the poor" (D&C 83:6).

Such teachings were not new then. They are not new now. Consistently the Master has taught, by example, His concern for the widow. To the grieving widow at Nain, bereft of her only son, He came personally and to the dead son restored the breath of life—and to the astonished widow her son. To the widow at Zarephath, who with her son faced imminent starvation, He sent the prophet Elijah with the power to teach faith as well as provide food.

We may say to ourselves, "But that was long ago and ever so far away." I respond, "Is there a city called Zarephath near your home? Is there a town known as Nain?" We may know our cities as Columbus or Coalville, Detroit or Denver. Whatever the name, there lives within each city the widow deprived of her companion and often her child. The need is the same. The affliction is real.

The widow's home is generally not large or ornate. Frequently it is modest in size and humble in appearance. Often it is tucked away at the top of the stairs or the back of the hallway and consists of but one room. To such homes He sends you and me.

There may exist an actual need for food, clothing—even

shelter. Such can be supplied. Almost always there remains the hope for that special hyacinth to feed the soul. ("The Long Line of the Lonely," *Ensign,* May 1981, 47)

———

Some years ago, in Salt Lake City, there lived two sisters. Each had two handsome sons. Each had a loving husband. Each lived in comfort, prosperity, and good health. Then the grim reaper visited their homes. First, each lost a son; then the husband and father. Friends visited, words brought a measure of comfort, but grief continued unrelieved. . . .

The years passed. Hearts remained broken. The two sisters sought and achieved seclusion. They shut themselves off from the world which surrounded them. Alone they remained with their remorse. Then there came to a latter-day prophet of God, who knew well these two sisters, the voice of the Lord which directed him to their plight. Elder Harold B. Lee left his busy office and visited the penthouse home of the lonely widows. He listened to their pleadings. He felt the sorrow of their hearts. Then he called them to the service of God and to mankind. Each commenced a ministry in the holy temple in Salt Lake City. Each looked outward into the lives of others and upward into the face of God. Peace replaced turmoil. Confidence dispelled despair. God had once again remembered the widow and, through a prophet, brought divine comfort. ("Building a House for Eternity," Los Angeles Temple Workers Devotional, September 19, 1993)

———

I express my sincere appreciation to one and all who are mindful of the widow. To the thoughtful neighbors who invite a widow to dinner; and to that royal army of noble women, the visiting teachers of the Relief Society, I add, may God bless you for your kindness and your love unfeigned toward her who reaches out and touches vanished hands and listens to voices forever stilled. . . .

Thank you to thoughtful and caring bishops who insure that no widow's cupboard is empty, no house unwarmed, or no life unblessed. ("The Fatherless and the Widows—Beloved of God," *Ensign,* November 1994, 70–71)

———

The nursing homes are crowded, the hospital beds are full, the days come and go—often the weeks and months pass—but mother is not visited. Can we not appreciate the pangs of loneliness, the yearnings of mother's heart when hour after hour, alone in her age, she gazes out the window for the loved one who does not visit, the letter the postman does not bring. She listens for the knock that does not sound, the telephone that does not ring, the voice she does not hear. How does such a mother feel when her neighbor welcomes gladly the smile of a son, the hug of a daughter, the glad exclamation of a child, "Hello, Grandmother." ("'Behold Thy Mother,'" Conference Report, October 1973, 27–28)

WOMEN
(SEE ALSO RELIEF SOCIETY)

———

Sisters, you are the epitome of love. You brighten your homes, you lead with kindness your children; and while your husbands may be head of the home, you surely are the heart of the home. Together, through respect for each other and sharing of responsibilities, you make an unbeatable team. ("Be Thou an Example," *Ensign,* November 2001, 100)

———

There are those of you who are single—perhaps in school, perhaps working—yet forging a full and rich life, whatever the future may hold. Some of you are busy mothers of growing children; still others are single mothers struggling to raise your children without the help of a husband and father. Some of you have raised your children but have realized that challenges have only multiplied as your children have had children of their own, and their need for your help is ongoing. There are those of you who have aging parents who require the loving care only you can give.

Wherever you are in life, your individual tapestry is woven with threads common to you and to all women. . . .

Each one of you is living a life filled with much to do. I plead with you not to let the important things in life pass you by, planning instead for that illusive and nonexistent future day when you'll have time to do all that you want to do. Instead, find joy in the journey—now. ("Joy in the Journey," BYU Women's Conference, May 2, 2008)

———

You are a mighty force for good, one of the most powerful in the entire world. Your influence ranges far beyond yourself and your home and touches others all around the globe. You have reached out to your brothers and sisters across streets, across cities, across nations, across continents, across oceans. You personify the Relief Society motto: "Charity never faileth."

You are, of course, surrounded by opportunities for service. No doubt at times you recognize so many such opportunities that you may feel somewhat overwhelmed. Where do you begin? How can you do it all? How do you choose, from all the needs you observe, where and how to serve?

Often small acts of service are all that is required to lift and bless another: a question concerning a person's family, quick words of encouragement, a sincere compliment, a small note of thanks, a brief telephone call. If we are observant and aware, and if we act on the promptings which come to us, we can accomplish much good. ("Three Goals to Guide You," *Ensign,* November 2007, 120–21)

WORK
(SEE ALSO EFFORT)

———

Work is basic to all we do. God's first direction to Adam in the Garden of Eden, as recorded in scripture, was to dress the garden and take care of it. After the fall of Adam, God cursed the earth for Adam's sake, saying, "In the sweat of thy face shalt thou eat bread, till thou return unto the ground" (Genesis 3:19). Today many have forgotten the value of work. Some believe that the highest goal in life is to achieve a condition in which one no longer needs to work. (Regional Representatives Seminar, April 4, 1986)

———

The best way to prepare for your future does not consist of merely dreaming about it. Great men have not been merely dreamers; they have returned from their visions to the practicalities of replacing the airy stones of their dream castles with solid masonry wrought by their hands.

Vision without work is daydreaming. Work without vision is drudgery. Vision, coupled with work, will ensure your success. ("Yesterday, Today, and Tomorrow," Weber State College Baccalaureate, May 31, 1968)

———

You have developed the skill to study—use it. You have learned the value of effort—apply it. You have pursued the quest for excellence—continue it. ("Guideposts for Life's Journey," BYU–Idaho Commencement, August 22, 2003)

———

In professional, business, scientific, and technological life there is a rule which can be a very good rule for ambitious young persons. The rule is, "Find a vacuum and expand into it." Ask yourself, "What is there that needs doing and is not being done?" Then assess your capacity for doing things and let it be your ambition to do the work that you can do best, in an area where it is needed most, and then put all your mind into it. ("Great Expectations," BYU Devotional, May 11, 1965)

———

What the public takes for brilliance is really the result of thorough, painstaking investigation and downright hard work. Were we to be deprived of work, we should be robbed of our greatest field of enjoyment and be forever condemned to mediocrity. ("Constant Truths in Changing Times," BYU Commencement, May 26, 1967)

Formula W: "Work Will Win When Wishy Washy Wishing Won't." ("Return with Honor," BYU Devotional, January 19, 1971)

WORLDLINESS

As we travel throughout the world, very often the members of the Church, and particularly the priesthood leaders, ask us, "What do you consider the greatest problem facing the Church?" I usually answer, "Our major challenge for the membership of the Church is to live in the world without being of the world." I would like to emphasize that in this day in which we live, the floodwaters of immorality, irresponsibility, and dishonesty lap at the very moorings of our individual lives. If we do not safeguard those moorings, if we do not have deeply entrenched foundations to withstand such eroding influences, we are going to be in difficulty. ("The Need to Add Men to the Melchizedek Priesthood," Regional Representatives Seminar, April 6, 1984)

One of the most beautiful scriptures in the New Testament talks about treasure. You've seen people polish a new car, haven't you? I know one man who every morning at 5:30 washes his car, except on Sunday. He loves that car with a passion. He parks it next to a pillar in the parking terrace so there is only one chance instead of two of a car hitting it. And when he goes home at night he takes a dust rag and polishes the top to remove any particles that may have gathered since 5:30 A.M.

Some people love clothing; they like to dress up and gaze at themselves in a mirror. Others like different hairstyles. Still others like certain ties or shoes. Some people love money and love to make money. That is all that whets their interest. In some way, all of these people feel they have found happiness.

But the Savior gave us the great formula for happiness. He said, "Lay not up for yourselves treasures upon earth, where moth and rust doth corrupt, and where thieves break through and steal: But lay up for yourselves treasures in heaven, where neither moth nor rust doth corrupt, and where thieves do not break through nor steal: For where your treasure is, there will your heart be also" (Matthew 6:19–20). ("Traditions," Dixie College Homecoming, November 2, 1986)

———

In cities across the land and in nations throughout the world, there has occurred a deterioration of the home and family. Abandoned in many instances is the safety net of personal and family prayer. A macho-inspired attitude of "I can go it alone," or "I don't need the help of anyone" dominates the daily philosophy of many. Frequently there is rebellion against long-established traditions of decency and order, and the temptation to run with the crowd is overwhelming. Such a destructive philosophy, this formula for failure, can lead to ruin. ("The Upward Reach," *Ensign,* November 1993, 48)

———

We have observed in recent years the accelerating erosion of many of the restraints upon human conduct which have guided the lives of past generations. Theology has stretched its boundaries to embrace thinkers who proclaim the death of

God, and God's orphans are freed to indulge their selfishness according to their whims.

There are those who declare chastity to be a state of mind rather than a physical condition. Integrity, which was once a fixed and absolute quality, has taken on a new flexibility; some seem to have accepted as their philosophy Oscar Wilde's dictum that the best way to get rid of temptation is to give in to it.

Our intellectual and moral condition has fallen hopelessly behind our technical progress. You can help restore the balance. ("Constant Truths in Changing Times," BYU Commencement, May 26, 1967)

———

We live in a world where moral character ofttimes is relegated to a position secondary to facial beauty or personal charm. We read and hear of local, national, and international beauty contests. Throngs pay tribute to Miss America, Miss World, and Miss Universe. Athletic prowess, too, has its following. The winter games, the world Olympics, the tournaments of international scope bring forth the adoring applause of the enthralled crowd. Such are the ways of men!

But what are the inspired words of God? From a time of long ago, the counsel of Samuel the prophet echoes in our ears: " . . . the Lord seeth not as man seeth; for man looketh on the outward appearance, but the Lord looketh on the heart" (1 Samuel 16:7). ("Yellow Canaries with Gray on Their Wings," *Ensign,* July 1973, 43)

———

The tenor of our times is permissiveness. All around us we see the idols of the movie screen, the heroes of the athletic field—those whom many young people long to emulate—as disregarding the laws of God and rationalizing away sinful practices, seemingly with no ill effect. Don't you believe it! There is a time of reckoning—even a balancing of the ledger. Every Cinderella has her midnight—it's called Judgment Day, even the Big Exam of Life. Are you prepared? Are you pleased with your own performance? ("Be Thou an Example," *Ensign,* May 2005, 113–14)

YOUTH

———

You are the sons and daughters of Almighty God. You have a destiny to fulfill, a life to live, a contribution to make, a goal to achieve. The future of the kingdom of God upon the earth will, in part, be aided by your devotion.

When this perspective is firmly in mind, you can appreciate the absolute necessity of diligence in this, your period of preparation. Neglect to prepare and you mortgage your future. ("Pathway to Life Eternal," BYU Devotional, February 27, 1968)

———

Youth is a time for growth. Our minds during these formative years are receptive to truth, but they are also receptive to error. The responsibility to choose rests with each [young person]. As the years go by, the choices become increasingly complex, and at times we may be tempted to waver. The need for a personal code of honor is demanded not only on a daily basis, but frequently many times in a given day. ("Who Honors God, God Honors," *Ensign,* November 1995, 48)

———

On occasion, we are asked, "What do you consider to be the greatest challenge facing the Church today?" I have pondered this question, as have my Brethren, and a simple answer will not suffice. My thoughts, however, turn to the tragic losses which occur as young men journey along the Aaronic Priesthood path and the effect of such casualties on the lives of so many. When a boy is lost, a future missionary is lost, a temple marriage vanishes, and another is added to the swelling number of prospective elders. This problem needs to be addressed now. The tender sapling needs support if it is not to be bent, then broken, by the winds of the world. ("Only a Teacher," Regional Representatives Seminar, March 31, 1989)

———

Consider the love your parents have for you and that you have for them. Instead of simply asking them, "Where are the keys to your car?" you might add, "I'll be a bit late tonight." Often the clock ticks more loudly and the hands move more slowly when the night is dark, the hour is late, and a son or a daughter has not yet come home. A telephone call, "We're okay; we just stopped for something to eat. Don't worry; we're fine," is an indication of true love of parents and of the training of a Latter-day Saint home. ("Three Gates to Open," BYU Devotional, November 14, 2006)

———

How long has it been since you looked into the eyes of your mother and, holding nothing back, spoke those welcome words, "Mother, I truly love you"? How about Father, who daily toils to provide for you? Fathers appreciate hearing those same precious words from the lips of a child, "I love you."

It is too easy to take parents for granted and to fail to

realize just how much they mean to you and you to them. ("Your Celestial Journey," *Ensign,* May 1999, 98)

———

During this time of your lives . . . hazards loom. I speak of temptings of the evil one, following the wrong crowd, doing the wrong things, and forgetting who you are and what God expects you to become. Remember, oh remember, the prayers of your parents, the teachings learned at home. And never forget the safety of personal prayer and your determination to stand firm for truth and righteousness. ("Dear to Our Hearts, Always," BYU Devotional, September 12, 2000)

———

There come thundering to our ears the words from Mt. Sinai: "Honour thy father and thy mother."

My, how your parents love you, how they pray for you. Honor them.

. . . There are countless ways in which you can show true love to your mothers and to your fathers. You can obey them and follow their teachings, for they will never lead you astray. You can treat them with respect. They have sacrificed much and continue to sacrifice in your behalf.

Be honest with your mother and your father. One reflection of such honesty with parents is to communicate with them. Avoid the silent treatment. . . .

Don't wait until that light from your household is gone; don't wait until that voice you know is stilled before you say, "I love you, Mother; I love you, Father." Now is the time to think and the time to thank. I trust you will do both. You have a heritage; honor it. ("Be Thou an Example," *Ensign,* May 2005, 112)

———

Maintain an eternal perspective. Let there be a temple marriage in your future. There is no scene so sweet, no time so sacred as that very special day of your marriage. Then and there you glimpse celestial joy. Be alert; do not permit temptation to rob you of this blessing.

Make every decision you contemplate pass this test: What does it do to me? What does it do for me? ("Be Thou an Example," *Ensign,* May 2005, 113)

———

My dear young friends, you have been reserved to come forth at this particular time when the gospel of Jesus Christ has been restored to the earth. . . .

You have been taught the truths of the gospel by your parents and by your teachers in the Church. You will continue to find truth in the scriptures, in the teachings of the prophets, and through the inspiration which comes to you as you bend your knees and seek the help of God. . . .

When firmly planted, your testimony of the gospel, of the Savior, and of our Heavenly Father will influence all that you do throughout your life. It will help to determine how you spend your time and with whom you choose to associate. It will affect the way you treat your family, how you interact with others. It will bring love, peace, and joy into your life. It should help you determine to be modest in your dress and in your speech. ("Be Thou an Example," *Ensign,* May 2005, 114)

———

Although there have always been challenges in the world, many of those which you face are unique to this time. But you are some of our Heavenly Father's strongest children, and He has saved you to come to the earth "for such a time as this"

(Esther 4:14). With His help, you will have the courage to face whatever comes. Though the world may at times appear dark, you have the light of the gospel which will be as a beacon to guide your way. ("May You Have Courage," *Ensign,* May 2009, 127)

SCRIPTURE INDEX

SUBJECT INDEX

A

Aaronic Priesthood
    significance of ordination
        to, 1
    as preparation for
        missionary service, 1,
        4–5
    leadership responsibilities
        of, 1–3
    leading, with patience, 4
    guides for success in, 5
    giving proper emphasis
        to, 6–9
    bishops and, 30–31
    home teaching and, 140
    missionary work and, 186,
        190
    oath and covenant of
        priesthood and, 239
    reactivation and, 251, 337
Abel, 68
Abraham, 204
Abuse, 8–9, 17–18
Accountability, 41–47, 255–56
Actions
    changing, 35, 89
    effort and, 99
    as example, 102–5
    faith and, 109–10
    showing love through, 149
    thoughts and, 265
Activity. *See* Church activity
Adam, 205
Addiction, 262, 308–9
Adversity
    universal nature of, 9–10

    common forms of, 10–11
    comfort in, 11
    faith to withstand, 11–12
    as test, 12–13
    See also Trials
Agency, 13–14. *See also* Choice;
    Decisions
Alcohol, 92, 262, 265, 308
Alibis, 25–26
Alice's Adventures in Wonderland
    (Carroll), 43–44
America, 14–17, 157–58
Anger, 17–19, 70–71, 216–17
Apostasy, 132
Appearances, 163–65, 264, 293
Ashton, Marvin O., 250
Atonement, 19–22, 125
Attitude
    joyful, 23
    when responding to trials,
        23–24
    positive, power of, 24–25
    and alibis, 25–26
    types of, leading to failure,
        26–27
    reassessing, 28
    changing, 35
    Nephi's, contrasted with
        that of brothers, 54
    enhanced, through Christ,
        89
Audubon, John James, 23–24

B

Bacon, Sir Francis, 166
Balance, 28–29, 57

missionary work through,
193
parents as, 208–9
Excellence, 105–6
Ezra Taft Benson Agriculture
and Food Institute, 320–21

F

Failure, 26–27, 100–101, 295
Faith
through trials, 11–12
of children, 39
decision-making and, 85
teachings on, 106–11
prayer and, 224
Family, 111–13, 194, 316. *See
also* Home
Family history work, 114–16.
See also Temples/Temple
work
Family home evening, 116–17
Family prayer, 224–25, 227–28,
229, 334
Fast offerings, 323, 325
Fathers, 117, 210–11
Faust, James E., 55
Fear
progress and, 26, 302
confronting, 98
faith and, 109
of leadership, 167
missionary work and,
186–87
of future, 207
See also Courage

Feedback, improving
communication through,
62
Fellowshiping, 118–19
Finances
in ward, 31
personal, managing,
79–83
of Church, 81
in times of emergency,
318–19
First Vision, 161
Food storage, 80
"Formula W," 333
Ford, Henry, 94
Forgiveness, 70, 119–21
For the Strength of Youth, 263
Fosdick, Harry Emerson, 167
Freedom, 122
Friendship, 122–23, 264

G

Garden of Eden, 205
Gemstones, polishing, 13
Genealogy, 114–16
Generalities, dealing in, 143
Gifts, 49, 51
Gladstone, William H., 148,
224
Goals, 123–24
God
love for, 16, 17, 173, 175,
176
Creation and, 75–76
as father, 117

Page #97 Effort. (See also Work.)

" " #116 & 117 Family Home Evening